THE SEA-GOD'S HERB

ALSO BY JOHN DOMINI

THE SEA-GOD'S HERB

ESSAYS & CRITICISM: 1975–2014

John Domini

DZANC
BOOKS

DZANC
BOOKS

1334 Woodbourne Street
Westland, MI 48186
www.dzancbooks.org

Book design by Steven Seighman.
Cover image: Ugo Rondinone, "soul," at Gladstone Gallery, Manhattan,
NY, summer 2013. Photo by John Domini.

Published 2014 by Dzanc Books

ISBN: 978-1-938103-78-0
First edition: March 2014

This project is supported in part by awards from the National Endowment for the
Arts and Michigan Council for Arts and Cultural Affairs.

Printed in the United States of America

10   9   8   7   6   5   4   3   2   1

Three Editors:

Kit Rachlis weekly,
Willard Spiegelman quarterly,
Joe Amato, starting every other month.

TABLE OF CONTENTS

Fresh Tide

Other Gravities

Coming Tide

Galactic Pole

THE SEA-GOD'S HERB

THE SEA-GOD'S HERB: ESSAYS & CRITICISM, 1975-2014

Preface

No honest assessment of what this book's about can ignore the vagaries of my DNA. Why should I take time and energy to write *about* contemporary literature, and other artforms, when what I care about most is bringing off imaginative work of my own? I can offer a rationale, to be sure. I can claim that the essays and reviews here—selected from a far larger assortment of publications—amount to an argument on behalf of latter-day non-traditional storytelling. That argument has been revised and re-revised for the sake of this book, though it went through many a revision, up late and up early, back when the pieces first appeared. Nevertheless, now when I look the effort over and ask myself *why*, some part of my answer must be a shrug. That's the way the helix doubles.

On top of that, I can get behind the usual complaints about putting in time as a critic. Writers engaged in creative efforts often grumble about how higher impulses get diffused when they have to generate the low-level noise of a book review. Consider, for instance, two compendiums of such stuff from two radically different sensibilities, John Updike and Gilbert Sorrentino. These writers couldn't have stood farther apart on most matters, but they shared a dismissive attitude toward critique and commentary. In Updike's introduction to *Picked-Up Pieces* (1975), he claims that what he feels for the "utmost favorites" of his reviews and such is no better than "a step-emotion" compared with his pride in anything creative. Sorrentino's "Preface" to *Something Said* (1984) concludes that the job "is a strange enterprise and one that I am happy to be involved in only at its periphery."

I honor my elders. I've got a couple of essays on Sorrentino here. As for Updike (and with all due respect for the bulging '70s scrapbook *Rabbit is Rich* and the bite of the Bech stories), he never needed my help. It's the idea of "help," you see, that drives the critic and essayist in me, when everything's said and done. Misgivings about the role may be hard-wired into my personality and buttressed by my reading, yet at the same time this argument keeps coming up. It keeps yanking me to the desk: a brief on behalf of the most modern and post-modern. Such work has been so badly understood that I feel I can be useful.

This sense of the useful, once upon a time, was spurred by critic-*cum*-novelist models. A single example will do: Robert Coover's thoughtful celebration of Samuel Beckett, "The Last Quixote." The essay appeared in *New American Review* in 1971 and opened with a sober challenge: "It is difficult to do this thing, to speak of Beckett." I read the piece even as I lay stunned across the floor by Coover's *Pricksongs & Descants*, and I discerned a fascinating line of thought within those central words, "this thing." In them, I detected an intuition about the present: Coover's thing was of the moment, and therefore difficult to speak of while still *in* the moment. Certainly "The Last Quixote" helped me suss out a few of Beckett's secrets, yet its greater gift may have been the essayist's openness to the timeless wallop of fiction, even when ancient business like identification or event or catharsis takes improbable new shape. Ever since, blocking the inroads of cynicism the best I can, I've taken up new story surrogates with faith.

Transformation would be another word for it, a word that gives me my title. The source is Dante, the first Canto of *Paradiso*, which begins a lot like Coover on Beckett. It begins in doubt, as the Poet frets that he can never get across the wonders he's seen. He must *trasumanar*, "transhumanize," in the *Divine Comedy*'s distinguishing neologism. Yet his guide Beatrice helps him achieve this altered state with a single long look:

> Gazing at her, I felt myself becoming
> what Glaucus had become tasting the herb
> that made him like the other sea-gods there.

The translation is Mark Musa's, but the myth referred to remains the same in any idiom. A fisherman notices that a certain shore grass revives his dead catch and so he tries the stuff himself; he becomes a god. What's more, Glaucus stays that way. He gets no comeuppance, making miracles and collecting lovers. Ovid, Dante's source, no doubt took pleasure in how the story upset expectation.

My own pleasure in the *Comedy* can also be found here in *Sea-God*. I believe that my explorations of Dante belong with the project I've just outlined—namely, a definition and celebration of the postmodern. That's Sorrentino's "strange enterprise" for you. If I sound glib, I'm not sure I should apologize, because any honest critic has to recognize how his or her arguments can become glib, a kind of shrink-wrap that risks suffocating the artwork under consideration. Granted, the most thoughtful review or essay will have an ameliorative impact, correcting misapprehension and enlarging the perception of beauty. That's the best outcome, and we have a good handful of happy examples. Where would Jackson Pollock and the Abstract Expressionists have been without their champion, Clement Greenberg? Nevertheless, essays and reviews also make some *particular* impact on creator, object, and aesthetic. The good critic works out of his hand just as the artist works out of his, and that hand leaves its own recognizable print. Mine reveals ancient narrative structures and satisfactions in contemporary storytelling. Not a bad revelation, perhaps, but by the same token, *Sea-God* has its limits too, and will in time tumble into one general consensus or another. "Oh, Domini," they'll say, c. 2095, "he's one of those who's always chasing ecstasy and archetypes." So be it. Anyway, I should be so lucky as to last that long, and for better or for worse that's why my Dante investigations belong. Therefore, too, the text as a whole amounts to a defense of artists taking chances.

This defense owes something to other theorists, naturally. With Karl Marx, it posts a manifesto against the industrial product that generally occupies the U.S. bestseller lists. I also detect Mikhail Bahktin and his carnival, Jacques Derrida and his grammatology. Still, my defense of the imagination intends to go beyond trends in analysis. It goes to the basic health of the storyteller. The ecstasy of narrative, an ecstasy gained by prevarication and sleight of hand, can be reached also in works that seem to reject such satisfaction. Artists cavalier about old-time novelistic virtues, like Carole Maso, share common purpose with those like Richard Powers, who have a clear reliance on the sturdy familiars of plot and character and so forth. Such a sharing, tricky to detect but central to the reading, defines the second, more important way in which my reconsideration of the *Divine Comedy* belongs among these pieces. Dante's work too appears to be something other than story: a theology, in particular. Seeing past such appearances also drove me to include a brief selection of pieces that consider other art forms. And not till I had the lead, "Against the 'Impossible to Explain,'" did I have the whole, the book. I couldn't abide bringing out a mere miscellany.

So I've got an argument, but at the same time I can't help but think of how it could ring tinny. I can't help but think of critics who never get over themselves. Harold Bloom would be the obvious case, wailing about *The Closing of the American Mind* even as he shoved his own dusty bookshelves against the door. More recently, there are the

New Yorker hatchet jobs of James Wood. The distinguishing mark of such stuff is the lack of receptivity. Earning an insight matters less than getting off, with a snicker of self-congratulation, a quip. Thus I've got to be receptive myself—and thus my argument has got to be *modular*.

I mean that *Sea-God* best embodies what it has to say in this form: a collection of modes (okay, *approaches*), rather than a monolith of My Way. I may have re-revised the pieces included, but their arrangement remains roughly chronological, and each one still bears the marks of their original occasion, of "this thing," the present. The monolith alternative, the single essay or "monograph," inevitably stumbles into some academic theory or other. And if the aversion for theory seems like a knee-jerk reaction, and weirder still like something I share with Bloom, let me assure you, there's more to it. Placing work into ideological camps, no matter how pretty you make the cabin curtains, takes away the immediacy and impact of first encounter with a novel or stories. My project, on the other hand, has everything to do with immediacy and impact. It honors, first and last, the spell cast as a narrative unfolds, a magic all the more powerful, in the best cases, when it doesn't begin with conventional abracadabra.

So too my critical vocabulary strives for American plainness. So too my analysis strives to discern humane purposes in the book at hand, the ways it aspires to art's enhancement while alert to the world's degradations. If that means my criticism flirts with yet another theory, the Transcendalist, so be it. The more important point is that every critic gets his smart mouth smashed, sooner or later, by core quality. Remarks aren't literature, no matter how sharp the quip might look in a magazine. Remarks fall away and good work emerges; *Moby-Dick* swamps every slick out there. The point is another rare case of agreement between Sorrentino and Updike. Both men argue that commentary disappears into general appreciation—general consensus, as I noted earlier.

I've seen this happen with one of the pieces here. The essay on Donald Barthelme and "The Indian Uprising" may be the most widely read thing I've ever done, and I've found it cited in MLA papers, PhD dissertations, and more. I've seen an anthology in which the story appears with footnotes, identifying T.S. Eliot here and Thomas Mann there, and my piece available for purchase on websites like E-Notes (not that I've seen a penny). By now, what does it matter that when I first worked up my ideas no one else had looked into Barthelme's pattern of Modernist allusion? Wasn't that pattern his doing, anyway? I know I got my first hint of what was going on when I studied with the author, as an undergrad.

Really, once more, the best response may be a shrug. I'm gratified to have added to the pleasures of the text, but I remember what Paul Valéry said about myth and story being "the soul of our actions and loves." When it comes to a vibrant artifact like "Indian Uprising," mine is anything but the final word. In *Hiding Man*, Tracy Daugherty's excellent critical biography of Barthelme, he gets my contribution right. He places it with others, then makes a canny suggestion of his own.

While the notion of contributor sits more comfortably with me than that of proctor or Super-Critic, I don't mean to pussyfoot around, either. My argument's wholehearted, as is my dedication, a salute those that have sustained whatever I've added to discourse. I've been lucky indeed to get an editor as savvy and attentive as Kit Rachlis, first at *Boston Phoenix* and then at *LA Weekly*; lucky again that Willard Speigelman, at *Southwest Review*, so often made space for me when I needed to go longer; lucky a third time to have Joe Amato in my corner, starting as editor of *American Book Review* and going from there.

Naturally I've got other angels. They'll understand that this isn't the occasion for drawing up a list, no more than for settling old scores. I'm working here. Any adjustment I made in my originals can be tracked down, if anyone's interested, and besides, that isn't the metamorphosis that matters. The one that matters occurs when we read more challenging pieces of fiction and "transhumanize." That's the change I hope to encourage with *Sea-God's Herb*, not only when others consider the texts and artifacts I do, but also in the future, when they encounter some as-yet-unimagined manifestation for this same inconfinable spirit.

John Domini
Des Moines, 2013

AGAINST THE "IMPOSSIBLE TO EXPLAIN:" THE POSTMODERN NOVEL & SOCIETY

Here's the problem. You decide to try some reading outside the ordinary, a novel that doesn't have the usual earmarks, and it proves interesting, satisfying, but you don't entirely understand why, and when you look for help, an illuminating review or something, you can't find any.

You've picked up Carole Maso's *Aureole*, for instance. This edition is dated 2003, from City Lights Books—didn't they do *Howl*? Indeed, the first riffle through the pages reveals a poet's typography, lots of white space. Is that *paragraphing*? Still, you take a flyer, and the upshot is pretty damn good. The book reads first like poetry, then like stories, then like a novel. The front matter lists no previous publications, and while between each titled story or chapter you find no obvious connections, hardly any names for instance, you do pick up recurring phrases, developing histories, consistent obsessions. Sexual obsessions primarily, and primarily lesbian, though the encounters have too strange an angle of view, and too many ellipses, to qualify as porn. The reading experience isn't difficult, exactly, not with so much flesh and heat, but you swing from one startling phrase to another:

> reminded by the fragile or the streamers, persimmons on a night table—or pomegranates, as I look up from the sumptuous beautiful body of another woman, what am I remembering?

Wanting you in this life—and all lives.

Without veils, where we might rest.
Where the plum tree?

The burning barge? And the swollen river calling?

Throughout, the emphasis isn't on sumptuous bodies so much
as on ruptured expectation, busted logic. A priest rebuffs a girl's infatuation but ends up a craven voyeur; two women tumble into sadomasochism, somehow needing the corruption. The cosmopolitan
settings, Paris and Provincetown and somewhere along the Ganges,
create a hothouse environment, but no one's wallowing in privilege.
Rather, the tensions recall Henry James, on tenterhooks between
sophistication and yearning. In later sections, featuring an older
protagonist, even her lovemaking suggests her passions' evanescence
(reminded by the fragile or the streamers...). By the time you finish
the centerpiece, "Anju Flying Streamers After," an elegy that's also
a resurrection, *Aureole* looks like poetry after all. It participates in a
tradition going back to Sappho (who turns up, naturally); it both celebrates Aphrodite's rare visits in the flesh and mourns her departures.
The aureole brightens, but also drains.

Pretty damn good, in short. The book's power resides, as well, in
all the questions it raises—like, how can she get away with this? How
can so unlikely a narrative hurt and tickle and signify? Yet when you
go looking for answers, some clarifying criticism, you discover the
truth of a quip I heard from Roseanne Quinn, a Maso aficionado
at Santa Clara U. In a conference paper (now published), Quinn
grumbled that the only decent explication of Maso's work comes
from Maso herself. This when the author has eight books by now,
including *The Art Lover*, reissued as a "New Directions Classic" in
2006. But for a number of her titles, it's difficult to find commentary
other than a squib in *Publishers Weekly*. Worse, regarding *Aureole*, the

Kirkus notice manages to get several details wrong in the space of 250 words.

That's the problem, the impetus for this essay. In the millennial US, for those who venture an unconventional approach to book-length fiction, criticism just hasn't been doing its job. In *Aureole*'s case, a fascinating alternative remains largely ignored. The lone fuller appreciation I found was written long after publication and for a small-circulation quarterly, *The Review of Contemporary Fiction*. What's more, what's worse, can be the sort of notice a novel receives, if it violates the norms. Another book I'm going to look at, Steve Erickson's far-from-ordinary *Zeroville* (2007), enjoyed high-profile encomiums; the *Times Book Review* hailed it as the author's "best." Yet the *Times* reviewer, Liesl Schillinger, went on to say: "It's simply impossible to explain the intent and direction of this…novel." Oh really? And this from someone described as "a regular contributor" to the *Review*? A better brief example of the problem with contemporary criticism would be hard to find.

The applause that greeted *Zeroville*, in any case, should be taken as an aberration. Far more commonly, when American book-length fiction strays from straightforward realism and structure—Erickson strays from both—and when one of the major review outlets gives it attention, the write-up will be vicious. It'll look as if the author has wandered into Sniper's Alley. Over half a century ago, Robbe-Grillet's *For a New Novel* traced recent developments in the art form, but those trying for similar innovation on this side of the Atlantic have come under repeated attack, in our most prominent critical forums. "Postmodern" sits comfortably with other media, whether a Danger Mouse mashup or *Angels in America*. But when it comes to novels, the term's a dirty word, even for a lot of novelists. John Gardner would be the most obstreperous; his call to the Old School barricades was *On Moral Fiction* (1978), a book that gets far wider play, these days, than his fiction.

Champions of imaginative freedom exist, of course. But vituperation toward all that's Po-Mo has been pretty much the rule across the most prestigious organs of our literary culture. I'm not the only one to have noticed; recently Zadie Smith too puzzled over the pervading ill will, and I'll get to what she had to say. But first, consider the history.

For starters, as recently as Robbe-Grillet's best years (*The Voyeur* appeared in '55), most US readers wore blinders. There was censorship, I mean; only in '58 were stores allowed to carry *Lady Chatterly's Lover*, in spite of Lawrence's implication that adultery could be good for you. In the '60s—the *'60s*, man—the homegrown novels *Naked Lunch* and *Last Exit to Brooklyn* went up before similar tribunals. It helps to keep this Puritanical background in mind. For not long after Burroughs saw print, Barthelme turned up in the *New Yorker*, and Barth brought out his essay "The Literature of Exhaustion," a brilliant piece but hardly combative, more established figures began to lash back. Gore Vidal, inverately combative, tore into Barth, Barthelme, and others in "American Plastic," a '76 essay that set the pattern for Gardner's screed two years later. Indeed, *On Moral Fiction* feels flimsy by comparison, little beyond its media-savvy title. In retrospect it's the least of these complaints.

The best would be Tom Wolfe's from ten years further along, "Stalking the Billion-Footed Beast." While ill-informed about the novelty it seeks to repress (calling Robert Coover a "Minimalist," for example), "Beast" nonetheless makes a rip-snorting defense of the social novel and the realistic tradition. It's a worthy polemic, especially good on the value of research.

Now, when Wolfe himself writes novels, he lacks the impact of a younger author who's staked the same claim. Richard Price has brought off urban portraits-in-the-round, in *Clockers* especially, with a depth you won't find in *A Bonfire of the Vanities*. So has Richard Powers, another novelist of the generation that followed Wolfe's.

Granted, there are sizeable differences between older writers and younger; Wolfe wouldn't be caught dead in Kearney, Nebraska, the locale of *The Echo Maker*. So too, distinctions must be drawn between the Baby Boomers. But the accomplishments of both belong in the social-realist tradition of novelists from Fielding to Steinbeck, and bear out its continuing vitality. *The Billion-Footed Beast* hardly lacks for vigorous young caretakers. Yet back on Sniper's Alley, there's been no letup.

The angriest fusillades came in '02, with Dale Peck tearing into Rick Moody in *The New Republic* and Jonathan Franzen attacking William Gaddis in *The New Yorker*. These harangues, though similar to Wolfe's, don't hold up so well. Franzen's core value was the slippery business of "reading pleasure," and once he got beyond Gaddis, he whaled away indiscriminately. B.R. Myers proved likewise blind to distinctions when he made the *Atlantic* cover with his "Reader's Manifesto," lumping Don DeLillo with Toni Morrison. To Meyers, both raised the same threat to storytelling. What's actually the same, if you step back for a long view, is the thesis behind the various broadsides. A thesis insistent as a chant: Po-Mo bad, meat-and-potatoes good.

Exceptions can always be found. In '79, *The Atlantic* made room for Barth's followup, "The Literature of Replenishment," and in '05 *Harpers* ran Ben Marcus's witty response to Franzen. Still, mainstream criticism held to its oppressive pattern, one that also puzzled Zadie Smith. In the fall of '08, in the *New York Review of Books*, Smith reviewed, at length, two very different novels. She looked at Joseph O'Neill's *Netherland*, the sort of social novel Wolfe would applaud, and at Tom McCarthy's *Remainder*, which eschews norms of realism and representation. Recognizing that the two fictions were "antipodal," Smith wondered at how "American metafiction" had come to be branded a "failure," by "our most famous public critics." She noted that David Foster Wallace's name had now been added to those of the usual suspects.

Her assessment, happily, rated the strange *Remainder* more highly than the familiar *Netherland*. Still, she left begging two questions raised by her considering these novels together.

Question #1 addresses the criticism, the entrenched response I've just summarized. This response would have it that the Literature of Exhaustion and Replenishment has long since proven something like a motel room in a horror movie. Once an author checks in, he's never seen again. Yet if that's the case, if in fact it's *been* the case for two generations now of novel-writing Americans, why go on posting the skull and crossbones? Why, when anyone can see the social novel remains durable? The answer's complicated, it entails more than books and their intrinsic qualities, but certain causes and effects need to be pointed out before getting into the more literary business of Question #2. That would be: What's at stake in the lengthy prose narrative that's *not* about a few recognizable men and women in a well-researched time and place? When we turn, as writer or as reader, to more esoteric fiction, are we entirely rejecting the qualities that distinguish, say, *The Electric Kool-Aid Acid Test*? Does the meta-fictional, the postmodern, the experimental—"Oh I wish there were some words in the world," cries Barthelme's Snow White, "that were not the words I always hear!"—does that sort of novel really have so tenuous a relationship to the rough and tumble in which we live?

The problem, it bears repeating, lies with the criticism and not the novel. Serious fiction has faced scary new difficulties over these past decades, difficulties I'll try to appraise, but the core process for its practitioners hasn't changed. Nor has it gotten any easier; a developing creative spirit still learns by trial and error, which includes trying out all kinds of older books—including those outside the learner's sensibility. An apprentice novelist may settle eventually into the mainstream, but on the way there, at some point, he'll call for madder music and stronger wine. Thus younger proponents of social realism have no problem, unlike Old Man Wolfe, expressing regard for members of the other camp. Richard Price told me he loved Gilbert Sorrentino's *Steelwork*, a collage without a narrative; half-joking, he said he had sections memorized. Richard Powers claimed that, when he was having trouble with *In Time of Our Singing*, few things helped so much as a fan letter, out of the blue, from John Barth.

By now Price and Powers represent the parents, in mid-career. Now it's their children who must embrace or reject wilder permutations of book-length fiction. Meantime, the business of publishing offers little help, in a terrific confusion, at once atrophied and lush. The tangle reaches to issues outside novels themselves, as I say, and so I'll trace just three of its roots.

Begin with commercial publishing, shrinking and fickle. As far back as 1980, Thomas Whiteside's *The Blockbuster Complex* chillingly detailed the slide among the larger literary agencies and publishing houses toward the lowest common denominator. In the thirty years since, things have only gotten worse. A "gentlemen's business" like Harper & Row became a conglomerate like HarperCollins, a media octopus concerned less with good books than with predictable quarterly profits. Also changes in tax law, under Reagan, swept away the publishers' backlist. For them, for decades, the backlist had been a cash cow; for novelists, it was perhaps their best opportunity to develop an audience. Now if their work felt like too much of a challenge, if it appeared unlikely to turn a quick buck, more than likely it had no place in Manhattan.

So elsewhere in the country, countermeasures got underway. The US has enjoyed a boom in smaller publishing, the second significant development a critic needs to understand. University presses and such had long been essential for American poets, but over the last thirty years or so they've mattered more than ever for novelists. A heartening number of such ventures have sustained a continuing contribution, from Coffee House in Minneapolis to FC2, shuttling from Tallahasee to Houston to Tuscaloosa. Success for a novel with one of these isn't measured by sales, so much, since most are not-for-profit (an exception would be the excellent Unbridled Books, out of Columbia, MO). But on the other hand, state or federal subsidies leave next to nothing for advertising. There can be distribution problems as well. If a reviewer's failed to do his homework, the proliferation of small-press titles will resemble a bewildering stretch of urban sprawl: cul-de-sacs of paperbacks. The clutter of a bookfair can leave a person overwhelmed.

Still, doesn't this new dilemma only raise another old challenge? Hasn't it always been a critic's job to wander the stalls and pick out what's deserving? As for the artist, their assignment hasn't changed either—call it creating something that can't be overlooked. But every artist also knows of worthy efforts that went overlooked, for most of a lifetime at least, in the pandemonium of the American marketplace. Two signal cases in fiction would be stylish Dawn Powell and scummy Charles Bukowski.

Putting these elements together, the collapse of former guideposts and the persistence of non-negotiable demands, the trouble with contemporary criticism can be understood as largely a problem of degree. *Too many* critics follow the money, uncritically; that's not my whole argument, but that's a lot of it. *Not enough* critics will cock an ear to any noise beyond New York, or take time to sample twenty pages of a novel that comes out of nowhere and demands extra effort. *Too often* reviews fall back on clichés about "characters that live and breathe" and "packed with Dixie [or Down East, or DUMBO] detail." It's as if everyone selected from the same menu in the software—a program that functions best with the social-novel template. But if the interface of individual and society takes an unfamiliar form, it robs *far too many* reviewers of their apparatus for passing judgment.

In this imperfect world, for novelists who work in an alternative mode and appear on an alternative press (the two sets overlap almost perfectly), a primary resource has become the internet. The web offers a solution when the career's gone DIY. The situation recalls the music scene of the '60s, when innovators from Dylan to Zappa could get around the musical establishment by manipulating new systems. In the present decade, literary websites have made a contribution to rival that of the small presses. Case in point, the Emerging Writers Network. Yet the growing importance of the internet, not just for publicity but as an actual venue for publication, also presents the third stumbling block to the appreciation of fiction other than social realism.

Conventional wisdom has it that the Web has become one of the worst distractions from the novel. Old print, runs the argument, can't keep up with our new toys. What's more, as computers grow smaller and speedier, a book presents that much more cumbersome a technology. Well—true. The argument's irrefutable, as far as it goes. Yet an informed critic should also understand the way in which Internet culture remains irrelevant to the evolution of narrative. Novels no longer claim the cutting edge in entertainment, granted, but their hundred-year run was over a hundred years ago. Besides that, their grip on the reading public was always less than unbreakable. Even the fiercely intelligent Elizabeth Bennett insists to Mr. Darcy, "I cannot talk of books in a ballroom; my head is always full of something else." That was in 1813, and these characters too contended with threats to their reading time. At least one of those threats, anxiety over their place in the class system, no longer exists. These days, there's no question that some potential readers will linger longer over a Facebook status than a good story. But, overall, literacy keeps increasing, and among those numbers there will be those for whom Austen seems harder to comprehend than, say, Percival Everett's *Glyph*.

Now, the pleasures to be had in *Glyph*, indeed in the whole lengthening shelf of American metafiction, are dwarfed by the issues around electronic communication. Most of those lie far beyond the scope of my essay. But that bookshelf, the howls of warning it raises and the way it keeps growing regardless, suggests that the web poses a threat other than simple distraction.

D.H. Lawrence argued that the novel was unmatched as a medium for "subtle interrelationships," but eighty years after *Lady Chatterly*, what offers more subtlety and interrelatedness than the World Wide Web? And if the new novel is Facebook, or World of Warcraft, then aren't novels that break from social realism even further behind the curve? The internet, in other words, makes the avant-garde seem retrograde. It suggests that the real artists are over in computer-based hypertext. The foremost champion of electronic narrative is Robert Coover, also of course a first-wave figure in American postmodernism. Coover's hypertext course at Brown, his essays in the *Times* and elsewhere, provide the most reliable crystal ball we have for the future of story. As he points out in an '09 *American Book Review*, this form of expression has already gone "from oral tale-tellers to clay tablets to scroll to codex to printed book." The metamorphoses (to cite a lovely antique) won't end there, not so long as the species has a need for myth and fable. Then why would any young imagination with a penchant for going outside the lines not explore a computer-based variant?

One answer is that they already are. Most postmodern novels render experience in ways not unlike a good session on the web. An example would be the plotting by association, by juxtaposition, in *Aureole*. Any longer story set in the present will feature the internet somehow, but books that push the envelope actually transpose the sensations into print (I say something about this later, with reference to two sample novels). Still, those sensations reach the reader via an older technology, and I say this with no disrespect for the newer one. I much admire Shelley Jackson's hypertext *Patchwork Girl*. But Jackson herself went on to a story in prose, between covers, with *Half Life*. Nor has Coover ever abandoned putting pages between covers. For him, as for most fiction writers, that challenge remains enough for one lifetime. The geek skills required for hypertext, not to mention the profound adjustment required by its open-ended narrative, still keep the form at arm's length.

Technological advances always put a fresh spin on the arts, and roughly a century ago, faced with the possibilities of motion pictures, Jean Cocteau made a useful remark. "Film will become an art," he claimed, "only when its materials are as inexpensive as pencil and paper." Since then, that point has very nearly been reached, thanks to innovators from Godard to the founders of YouTube. The more we live via thinking machines, the more our stories will take on elements of the experience. The process already has a number of benchmarks, in novel form—and I'm not even talking about graphic novels. Many an American experiment in long fiction includes visuals, but they aren't comic books any more than they're software. *Barry Weem, Boy Genius* strikes me as terrific, as do several other graphic novels, but it uses fundamentally different tools.

Meanwhile, over in print, the artists keep notching benchmarks. Still relying on subtle interrelations between language and pattern, novelists have matched the bewildering changes thrown at us with surprises of their own; their artifacts expand perception and suggest fresh forms of order. Such as? Specific cases? I'll get into three, next, but each underscores how alternative storytelling is hardly withering in the shadow of computer culture. Rather the two media share the light, affording greater mutual illumination. It's enough to make you think the postmodern novel has a social function.

Naturally, other pressures shape contemporary American fiction. For one, there's the ferocious growth of creative writing programs. But surely the CW curriculum has had its greatest impact economically, as a means of earning a living. So far as the art and its development is concerned, the academic arena presents the usual moil of good and bad, along with the same major actors: the dwindling bigs, the mushrooming smalls, and the roar of the communications revolution. It tells you something when one of "our most famous public critics" takes on creative writing and sounds as truculent as if the subject's metafiction. Louis Menand's "Critic At Large" piece in the *New Yorker*, summer '09, railed against the Associated Writing Programs in pretty much the same terms Gore Vidal used almost forty years ago.

In either case, the attack's a frightened one at bottom. Frightened and lazy—that's the baseline motive, behind the critics' continued attacks. From Vidal to whoever's next, they keep raising alarums because the barbarian hordes keep coming. They just keep coming, and for an armchair general, it's too much work to figure out their mall-rat tactics, their kitchen weaponry.

But that's my job now, my Question #2: how the Vandals do it. Remember, also, that I come in peace; my analysis intends to reveal how John Barth and Tom Wolfe might shake hands. Thus my own generation of novelists provides the most useful examples. If I got out William Gass again, the text-bending Gass of *Willie Masters' Lonesome Wife*, I'd leave the postmodern stuck in the past. Better to look at those who began when *Willie Masters'* had already changed the landscape, and who have since brought off alternative structures of their own, and whose best work may yet lie ahead. That's the career juncture at which Price and Powers stand, after all. If they exemplify the continuing vitality of the social novel, my representatives of another aesthetic should be more or less coeval. So I'll return to Maso's *Aureole*, then look at *Michael Martone by Michael Martone*—by Michael Martone, and published in '05—then at Erickson's *Zeroville*.

The sequence has nothing to do with ultimate worth. Each of the novels strikes me as inspired and finely wrought, and each in a different way, providing different illumination. But it won't serve my purpose to award stars and half-stars. Rather I should begin with a couple of points all three have in common. First, while the authors have had some success with commercial houses (Erickson especially), their novels are now on smaller presses. *Zeroville* appeared with the new Europa Editions, an offshoot of an Italian publisher, and *Mar-*

tone/Martone is on Fiction Collective 2. Second, while each book has an idiosyncratic take on "story," even a browser will see that they're socially relevant in their subject matter.

Maso's characters may move in a privileged milieu, but as I say, her stolen moments of ecstasy prove eventually as fragile as the golden bowl of Henry James. Erotic strategies, as in James, must adjust and adjust again for the lovers' relative status and for local mores, now in New England and now New Delhi. In *Martone/Martone*, every "chapter" (as in *Aureole*, the term doesn't quite fit) begins in Ft. Wayne, Indiana, and nearly all address the quotidian realities of Middle America in the late twentieth century. Martone's so savvy about heartland economics, Sinclair Lewis could learn a thing or two. As for *Zeroville*, it turns a kaleidoscope on a kaleidoscope and yet seems the most real-world of the three. Erickson's is a tale of the movie industry, told in straightforward chronology, and he doesn't neglect to expose Hollywood enslavement to money and status.

Of course, a browser can also see that *Zeroville*'s author is no plodding realist, no more than the other two. But my thumbnails play up the books' social materials for good reason. One measure for how criticism has lost its bearings, when it comes to the New and Newer Novel, is how often reviews ignore just such basic considerations. You see it *too often*. A reviewer will harp on formal issues, but leave out matters like where the money comes from. More galling still, the critical establishment isn't so blind when the experiment comes from abroad. John Updike could be a conscientious reader, and he swiftly grasped how contemporary Italian compromises were central to Italo Calvino. But when Americans tried something similar, Updike's response was silence. He did deign to look at DeLillo's *Players*, but couldn't locate its reality, and sniffed at the "spindly motivation." Reviewers give foreign writers credit they won't give those from the States; the latest example would be Roberto Bolano.

————

Yet though Carole Maso intends a drama of private discovery, in *Aureole*, the book's by no means indifferent to the larger world. As stories cohere into narrative, the catalytic element is what the cosmopolite protagonists might call the *Leibe-Bildungs-roman*: the love-formation-novel. In the opener, girls meet during a student year abroad: "They're so young they haven't become anything." Subsequently, the encounters enact their becoming, a growth that leaves behind occasional victims like the tormented priest. The extremes of lovemaking, the S&M, amount to a necessary risk, a testing of passion's limits. Also the coming of age doesn't neglect the ordinary. Problems of family and economics cast their shadow over the hothouse, the crucial example coming just after the great "Anjou Flying Streamers After."

At that point, where a conventional novel would have its climax, there's an untitled two-page insert in long paragraphs and italics—a unique format for this book, as is the perspective, first-person for once. Here a college-age Punjabi girl relates how she changed her life, getting free of her oppressive birthplace, after she met a white woman walking along the Ganges. The seminal meeting at water's edge reprises others in *Aureole*, and it seems to result in another transgressive affair. But if so (the passage makes no explicit reference), the sex comes much later, in America, by which time the whole point of the exile's brief tale is her desire to return. In our leaving is our return, just as, when this girl had her long-ago vision, the light hair of the wandering "Princess" made her seem at first very old.

Martone's *Martone*, as you might imagine, comes across as considerably more lighthearted. The book pretends to be a collection of third-person "Contributor's Notes," such as appear in literary journals (many did, according to the actual Acknowledgements). Each begins with the same humble birth notice—"in Fort Wayne, Indiana"—and thereafter most stray far from what you'd call real life. A minute on Google will turn up the facts (Martone studied under Barth, at Johns Hopkins), but one stand-in has a career in earthmoving, and another runs through multiple wives before returning to his "ancestral home" outside Naples. Most Notes unspool over two or three pages, the prose unbroken, the detail well beyond publishing credentials: "At the age of nineteen years, four months, three days, twenty-two minutes, and an indeterminate number of seconds old he first experienced sexual intercourse."

Three entries do have different titles, and one of these, like Maso's odd-woman-out, comes at more or less the climax point (the thirty-fifth entry out of forty-four). But the variants wink at differences. Titled "Vita" or "About the Author," they have the same substance as the others. Each has a loose coherence, clustering related details and incidents. The Contributor moves via associative leaps, as if via hyperlink. Unlike web pages, though, nearly all those in *Martone/Martone* move from youth to maturity.

So the Note that features his deflowering also speaks of a time when, as a child, he surprised his mother and father in the act. That isn't the narrator's own recollection, however. Martone's mother tells him, after she herself has stumbled upon her nineteen-year-old and a girlfriend. Mama savors the irony, too. She's by no means springing the kind of terrible secret that, in the common run of novel, would change everything. What changes everything, perhaps invests it with meaning, is the passage of time. The mother's jovial recollection first carries the action of the Note closer to the present and then prompts its conclusion, when the adult writer visits his mother's corpse, in the funeral home. There he catches an employee in a different form of *flagrante delicto*, "furtively applying rouge to his mother's bloodless cheek."

The episode's final irony delivers the chill from which no irony can distract us. A substantial majority of the Notes work toward the same, the mother's death. Her bony finger taps even the romantic picaresque that winds up in Italy, the last sentence of which enters a dead city, an "Etruscan dig." Yet the pervading affect remains anything but gloomy. Nor could it be further from Maso's, hot and bothered. *Martone/Martone* prefers to play Hamlet with Yorick's skull. The novel concludes in a surrogate graveyard, the Contributors page of a magazine gone defunct, and there too sustains the tension between Joker and Reaper. The names and credits seem "like a party," but a number are already lost to oblivion, "a fossil record of some life's life-story."

The syntactical stumble, the redundancy, eases the scare of "fossil record." Similar corruptions riddle the depictions of Fort Wayne and its arcana (Martone has always turned such stuff to use, fond yet clever, starting with *Alive and Dead in Indiana*, in '84). The Note concerning a local cartoon show gets off poker-faced jokes but ends in "a kind of immortality," the TV station's archives. Not that the Contributor himself can enter this Paradise—where he lives, it's "impossible to see."

An identifying trait for postmodern art would be its subversion of "metanarrative." That last word applies to the great majority of novels since Samuel Richardson, in 1758, launched the form's halcyon moment with *Pamela*. That book's metanarrative makes Pamela correspondent with her status group, her times; if she can keep her virtue then so may her society. Tom Wolfe's metanarrative, his Beast, would be much the same—but he never questioned his central assumption. He never doubts that a novelist can know just what his life and times are up to. Martone's *Martone*, in large part because it's loaded with Americana, raises the question. It's a clown wagon, and every painted face against the windows presents an unsettling doppleganger. Which history can we trust? If *Aureole* harks back to an audience with the Goddess, *Martone/Martone* recalls meeting the Sphinx.

Zeroville's defining mythic encounter would be with Teiresias, the blind hermaphrodite who tells a person's destiny. In these rough terms, the search for self-knowledge, the novel easily fits my defense of younger American postmodernists. But Steve Erickson sets up his own allusive framework. He reaches back to Genesis at its most intimate and terrifying: the sacrifice of Isaac.

The allegory received no mention in the *Times* review, nor in all but one of the others I read. Yet it's everywhere, even in a horror-show flashback to the childhood of *Zeroville's* protagonists. Still, this novel dwells no more on family scars than *Martone/Martone*. Mostly it hurtles forward, following the improbable Hollywood career of its central naïf/savant, the seminary dropout Ike. Ike arrives so clueless about anything beyond his Bible training and a few classic movies that he falls briefly under suspicion for the Manson murders. Over the next decade-plus, however, with the luck of the innocent and the focus of the insane, he rises and falls as Vikar, the only industry player to ride the bus and avoid talking on the phone—as well as the legend behind a one-hit-wonder called *Your Pale Blue Eyes*. It's a classic plot parabola, from Best Boy to *Auteur* to Zero, but it's never bristled with so many references to Abraham and Isaac. Not for nothing does the protagonist prefer to get away from his full given name. He sees the Genesis episode especially in the movies, and nine times out of ten, no angel appears to spare the child. To Vikar, *Chinatown* reveals that "God has seeped into Los Angeles…and found His instruments there by which to sacrifice his children."

Such strong material seems to suggest that *Zeroville* doesn't belong in this essay. The last third of the book actually features a damsel in distress, a vulnerable teenager, and delivers no surrogate climax. As you read, you're never required to fill in wide gaps, as in *Aureole*, or to return repeatedly to Square One, as in *Martone/Martone*. Erickson, in fact, has distanced himself from novels like those. "I hear the word 'experiment,'" he told a *Bookslut* interviewer, "and I reach for my revolver." Also, as I've noted, *Zeroville* hardly went unnoticed. I applaud, too, Christopher Sorrentino's thoughtful reading for the *L.A. Times*. Still, when your most powerful friend, your New York friend, describes the work as "simply impossible to explain"—who needs enemies? That is, what frustrates me goes beyond problems of degree (*too many, too often…*) to what smacks of dumbing-down, refusing to grapple with how an author freshens his or her form and takes the experience to new vulnerability. Note, in sorry particular, how dismissively Schillinger characterizes Erickson's oeuvre: "likes to mess with readers' heads."

Let me say, more usefully, that I'd pick *Tours of the Black Clock* (1989) as the greatest of his nine previous efforts, and that this messing with heads takes a specific form, that of a familiar world turned perverse. LA often serves as the turf, but whatever the setting, it's either blasted by apocalypse, off in an alternative history, or both. The strangeness owes something to a rhetoric that indulges the lurid coloration of Raymond Chandler and the noir tradition. Erickson's poetics go further, though, veering into snarls and psalms. Till this novel, plots tended to veer as well, highly discontinuous. *Tours* for instance leapt from Hitler's screening room to tundra swarming with silver buffalo. Certainly the novel earned its place on a *L.A. Times* list, published in '09, of "61 Essential Postmodern Reads." So *Zeroville* deserves to be understood not just as some vague "best," but—while keeping a weather eye on the author's firearm—as an experiment.

Erickson perverts more than the setting, in his latest. Its title derives from *Alphaville* (the text itself supplies the citation, another device straight out of the postmodern playbook), and just as Goddard warped the detective story, so *Zeroville* plays havoc with two respected modes of narrative. He tweaks the historical drama and the parabola of rise and fall.

The history here is a Golden Age for cineastes like Erickson, a movie reviewer since Vikar's era. It's the '70s, Hollywood's celebrated "Decade Under the Influence," and *Zeroville* not only awards Scorsese a flitting cameo, but also includes just about all the period's movers and shakers. You could put the research up against anything in Tom Wolfe. One detail that helps establish Vikar's character comes when he notices a reticent young actor studying him intently, then thinks ahead to this man's performance, a few years later, "in a movie about a cab driver who goes crazy." The moment zips by so fast, and massages such a worn cultural touchstone, that you don't notice its disjunctive nature. Erickson jumps out of his sequential chronology while also knitting together imaginative worlds (*Taxi Driver* and the novel in hand) and real (DeNiro in the flesh, you in the theater). Crucial to this trick is the point of view, which till the book's last pages is in close third person. Close, that is, to a more sympathetic Travis Bickle. Early on, Vikar is described as "*cinéautistic*," and the coinage works.

The protagonist's psychology, barely functional, drew a lot of comment in the reviews. None, however, noted that similar issues afflicted nearly everyone in *Zeroville*. Nearly everyone's an obsessive, so that the feel is stylized; the repetitions, the movie chatter, actually contribute to the pleasure and momentum of the reading. More than that, with so many one or two-note characters, and with the settings of some later episodes quite out of this world, the two people of genuine depth can't help but insinuate something like, yes, a social value. These are two women: first Vikar's mentor in the editing booth, sick and old and drinking more each time we see her, and later the teenager at risk, a punk girl with family issues and perspicuity. Vikar has a personal agenda in taking the girl under his broken wing; his own obsessions included her mother, also broken. More than that, the struggle of both the actual parent and the stand-in dramatizes how these halcyon '70s could be anything but for women. Says one of the more reliable fanatics in Vikar's circle: "It's really not a business for broads."

And it's really not a business of feminist revisionism, this novel. It's not that simple sort of history, either—though the feminist sympathies deserve to be noted, and so far as I can see they weren't. Nevertheless, the protagonist's furious single-mindedness keeps things on the verge of hallucination. With its persistent links to dream, to the fabulous, *Zeroville* both has the social novel and devours it too.

Related is a structural gambit that might've been cooked up at a meeting of the arch-experimental Oulipo. I mean the numbering of the chapters. These can be very brief (one is a blank) but more often run a few pages, and Erickson counts first forward to chapter 227, then backward to 0 again. The turning point falls midway along the overall length, too, and calls attention to itself in the voice of the same unnamed Author who engineers the skillful flashes forward and back. Now, if the watershed number has some special significance in filmmaking, it eludes me. But I do think of the loser's bookkeeping in Allen Ginsberg's "America"— "America two dollars and 27 cents January 17, 1956"—because I do see how the reset occurs at the peak of Vikar's success. He's just been handed the *Blue Eyes* project, and the film's to be featured at Cannes. What follows is the downside, inevitable it would seem, given his tenuous connection to the practical. But in *Zeroville*, the fall is complicated, first by a rise in nobility. Vikar sacrifices himself to save the girl. Moral growth like that allies the novel to a classic tradition, but its latter half also makes an audacious move into the surreal.

As chapters return to zero, cinema history enters the Collective Unconscious. Our hero says as much, in his way: "All stories are in the time and all time is in the stories." This statement recurs in various forms, and may illuminate the chapter structure, in which movement forward is also movement back. More than that, it emphasizes how Erickson's at play with his research, as befits details that anyone can find, these days, on IMDB.com. His key cut-and-paste concerns the lost master print of *La passion de Jeanne d'Arc* (1928) and his own story's darkest obsession. St. Joan after all was a child-woman sacrificed to a God of murder, and so Dreyer's original conceals a destructive latter-day archetype; Vikar must track down the print and snip the threat from the loop. The effort leaves him drinking with the Angel of Death, its embodiment another highly playful touch. Only by such ambivalent means, and only in an alternative theater or Testament, do the final edits of our *cinéautistic* restore the balance between patriarch and child, man and woman.

This ambivalence also suggests how the shared dream we call the movies may have come to the end. *Zeroville*'s tokens for history include many graves and ghosts, the oldest being D.W. Griffith, another patriarch. These days, Griffith's narrative machinery no longer rules the *zeitgeist*. Even Vikar notices how LA theaters have lost their grandeur, and no doubt the places he visited have since been razed. No movie is so big, these days, that it won't be cut to fit far smaller screens.

So the '07 novel is an act of reparation, a giving back to the vanished world that made the work possible. Outstanding past examples in the artform include, well, where would you start? *À la recherche du temps perdu?* An impossible comparison for any novel, especially now, a hundred years after its hundred years as Top Story. Still, both *Aureole* and *Martone/Martone* are, like *Zeroville*, firmly grounded in the society that made them: Maso the demimonde and Martone just the opposite. That the authors' view of the old home includes an acute awareness of its faults seems to me of a piece with their effort to invent original shapes and perspectives for its staging.

Hand-me-down shapes, cookie-cutter, would degrade and misrepresent the passions they seek to present. The point would seem almost to go without saying, except when John Barth said it in "The Literature of Exhaustion," he set off bellows of objection that still echo round the yards. Maybe I'd do better to cite Milan Kundera, considering how the best-known American critics prefer their postmodernists to live abroad. "Kitsch," according to *The Unbearable Lightness of Being*, "is the stopover between being and oblivion." The line, fittingly, was composed in exile from a regime that no longer exists—which ruled a country that no longer exists. What I've sketched here, then, might be considered a map to the new Republic of the Long Narrative. A map with lacunae, to be sure. In my eagerness to take down more prominent reviewers and their forums, I've left out the smaller places that make a point of keeping up with innovations. The exemplary *HTMLGiant*, for instance. Also the examples I chose for a more inclusive reading, one that marries social responsibility and high-wire artistry, are all relatively upbeat. All three novels reach a kind of Heaven, and two deliver plenty of laughs.

Still, what Maso, Martone, and Erickson offer falls well short of unalloyed happiness. Then too, since the works stand so far apart from each other, the conclusions I've drawn from them would apply to gloomier visions. Brian Evenson presents a salient case, full of blood and trouble. But I'm not going to draw up a list of other worthy names, either. That wouldn't serve my purpose, a column of names stark as a girder. I'm arguing for the opposite, fiction elastic and fertile as Schopenhauer's notion of self, explaining itself to itself—and in the process explaining itself to another.

—*Quarterly Conversation*, 2010

EARLY TIDE

THE HUMANIST MODEL:
WILLIAM GASS & THE WORLD WITHIN THE WORLD

Among Humanists of the Renaissance, the first principle of literary scholarship was absolute fidelity to the grammar and syntax of classical models. Their argument, first outlined by Petrarch, ran that a sentence of Cicero did not exist merely as a vessel for fourteenth or fifteenth-century theories, but rather as a unique and precious chamber, sealed at one end by etymology and at the other by rhetorical convention, in which the spirit of antiquity remained alive.

The criticism of William Gass is a throwback to these standards of scholarship, now generally abandoned; it proceeds only by slow degrees toward revelation, and only through strict adherence to the grammar, structure, and vocabulary of the original. The very title of this, Gass's second and best collection of essays, both slows the tongue with its stately assonance and raises succinctly this issue of the preservation possible in language. Gass the critic presses his ear flat against every sentence he studies, trying to catch the precise intonation the author breathed into it, believing, as he says here, that "The sounds of any sentence are its bones." And believing further, as he put it in a recent *Paris Review* interview, that "talk is essential to the human spirit. It *is* the human spirit."

Therefore, although style is the subject Gass always comes to eventually, his procedure varies considerably from essay to essay. For he is never satisfied with mere gloss; that would be tantamount to shushing whatever voice is trying to emerge from the sentences under discussion. No, Gass must always *demonstrate*. In "Carrots, Noses, Snow, Rose, Roses," the penultimate essay and the clearest definition we have to date of his aesthetic principles, Gass explains his motives when doing criticism:

> ...prose, in essays such as this, experiments with the interplay of genres, attempting both demonstration and display...

So in the article on Freud (which incidentally gives evidence of copious scientific reading) there are lettered formulas demonstrating the genius of Freud's all-encompassing "language model" which imagines that...patterns of behavior are sentences," such as:

WW(I-+P—>Ob, Or)

Similarly, in a different but equally convincing demonstration, Gass momentarily adopts Henry Miller's attitude toward women in order to make unmistakably clear how Miller had at heart something of "the locker-room brag:"

> like servants,...[women's] awareness is belowstairs, and like slopeheads and gooks, who cares?

The authors Gass considers in this volume are all very much modern figures (from Freud and Colette to Sartre and Sylvia Plath), and though his three closing essays take no single writer as their occasion, as their occasion, their attempt is if anything an advance beyond even the most modern thinkers discussed in the first twelve pieces. In these last essays Gass attempts nothing less ambitious than definition of words' precise function and effect in literature. Yet throughout, the philosopher to whom Gass refers most often is not a modern, but the seventeenth century's Thomas Hobbes. The preference is revealing, for the author of *Leviathan* was, as his contemporary John Aubrey observed, "in love with geometry," and the *quod erat demostrandum* of geometry not only informs all of *World Within the Word,* but also serves as the shaping metaphor for the far-reaching final essays. These pieces contain some of the most difficult logic Gass has ever set forth, but when the lines of argument at last come clear, their insights can seem as sound as a postulate of Pythagoras. Take for example this sentence from "Groping for Trout," a discourse on metaphors that begins where Hobbes began his *Short Tract on First Principles,* with the laws of bodies in motion:

> I ask you finally...to think of every English word as Euclid for the poet, a wildly ordered set of meanings...maybe, but... right at home there nonetheless, to see that each one is...the center of a network of astonishing relations.

Yet despite the mathematical exactitude of his investigations, Gass is by no means interested in reducing literature to numbers. No: numbers, as "Groping for Trout" goes on to say, "are morally and metaphysically neutral." And: "words," on the other hand, "are not blank." Gass is as familiar with that side of the philosopher's coin which bears a human face as he is with the side on which all the numbers are printed. What I find most astonishing, and finally ennobling, about these essays is how their geometrician's attention to detail in no way interferes with the author's enthusiasm or the profound sympathy for the personal and more often than not painful demands of a literary artist's commitment. Thus the examination of a new Valéry translation, while it carefully distinguishes between shades of meaning in two lines from the poem "The Rower" (shades of meaning found only in the original French) also affirms that the form of a poem is "not an object...designed to trap...but...made to be because the soul is finally satisfied by what resembles it in its supremest dreams." The volume opens not with some clever bit of explication but with a description of Gass's mother drunken, hostile, near death. And the magnificent essay on Gertrude Stein admirably combines scholarship with uncommon sensitivity to the problems caused by her sexual predilections. Gass may describe literature as "passionately useless rigamarole," but he remains as attuned to its passion as to its rigged-up rolling.

Perhaps it is inevitable, then, that a collection with such scope, from the emotional to the mechanical, should in some places suffer from overreach. The demonstrations Gass makes do occasionally belabor their points (the lengthy Mr. Feaster passages of the Faulkner essay might be the best example)—though the author more than once freely concedes he has a tendency to overwrite. In each of the last three discourses, for instance, he follows up his most tedious and labyrinthine arguments with a kind of apology, such as, "words... leave us the mess I've just made us wade through." Still, the explanation does not always dispel the earlier obscurity. The wide use of pronouns generally causes the worst confusion, perhaps because he is striving for perfect sound, Gass tends to shy away from repeating the subject noun of a sentence.

Yet to a large extent *The World Within the Word* is belles lettres unlike any other, and hence beyond ordinary criticism. True, Gass does wish to perform the usual critical functions—one indication of how he perceives his role and his tradition is how, on three occasions, he takes time to respond directly to points raised by Edmund Wilson. But Gass also has a rare, special love for paradox, a trait in general more compatible to the creative spirit than the critical. Repeatedly (and once in a while obtrusively), Gass's thinking takes him to the theoretical extremes of his material, and in the final essay here, "The Ontology of a Sentence, or How to Make a World of Words," one suddenly finds him describing this characteristic in particularly strong terms: "a sodomous love of limits and a thirst for contradictions like a thirst for wine." Nonetheless this fascination with paradox may be in the end his finest quality as an essayist, because of the prodigious tasks it forces him to set himself. For when Gass succeeds, when he manages to visit each end of a given world and communicate them both, then he demonstrates a finer subtlety and as great a cogency as any critic now writing.

—*The New Republic,* 1976

WOBBLING WHEELS OF GENIUS & HISTORY: GUY DAVENPORT & DA VINCI'S BICYCLE

Throughout this odd collection of ten stories, Guy Davenport is careful to describe what he's up to. Consider this sentence from "Au Tombeau de Charles Fourier," at once the most strictly controlled and the strangest story here: "All of nature is series and pivot, like Pythagoras' numbers, like the transmutations of light." Yes: mathematics applied to the unpredictable changes of sunlight. That's the model, not "stories" in any normal sense. Rather Davenport's pieces work like interesting modal progressions, played wherever the mood strikes him, on an ungainly instrument constructed of history, literature, and occasional graphics. Yet though this author can speak with the tongues of men and angels, his fiction often ends up as stale-sounding brass.

The problem isn't just that much of the history and literature here is obscure. Who, for example, can identify C. Musonius Rufus? A first-century Roman philosopher, he provides the title for Davenport's best piece, as well as the central metaphoric balance between digging for water and seeking to fly. Who knows the poetry and novels of Swiss-born Robert Walser (1878-1956)? In fact, Walser deserves wider readership, despite a disorder we'd now probably diagnose as schizophrenia, and Davenport does a respectable job by him, adapting an assortment of his ramblings to make up the funniest story, "A Field of Snow on a Slope of the Rosenberg." But both these fine pieces toss in history as an unnecessary distraction. In mid-tale (indeed, in mid-paragraph), the fiction will leap from the unknown of one century to the famous of another. From Rufus we go without warning to Mussolini, to Victor Hugo, to primitive African tribesmen—and then, more than once, to Da Vinci and his bicycle.

This Renaissance invention was confirmed only during the 1960s, and apparently Da Vinci came up with it in a year rich with coincidence: 1493. In Davenport's stories, soon enough one gets the connection. The small gear of genius, he strives to demonstrate, drives in secret the larger wheel of history. Yet both are guided by a more wobbly wheel, call it accident or fate. All nature, all thought, whirl together at key junctures...

All well and good. To make drama of such moments seems a promising fictional purpose, and no doubt the fat dollops of historical minutiae are entirely accurate. Davenport earns his living, after all, as a scholar of literature and classics. Yet the total impression falls short of its inspiration.

Though he never writes badly, no. On the contrary, within the confines of a sentence the man proves at time exquisite, achieving a stately rhetoric that recalls Modernist masters like Wallace Stevens: "Into the eye of the wind it flew, lollop and bob as it butted rimples and funnels of air until it struck a balance and rode the void with a brave address" (from "The Wooden Dove of Archytas"). This author can sprinkle dictionary words all over the page and remain, nonetheless, admirably musical. If a refined vocabulary and a balletic flexibility of syntax were all we sought in fiction, *Da Vinci's Bicycle* would be more delight than disappointment.

Despite his world-gathering ambitions, however, this author remains unrelievedly a bookworm. He seems incapable of imagining on his own. Instead of emotional development—in whatever form—he'd rather insert the history of the Great Wall of China, and then perhaps a near page of conversation in German. The upshot is an effect odd for so brief a book, namely, that of overwriting.

Myself, I adore Mediterranean history, yet I ended up forcing myself through "The Antiquities of Elis," set during the reign of Marcus Aurelius. When I stand back from the finely filigreed individual pieces of the mosaic, the outlines seem right for me: a Greek travelogue, raising questions about the conflict between science and religion, with several bizarre touches of paganism and moments of erotic longing (both hetero- and homosexual). Yet the potential of these materials were again and again rendered flat backdrop, under brickloads of names (Pythagoras, Thales, Anaxagoras, Simonides…) and blocks of finicky research.

References such as those in "Elis," though spread all over the map and timeline, do sometimes come together tellingly. The first four stories, "Rufus" in particular, have an impact in the nervous system as well as the centers of cognition. Throughout, too, one spies the occasional glittering insight into the ambiguities of growing old. But what this reader took away from *Da Vinci's Bicycle* was, above all, a clearer sense of what makes other experiments in faction succeed. A telling contrast that kept coming to mind were the splendid stories of Jorge Luis Borges. These offer the same erudition, the same pervasive concern with history, and yet the narrative always has a natural shape, its book-learning in service to the exposure of some mystery or other of our existence. Guy Davenport, alas, seems instead to have put together nothing better than an academic farrago—a dozen encyclopedias spilled open on the floor. I can't find enough good for reading them in his order and not in their original, more ordinary one.

—Boston Globe, 1979

LETTERS & ETHICS:
THE MORAL FICTION OF JOHN BARTH

"Letters?" one of the characters here writes to John Barth, one of the other characters here. "A novel-in-letters, you say? Six several stories intertwining to make a seventh? A *capital* notion, sir!" Capital: the word in either spelling connotes great size, firm and classic structure, the forums where decisions affecting nations are made, and of course letters themselves. And this "old-time epistolary novel," as the subtitle has it, contains all four senses of the word. Spanning seven increasingly more complicated months in 1969, it manages to recapitulate all American history, rising in the end to a drama of the conflict between those who make events happen and those who stand back to see their effect:

> But tho savagery was savagery, the Baron maintained that all were not tarr'd with the same brush...Neither [side in the American Revolution] were yet routinely dismembering & flaying alive, or...impaling children on pointed stakes—had not done so, routinely, since the Middle Ages. Differences in degree were important; this was the 18th century, not the 12th; the fragile flower of humanism, of civilization—

Comprising eighty-eight letters from two fairly limited areas along our eastern coast, the novel brings into its near–nine hundred pages enough extravagant physical detail as to suggest the entire range of sensibility, ascending finally to a grandiose allegory of the struggle between the human spirit and unconscious nature:

> Nature bloody in fang and claw! Under me, over me, round about me, everything killing everything! I had dined that evening on crabs boiled alive and picked from their exoskeletons; as I ate I heard the day's news…Horrific nature; horrific world: out, out!

At the same time, *LETTERS* is belle-lettres, rife with allusions, multilingual puns, and other "literal" games. Its author's seventh book, it contains seven characters, and the title seven letters:

> Left to right…like files of troops the little heroes march: lead-footed *L;* twin top-heavy *T's* flanked by eager *E's,* arms ever-ready; rear-facing *R;* sinuous S—valiant fellows, so few and so many, with which we can say the unseeable!

Codes, especially, abound. According to one each letter must begin with some symbol or letter of the alphabet, in order eventually to spell out the book's subtitle. According to another, the date of each letter comes to figure in part of a still larger cryptograph. The novel's an enormous, multiple undertaking. Indeed Barth has always been one of those rare authors who labor to meet the greatest demands of aesthetic achievement. As he himself put it in his widely anthologized 1967 essay on Jorge Luis Borges, "The Literature of Exhaustion,"

> What makes…[Borges an artist] of the first rank, like Kafka, is the combination of that intellectually profound vision with great human insight, poetic power, and consummate mastery of his means, a definition which would have gone without saying, I suppose, in any century but our own.

But as it happens, that essay has been badly misunderstood. It is not about exhaustion; on the contrary, it argues that great artists and their work are forever inexhaustible. Nonetheless, unequivocal as the passage quoted seems, John Barth continually has to explain and re-explain his point—most recently [that is, as of 1980] to a member of the audience during a colloquy between himself and John Hawkes, published in the *New York Times*. Likewise, although common sense would argue that any author who aims so high should be honored for the attempt, if anything Barth's ideals have got him into trouble.

Over the last ten or a dozen years, his name has become almost a battle cry among critics and writers. On the one hand, William Gass effused, in a recent *Paris Review*, "Several of his books, in particular *The Sot-Weed Factor* [1960], are the works which stand to my generation as *Ulysses* did to its." On the other hand, John Gardner, reiterating an earlier argument of Gore Vidal's, dismissed Barth as "ambitious and fake"—though unfortunately *On Moral Fiction,* where Gardner made this argument, also reiterates the hastiness and illogic of Vidal's earlier "American Plastic: The Matter of Fiction." Barth's *Chimera* wins the National Book Award for fiction in 1972; yet Robert Scholes, long one of his supporters, expresses his disappointment with the book in *fiction international.* These examples are by no means definitive, granted, but they convey the right impression. The great bone of contention, generally, is Barth's penchant for what he calls "self-reflexive literature." "Metafiction" is the more common name for it, and in the Borges essay Barth describes the mode as literature in which the story is "a paradigm or metaphor for itself." Now, this self-concern—this yen to make the theory behind the drama *part* of the drama—is undeniably integral to his art; the approach is most pronounced in his book of short stories, *Lost in the Funhouse* (1968), and in the three linked novellas which make up *Chimera.* Yet those books are already sinking into the past, their brighter bits sticking to our better anthologies. Thus before addressing them. I will consider the new work. There will be time to circle back later, to reflect upon

Barth's career, and, ideally, to attempt a reconciliation of those opposing critical camps.

LETTERS immediately makes clear that it is a departure. The setting is not the timeless era of Scheherazade and the Greek gods, as in *Chimera,* but the Eastern Shore of Maryland and the Canadian border in and around Niagara Falls, lushly evoked. The novel has an attention to natural detail such as this author hasn't demonstrated since *The Sot-Weed Factor.* Moreover, political colors are painted in:

> A seven-year battle between the most conservative elements in the state…as you know, Mason and Dixon's line may be said to run north and south in Maryland, and the Eastern Shore is more Southern than Virginia—and the most "liberal"…who in higher latitudes would be adjudged cautious moderates at best.

Politics in Barth! But within the first twenty-five pages we have also Indian tribal rites, within the first thirty-five some madness about abducting Napoleon from St. Helena, within the first hundred a fevered love affair and a sprawling, tension-ridden scene in which some radicals attempt to blow up a bridge. Any reader with patience to go that far should be firmly hooked. This is Barth at his most rollicking, his most energetic, the Barth who has been praised, by Hawkes, as "a comic Melville." While comparisons to *Moby-Dick* generally do more harm than good, it can be said that *LETTERS* is less an unmoving funhouse mirror than a riotous Nantucket sleigh ride, booming over the waves after the biggest game.

And—thinking again of *Sot-Weed,* that book's parody of seventeenth-century prose, otherworldly as it might once have seemed, should not keep us now from the perception that many strengths of the 1960 novel are, in the best sense, conventional. Few books can match *Sot-Weed's* headlong dramatic pace, for instance, or, above all, its way of following through on philosophic speculations until wholeness is reached. Similarly, some of the essential workings in *LETTERS* are unabashedly plain. The conceit is that six characters are corresponding with "Mr. John Barth, Esq., Author"—that is, with another character, who bears only a passing resemblance to the twice-married father of three, forty-nine years old when this novel saw print, John Barth. Some of the other characters write directly to this character; others have their mail forwarded by lawyers, lovers, surviving relatives. Therein lies the book's straightforwardness: the characters must carry it. None of them are young. All soon reveal themselves nearly hamstrung, furthermore, by unnerving hints that their experience is recycling as they age. Indeed—most dangerous, so far as their carrying the story is concerned—with one exception, all are drawn from Barth's earlier fiction. But that exception, importantly, is Lady Amherst, the book's greatest creation.

Erstwhile lover of James Joyce and several other of this century's literary eminences, still heartsick over those love affairs and, especially, over the mysterious disappearance, thirty years previously, of her great American love and the child she bore him, nevertheless Lady A. remains full of delicious, nasty asides about her adopted country, spunkily hopeful of rediscovering her lost family, and genuinely a connoisseur of all that sensual experience has to offer, from a well-broiled trout to the heft of her lover's slack genitals. It is the Lady who initiates the action, during the first week of March. By mid-month, it is she who has that fevered love affair, with one Ambrose Mensch, a reincarnation from the more recognizably realistic episodes of *Lost in the Funhouse*. Mr. Mensch, though an avant-garde writer, is most profoundly concerned with things very much *rear-guard:* his family. His thirty-page story of their struggle up from German immigrant beginnings—humble domestic realism, for the most part—is the novel's first tour de force.

Thus these circlings intersect: juicily. Their route in previous novels is always clearly described at once, so that newcomers to the game may easily join in. That said, however, no summary can convey the whole septagonal plot. In fact the principal narrative throughout the first half is the heating up—as spring heats up into summer—of the Amherst-Mensch affair. Be that as it may, the four remaining characters demand some attention, and two of them in particular.

As for Todd Andrews and Jacob Horner, they are more or less the same as in *The Floating Opera* (1956, Barth's first novel) and *The End of the Road* (1958), respectively. Attorney Andrews finds himself falling in love at age sixty-nine, while also getting tangled up in a probate case similar to the one that nearly led him to kill himself in *Floating Opera,* when he wasn't yet forty. Horner, long ago a university comp dog, has his near-catatonic fifteen-year retreat in a Canadian asylum disrupted utterly by the reappearance of the man whose wife he, Jacob, killed. The almost-septuagenarian Andrews is, after Lady Amherst, the book's most sympathetic character; dispassionate and canny about the law, he is nonetheless fiercely humane where it matters, and soon comes to function as something akin to the novel's conscience. Horner on the other hand is the story's weakest link, humorously handled but just not that interesting.

With Andrew Burlingame Cook IV, however, descended from the protagonists of *Sot-Weed,* and with Jerome Bray, a relative to the Henry Bray of *Giles Goat-Boy* (1966), we enter a more troubling, more deceitful world. The letters of Andrew B. C. IV are, ostensibly, written in 1812, and they purport to explain how the author himself was responsible for the war with England that began that year. Yet in the present, 1969, we again and again encounter an unsettling character named Andrew Burlingame Cook—*VI.* This man proves by turns fatuously rednecked and disturbingly well-informed on everyone's movements and motives; he's a shadowy power in those conservative Maryland politics, and in the university where Lady Amherst works. That university has grown no less than 350-fold, hmm, 7X5X10, in seven short years. Then has Andrew VI (nearly seven...) got Something Going? And if so, is his plot on behalf of the rednecks, or on behalf of the radicals and angry blacks in nearby

Cambridge? During the novel's first half we get no straight answers, but we are presented with four letters from the contemporary Andrew's namesake ancestor, and they are replete with plot and counterplot. Apparently Andrew IV was a master player of "the Game of Governments," a spy and diplomat and more, who strove to bring down his hated "U. States" by means of something that was as much on the national mind in 1812 as in 1969: a second American Revolution. His best gambit, always, was pretending to work for the enemy, in this case the conservative elements in the young country, the rednecks of 1812 you might say…and this work keeps him away from home for long stretches at a time, so long that from that distance it's not always clear just which side he's on…

But the most astonishing character of *LETTERS*, both in itself and as an example of making piecework from older material serve admirably, is the bizarre flying insect-man who generally goes by the name Jerome Bray. In Bray's letters, Barth most fully indulges his affection for the playful aspects of literature. This insect-man "writes" on a bewildering computer, which among other problems can't restrain itself from flashing RESET every time it spots a pattern developing; the results may be the funniest writing Barth has ever done. More interestingly, Bray's letters soon reveal themselves to be a parody of the self-reflexive impulse. For if someone expects a computer to write a novel for them, as Bray is trying to, they might in fact get the references and the proper echoes at the flick of a switch, yet the upshot is nothing more than ream after ream of paper covered with binary code—*devoid* of inspiration or most (6/7's at least) of what a reader would call art. But at the same time, this computer-novelist exercises strange powers, particularly over women he happens to fancy. Also he keeps promising that all those who betrayed him will pay, will RESET.

The point of the summary is this: not only that each character lives in this novel as satisfyingly as in any earlier one, but also that he or she or it comes soon to signify some grander idea. Another essay could explicate each of the symbolic items held by each of the figures in this frieze. But my intention here is to assess *LETTERS* more generally, as part of Barth's whole oeuvre, so I'll only point out that in the letters from "John Barth, Esq." the Authorial figure of this novel intrudes, as all such figures have done since Cervantes. He makes clear, for example, that Lady Amherst is intended "to represent letters in the belletristic sense," and that the Burlingame-Cooks speak with the voice of History itself. The explanations are always brought off with a light touch, addressed to other characters rather than, overbearingly, to the reader. More illuminating, though, is how a structure of such size soon takes on the further support—in addition to its vividness, its emotional involvement, its plots within plots—of allegory.

LETTERS cannot long remain primarily the love story of Ambrose and the Lady. Their tale is, indeed, poignant and rambunctious. Ambrose has one child, a retarded teenage daughter, and though Lady Amherst is pushing fifty, both by mid-summer are committed to having a baby. Yet any map of tranquil Chesapeake Bay soon "turns into a catalogue of horrors." After the numerical code for certain Bay locations, we find grim warnings posted by the Armed Forces: "*204. 36: Shore bombardment...area. U.S. Navy. 204.40: long-range and aerial machine-gun firing...*" And as Todd Andrews reminds us, it was in Cambridge, Maryland, in 1967, that H. Rap Brown made his famous pronouncement, "Violence is American as apple pie." In the story's fourth section—the second *T*—we find a series of letters making reference to either Lake Chattauqua, in upstate New York, or the small town of Chattaugua, Maryland. We learn that the word (again, in either spelling) is an Algonkin Indian place-name, meaning, "a bag tied in the middle." An emblem, characteristically all-American yet erudite, for what's going on in the novel's structure: here in the middle the grab-bag narrative is tied. Here too, as the emphasis shifts to the unfinished business of American history, let's look a while at John Barth's career.

His own artistic "combination," recalling what he said about Borges, is clear enough. His belletristic leanings have much in common with the art of Vladimir Nabokov—in fact, Barth was one of the very few contemporary Americans Nabokov singled out for praise in the essay, "On Inspiration." On the other hand, this author's prolixity, and his way of developing each character to represent a philosophical issue, recalls the methods of the later Thomas Mann. Both of those earlier novelists, too, are notoriously cool, and Barth likewise gives us fiction more dispassionate than that of most Americans, preferring to wring his best effects from irony, or by forcing a hard decision out of some unlikely coincidence. Yet unlike Mann or Nabokov, he has a grinning glee about sexual matters—sometimes verging on the juvenile, as in the "Frig we must" joshing that undermined parts of *Chimera*. And his most pervasive quality, while at the same time his least appreciated, is the penchant he has for the big scene.

When Todd Andrews first tried to kill himself, it was not merely by poison or razor, but by blowing up a showboat on which he and nearly the entire population of his hometown were attending a performance. Ever since, with the exception of the most inward-looking tales from *Lost in the Funhouse,* Barth's fiction has seethed with battle action, high-wire litigation, even sex at the point of a knife. In this regard, it is significant that in the ten years since *The Sot-Weed Factor* first went into paperback, the book has enjoyed nine reprintings.[1] The information is readily available on *Sot-Weed's* title page, and from it anyone can draw common-sense conclusions about this author, yet if any critic has made the point it has escaped my attention. Clearly, it would

---

1. True in 1980, and for about another decade. The novel remains in paperback, on Anchor, and while I've trimmed the paragraph, I've let the point stand.

require an incredible amount of classroom assignment to demand a new printing of a 600-page novel nearly every year, even at lower reprint rates (roughly 25,000 copies). And while a horserace between Barth and his contemporaries up and down the bookstore shelves would serve little purpose, it is worth noting that the shorter books, the ones more often assigned, have up to twice as many printings, and that the most closely comparable reprint rate I found was for Thomas Pynchon. Therefore Barth must have won a modest but stable general readership, on his own merits. Not even Gore Vidal accused him of churning out potboilers, with gratuitous sex and gossip. Rather, what appeals to the rank-and-file book buyer must be classic qualities of story and scene.

The rest follows. Since Barth will abide no small-bore initiations and climaxes, likewise he won't sit still for those inarticulate boys and girls who generally stumble into them, and so we have that phenomenal array of human mercury, his characters. Even the naive ones can be light on their feet as Chaplin, conniving as W. C. Fields; even the family of Ambrose Mensch proves far-from-stolid German burghers. Since most of Barth's people are so quick, their problem is repeatedly the same: *How to make a decision?* The best of them are Hamlets, too brainy for their own good, and thus Barth's voice adapts from book to book like that of the Player King. He has no one instantly identifiable tone, like Faulkner or Lawrence; his rhetoric, his metaphors, are made subservient to the dramatic situation. He can rise to poetry when it's called for, as he does with conspicuous success during the burning-of-Washington episodes in *LETTERS,* and all his voices demonstrate a flexibility, rather Jamesian, which allows him to contain several ideas in one sentence without losing syntactical force. But soon enough, the problem of making a decision and the problem of finding a voice drew closer, and so the author was brought to metafiction.

Therein lies the best defense of Barth's self-reflexive explorations: that he was brought to them by the honest pursuit of his creative obsessions. Certainly, with the publication of *LETTERS*, more grounded in the actual, we can appreciate better how genuinely *strange* these stories are. A piece like "Title," for example, from *Funhouse,* is far stranger than most of what's out there. It's stranger even than Walter Abish or Raymond Federman, because it is more austere—all but devoid of sensual detail, "Title" poses the Author as a numb interlocutor between the vaudevillian Tambo and Mr. Bones who bedevil any artist, one arguing that the effort is worthless, the other wishing to struggle on. In its dozen pages, "Title" doesn't merely upset one or two of the reader's expectations; it challenges the whole notion of meaning existing behind words. "Title," like all the pieces from *Chimera* and *Funhouse* which linger in the mind, is exemplary: a rippling mirror that shows us, by its very form, the formlessness that underlies our most thoughtful decision. *"Drolls & Dreamers that we are,"* Andrew Burlingame Cook IV meditates, *"we fancy we can undo what we fancy we have done."*

This latest novel therefore is Barth's undoing of the fancy, his return to the world of social conscience and physical pain. If our imagination can turn a mirror into a monster, it is only in part because we perceive ourselves as nothing more than reflected light; we also see monsters because the tortuous history of mankind has proven time and again what rough beast confronts us in the glass. Take, for example, this reprisal for Iroquois atrocities committed under the leadership of an early Burlingame-Cook:

Colonel Bouquet's counter-expedition that year was Senecan in its ferocity. The English scalpt, raped, tortured, took few prisoners, disemboweled the pregnant—even lifted *two* scalps from each woman, and impaled the nether one on their saddle horns…

Who is Andrew Burlingame Cook IV? Using a bizarre family gift for transforming his voice, even (to some extent) his features, he can instigate slaughters like the one above, ostensibly intended to spur the natives to revenges even more viscious. Yet the man also insinuates himself among the highest levels of government and society, supping with Aaron Burr or Madame De Stael, indulging in parlor talk with Lord Byron. These meetings have an ostensible anti-American purpose as well; they seem to undermine the young nation's leadership. Cook claims to be proud of his Ahatchwhoop Indian blood, and has sworn vengeance on the entire white race. Yet the one act of revenge he carries out flawlessly is that of killing the harmless, aging poet who may be his long-absent father. This is Joel Barlow, whose poems turn up in American Literature anthologies. He and Andrew find themselves fleeing across Russia with Napoleon's decimated army (an echo of *War and Peace*? why not?). The younger man slips the older a blanket infected with pneumonia, a trick he learned from Indian-killers.

Not that Cook IV reveals his assassin's game; a reader has to recall one or two earlier letters, furious, which got into the depredations carried out against his native brothers. But then, what on earth does the frontier genocide have to do with dragging an aging cosmopolite dilettante over to Russia? And then killing the man? Every uncertainty leads to more—who is Andrew Burlingame Cook *VI*? From the first, one doubts the authenticity of his ancestor's letters, supposedly written in 1812. Soon they start to seem like another disguise, forgeries composed in a last-ditch attempt to win back the current male heir to the dreadful family business. This son is a '60s radical, in his early twenties now, and he despises *his* father. Chances are he harbors dreams of patricide.

In a letter sent mid-summer, from ABC VI's home in Chautauqua, MD, to "John Barth's" home in Chautauqua, NY, we have tied together the whole history of the Burlingame-Cooks: from Andrew

IV's middle age, in about 1812, to Andrew VI's, currently. Thereafter we hear no more from the ancestor; Andrew VI writes directly to his son, though he doesn't quite drop the pose of passing along family history. Instead, Cook IV summarizes later letters from his namesake, letters that he claims were originally set down in a code of numbers (suggesting, to be sure, Jerome Bray's ambition to have a computer do the work of the heart and mind).

But is it *true* that Andrew IV did all the later dirty work that his amanuensis claims, like causing Washington to be burnt in 1814, and abducting Napoleon in 1821? True? False? Whatever: "It is an age," Lord Byron is reported to declare, "in which the Real and Romantic are, so to speak, fraternal twins." Bonaparte himself was "that man… who play'd as none before him the Game of Governments, & convinced a whole century, for good or ill, that one man can turn the tide of history." The Burlingame-Cooks have spun a similar Romance out of *their* reality.

Precisely which episodes of '60s history Andrew VI is responsible for, we never do learn, but between his long yet swift-moving paragraphs of history, we perceive enough to make us shudder. His deeds are not quite so monstrous as his ancestor's— differences of degree are important; this is the twentieth century, not the eighteenth. Still, bad enough: Andrew VI's own father was "vaporized," oh quite accidentally, at Alamagordo, New Mexico, in July of 1945. Coolly, too, in the late-'60s Burlingame-Cook helped to quell riots by students and blacks, since he considers them an interference with the larger goal of a Second American Revolution. Also he's had his abusive way with Lady Amherst, first thirty years ago and now again this summer of '69, when Andrew VI manipulated her into a drugged rape at the hands of that Caliban, Bray…. All of this shadowy dealing on behalf of the Cause…. And eventually A. VI and his skullduggery raise the same questions as did his ancestor A. IV. What cause? Who *are* these people?

The best answer is the simplest: both Burlingame-Cooks are growing old. Indeed, the reader can stomach the outrages their letters portray largely because the sensibility we see through is, to choose a reference both men make good use of, past *mezzo cammin*. Yes they've been well educated; they know their Dante, their Indian languages, and anniversaries both personal and national. But now these minutiae have become precious to them, as precious as all their high-minded ideals. Andrew VI may claim that he has

> turned (to cite the motto of this border state) from *parole femine* to *fatti maschii:* from "womanly words" to "manly deeds," or from the registration of our times to their turning.

Yet the statement, like most of his, is the opposite of the truth. He has reached "the border state" in a sense other than settling by the Chesapeake. More than that, deed and word, this cause and that one, have grown blurry to him. As a young spy and provocateur he'd sought war and destruction, and now, yes, "the battle is joined," whether outside Washington in 1814 or on Hamburger Hill in 1969. But what's the result? "Men begin to die." As the Burlingame-Cooks grow older, they begin to notice there are ways to serve humanity better than conspiracy and murder:

> Their way takes them through the Piazza di Spagna. One wants to call across the fifteen decades: "Stay! Put by a moment these vague intrigues, this nonsense of Napoleon: young John Keats has just died here!"

Who is ABC IV? Well who are the ABC's for? Letters are fickle, are they not, changing to suit any need, any passion? Both ancestor and contemporary endure breakneck cross-country runs and sea-chases, and their descriptions of battle once or twice achieves detail and orchestration to rival Tolstoy at Borodino. But both are eventually stunned by the same simple emptiness that Ambrose Mensch once spotted, alone, in a certain dark funhouse mirror. The Burlingames' boiling game, one might say, has at last blinded them with its steam. And so stunned, they can't decide what next. They have offspring of their own after them by now, kids incensed by how they were abandoned, but the fathers lumber on, struggling to repeat, redo, make amends…

It's Oedipus, to be sure, and speaking of Freud, *LETTERS* also makes ample mention of his "compulsion to repeat." Then too, every character here cites Marx's famous observation that history repeats itself first as tragedy, then as farce. Yet the novel implies, in the end, a deeper reason for our recapitulation. The implication grows as the Bs here (Barth, Bray, Bonaparte, Burlingame, Barlow and many others) gather and hum; "mother of letters," Ambrose Mensch says of B, "birth, bones, blood & breast: the Feeder." And the point is underscored by means that have little to do with literature. One summer night Todd Andrews moors his Chesapeake skipjack in a ferny, isolated cove, and there he makes love with the woman who may be his grown, illegitimate daughter, a woman who urges him: "No obligations. No problems. Feel." We recycle, in other words, because we are part of that pervasive, unconscious embodiment of pure feeling, Nature. In our makeup we carry the remembrance of the mollusk we were billions of years ago, and no metaphor crops up so often in Barth's fiction as that of the mollusk shell, which excretes an entire circle in reverse in order to grow. So in *LETTERS*, as the furious plot unwinds—the probate case draws everyone into the Burlingame-Cook web, so they play some part in a re-enactment of the bombardment of Fort McHenry—as all this develops, the character that looms largest is the "bug," the "nut," the "disturbed, unearthly boy, more like a bird or bat or bumblebee," Jerome Bray.

"We did not know that slang expression," his computer writes, "nothing foreign is human to us." So his letters run, murky as a strobe-lit disco floor, and to describe what Bray does in direct language would do no justice to the affect. A large portion of his menace is in its scattershot presentation. Horrid things are done, and Lady Amherst isn't his only female victim—indeed, this "character" embodies such Alpha-Male nightmares, he clarifies how this novel is, among many other things, a long outcry against the abuse of women. But we glimpse his rapes and entrapments only round the corner of a punning phrase, or in an offhand reference using some code-name of his own devising. Thus it is only after about five hundred pages of these interdependent correspondences that Bray comes to terrify. At first, reading that he refers to all women as "females" is ludicrous, as is the name he's chosen for his farm, "Comalot." But then we realize that he drugs the farm's women into a drooling animal state. The laughter turns hideous, the grim equal of anything to be found in the current generation of so-called Black Humorists: grim as Vonnegut digging up Dresden, grim as the most scabrous conversation in William Gaddis's *JR*.

Bray's continually RESET-ing computer, we learn, has the name LILYVAC; it links the moral vacuum of numbers with that of nature. *LETTERS* is no novel for sentimental notions of birds and bees, not when the lily symbolizes fertility, precisely what Bray wants his females for. When at last the computer is glimpsed, when Todd Andrews arrives to save a woman trapped at the farm, the thing combines a numbers-based machine and an insect or animal:

> At least some of what you'd taken for metal or plastic was a scaly, waxy stuff, unidentifiable but vaguely repulsive; some of those wires were more like heavy beeswaxed cord, or dried tendons.

As autumn comes to the Maryland's Eastern Shore, Bray conducts a kind of harvest, carrying out threats that once seemed comical. By then we know that his grandmother was a Tuscarora princess named Kyuahaha, yes ha-ha—but in Algonkin her name meant "unfinished business." Now he not only "seeds" a female or two, but also drops on his enemies like a buzzbomb. When he surprises even the Burlingame-Cooks, the family that has dominated the second half of the novel, it would seem nothing can stand up against his vengeful "7-Year Plan," his braying triumph over humankind: fellow creatures, but they've developed such odd codes, they've so complicated what was once a naked business of breed, feed, and die. And yet...

Lady Amherst has remained with us all along, and the child she carries come autumn may not be Bray's after all, but rather the one she and her new husband Ambrose have been hoping for. Indeed, if Ambrose and Amherst take on the parenting, if they treat their progeny as happy proof that life can begin again in middle, then it hardly matters just what the boy, girl, or thing is made of. Can't we rise above our nature and make ourselves over? Similarly there is unfinished business in the courts, in Washington, and elsewhere; there's time enough, still. Bray and the Burlingames have been so busy they've forgotten someone, and Ambrose Mensch could show up with time enough, still, to prove himself—a man. He could still help one woman find fulfillment. "Entropy may be where it's all headed," Mensch writes, "but it isn't where it is." And thanks to his family's former business, he knows of a place where he could get the jump on Bray. And there's Todd Andrews in the mix, too, another participant in the re-enactment of the Siege of McHenry. The Burlingame-Cooks may have arranged for the rockets' red glare to turn bloody, but ever since *Floating Opera*, when Andrews has been on hand, explosive plans have fizzled out harmlessly...

Complexities of machine and of spirit; big scenes in which capital notions contend: letters and the fickle, fragile human element; repeating numbers and the heartless hum of nature. But it should not be inferred that because *LETTERS* ends with such headlines (it does, literally: "*On this date in history:...*1814: Fort McHenry bombardment ceases; F.S. Key reports flag still there"), it resolves with a mere big bang. No; *Giles Goat-Boy,* regrettably, proved that sort of single-note book. Its allegories stacked up into a stale layer cake, while *LETTERS* is weighty in quite another way. Setting aside what it has to say about shameful chapters of American history that haunt us still, setting aside its powerful feminist argument, setting aside even its aesthetic investigation—weighing life experienced against life imagined, with the scales teetering first one way and then the other, from letter to letter—setting aside all this, the attentive reader will discover more: a profound ethical question. The resolutions of its final, sinuous S are ambiguous as the snake itself: offering wisdom, threatening a Fall. John Gardner's broadsides notwithstanding, the decision to taste the fruit of Good and Evil is never simple. An end, a cause, may seem clearly to justify any means until we have *already* bitten the apple, until we have grown older and suffered a second education. Thus these six several stories intertwine to make a grander seventh, an American allegory of the Fall. Within their apple, its peel scarred by a thousand codes, these characters have discovered an enraged bee, bringing painfully home to them how accidents of nature can undo in a moment our most intricately thought-out decisions.

Yet that summary, too, seems over-simple in retrospect. Much else crowds the mind, much. For example: what the novel shows us concerning love (another experience fraught with the compulsion to repeat) suggests no *Pilgrim's Progress,* nor any computer manual, but rather the seven intertwined novels of Marcel Proust. Which suggests further: to even bother bringing such subtlety into print, these days, when most of us, buzz-happy with the media, can't take time for letters, lowercase, let alone in capitals—well it seems quixotic, and therefore of course noble, in the best, paradoxical sense. Which suggests…which suggests, further…but let those three dots by themselves make, so to speak, my final point. To write a mighty book, Melville reminds us, you must choose a mighty theme, and with this novel John Barth establishes emphatically that his themes are *not* just literary or academic, as has been too often and too hastily assumed, but rather ethical, philosophical, historical. It is tempting, on the basis of such vast issues rendered in so striking and multifaceted an idiom, to place him with the great myth-destroyers and -remakers of the present international generation: Gabriel Garcia Marquez, Gunter Grass, Italo Calvino, and Pynchon and Gaddis in this country. But whatever the eventual standing of his stock, it rests on a corpus of work that demonstrates, gaily, that the world is indeed a university. For what is lifeless, what dry-as-dust, about seeking Truth? His characters continue...continue as these three dots continue while ending...they sift through the documents of their lives, getting stung whenever they bang up against the hard facts of nature, and so with their bruises multiplying and changing color, with their crumpled heap of discarded lies growing larger around them, they produce unknowing a new image for the face of God.

—*Fiction International*, Fall 1980

PUBLIC EXPERIMENT, PRIVATE DESIRE: JOHN HAWKES & ROBERT COOVER

Both John Hawkes' *Virginie: Her Two Lives* and Robert Coover's *Spanking the Maid* present an endless, timeless outrage. In Hawkes' novel the narrator burns to death while still a child, still a virgin, in two incarnations two hundred years apart. First in 1740 and then again in 1945, this twice-born child chooses to burn—in fires set, worse still, by her own mother—rather than give up her innocence. Likewise, the protagonists of Coover's novella keep up their hideous behavior over an impossible stretch of time. As the master thinks, early on: "[The maid's] endless comings and goings and stupid mistakes are a trial, of course, and he feels sometimes like he's been living with them forever, but…he knows he must be firm…severe if need be." So he must spank his maid, repeatedly, perpetrating a wickedness not unlike that of Virginie's "Maman" setting fire to her child.

The master whales his servant on almost every other page during the latter half of Coover's very brief book, drawing blood that mysteriously disappears by next morning, even when he's lit into her with the "leathery elasticized bull's pizzle." Thus both these books make litter of what's literal. Both put the match to time and space, and to ordinary morality as well, and then color the flames with pain and desire. America's literary avant-garde, in which both authors can he placed, has rarely so goosed the mundane. Yet each book leaves an impression more of delicacy than depravity, more of art than of outrage.

John Hawkes has managed that balancing act, art and outrage, for a generation now. His ten novels to date constitute a wax museum dedicated to crimes of passion, often extraordinary in their horrific elegance. An outstanding case would be the scene of a thug torturing the young wife he's kidnapped in *The Lime Twig* (1961), and *Second Skin* (1963) meditates hauntingly on the suicides of a child, a wife, and a parent. What's more, as a true sensualist, he doesn't confine his highly developed sensibilities to high-voltage experiences. One passage in *Virginie* makes poetry of dishwashing. Another turns a beehive into the Taj Mahal: "…feeling and hearing the engines of its darkness, and smelling antiquity in its thick crusty walls, and thinking to myself that it was an airy mausoleum." The thoughts are those of that eleven-year-old title character, our narrator, and though the syntax and vocabulary seem over her head, the wide-open receptiveness feels just right. Again, the point's not realism—it's amazement.

Virginie should be amazed. She's an eyewitness to preposterous sexual escapades, played out two hundred years apart. In 1945 she is the sort-of sister of a libertine French cabdriver, Bocage, and when their sort-of Maman suffers a paralyzing stroke that leaves her mute as well as immobile, Bocage rounds up five women and four men to join him in "charades of love." In 1740, Virginie sits by at an isolated country chateau while "Seigneur," her guardian, educates another five women, more perversely though with an explicit purpose, in "the Art of Giving Pleasure." The chapters alternate centuries and tones. We're treated first to bawdy haggy-pants encounters, then to more exotic variations performed before a chaste and highbrow Seigneur. Hawkes distinguishes the flavor of each time with admirable precision, moving adroitly from Fellini among his clowns to de Sade among the nobility. The couplings and triplings that result have nothing to do with nuts and bolts. Every combination's unpredictable, and several entail no actual intercourse. In one particularly bizarre sexual substitute, c. 1945, a man's erect penis is sheathed in strips of flannel steamed in rose water. Similarly, we discover again how fascinating a euphemism can be; Virginie learns that a man carries a "zizi" or a "scepter," a woman a "fougasse" or, better still, a "sphinx."

Yet inventive circumlocutions won't justify a novel. Unlike the brilliant *Lime Twig*, *Virginie* is nearly all ecstasy, and that can become wearing. Hawkes does what he can, differentiating between his women cleverly, assigning each a color and a conversational tic. But his situation of course allows for little by way of character development or change; much of the time, we can wonder only what trick will be turned next. The book risks slipping into mere exquisite XXX—except for the presence of Virginie herself. The strangest of the outrages here is the child in the audience. Once we pass through Hawkes' looking-glass, Virginie lends humanity and art to acts that would otherwise be depraved. The novel's last chapters concentrate on this paradox. Closing scenes in both centuries thrust innocence and wickedness into conflict, with a masterful inevitability, and the climactic choices amount to a parable about art's making. Whether that parable invests the previous "charades" with meaning is, in the end, the question any novel of outrage and ideas must answer.

A question also posed by the oeuvre of Robert Coover. The best-known of his books to date, *The Public Burning* (1977), is an often obscene fantasia on the Rosenberg executions, largely narrated by Vice President Richard Nixon. That novel, however, went for big scenes, explosive revisionism spread out over hundreds of pages. In *Spanking the Maid*, Coover narrows the focus to a single archetypal moment, a wet dream outside history (as were the sexier bits in his superb story collection *Pricksongs and Descants* [1968]). The spanking episodes are floridly drawn, but their reiterations hardly amount to a "novel," no matter what its publishers say. Barely a hundred pages, the book can be polished off in a couple hours. The few sticks of furniture and fewer characters seem to have more in common with a barroom song than a best-seller. But this broken record of a narrative proves so finely imagined, it transcends quibbles about genre.

An unnamed master lies troubled, at the opening, by strange dreams; meantime an unnamed maid straightens his bathroom. Soon she must wake the man, in order to make up his room and allow him to prepare for the day. But alas, the girl's incompetent:

> Peering over her shoulder…her eye falls on the mirrored bed; one of the sheets is dangling at the foot, peeking out from under the spread as though exposing itself rudely. She…tucks it in, being careful to make the proper diagonal fold, but now the spread seems to he hanging lower on one side than the other. She whips it back, dragging the top sheet and blankets.

The master stands in the doorway, slapping his palm with the bull's pizzle. Soon enough she must bend, raise her skirts, lower her drawers. She proves a feeb, and then she's spanked—that's the entire story.

But note the ripple effect of the girl's incompetence. First sheet then spread, then sheets and blankets both: with the same brisk widening of focus, the paragraph-long snippets of "plot" replay their central incident. And as it widens, each repetition has some fundamental (the pun is Coover's) difference. At times the problem seems not to be the maid's, since more than once she discovers grotesque leftovers under the master's bedclothes, now a bloodstained belt, now an aborted fetus. Or we might share his point of view, realizing with him that he *must remain firm, even severe if need be.* "Am I being unfair?" he'll ask as once more he raises the rod, or the pizzle, or the… Then too, though nothing in the room gets tidy or ironed out once and for all, time does pass. The threat of punishment exists from the first, but the man doesn't actually lay on the strap till about midway through, and when he does the light in the bedroom window tells us it's almost noon. Thereafter the shadows lengthen along with the welts and bruises. Each partner begins to suffer doubts, then later still each gets past these doubts. In the process the repeated sentences and questions take on accumulative weight, unexpected colors. Hilarious to begin with, they first turn threatening and then start to sound both eloquent and mournful. Has there never been, can there never be, any "holiday from this divine government of pain"?

What Coover's working with is an expanding multiple metaphor, much as in Kafka's novellas. Master and maid in time flirt with the roles of God and humanity, ruler and ruled, the artist and his recalcitrant art, all while also keeping up their gender functions. At the start of the final long paragraph, we enter the master's dream—a touch of Finnegan while night falls. So Coover rounds off his syncopated etude with a moment's clear sounding of its principal theme: "Distantly blows are falling, something about freedom and government."

Of course, that phrase's placement has been calculated, and the words themselves honed, with the result that all this hanky-panky gets refined into a gem. *Spanking the Maid* proves itself a diamond from first cut to last, and *Virginie* achieves that hardness at least in its conclusion. But then why else investigate what's pornographic, bestial, *outside* reason, as the word "outrage" implies? If these two books wear their ideas on their sleeves more than a popular novel would, it's because they don't want the smug voyeuristic distance a popular novelist maintains, rather pursuing the wholehearted commitment of senses and mind a real artist must have. A glimpse of a child jumping into a fire would shock anyone, just as, once upon a time, any callow adolescent might get off on saucy Victorian stories of a man and a maid. But the committed acrobat of the avant-garde leaps into the inferno beyond reason in an honest attempt to fly.

—*Boston Phoenix*, 1982

DYING ON THE VINE:
THOMAS PYNCHON & VINELAND

Here and there, this is a wonderful book. In the traffic-jam poetry of an occasional sentence, in the skewed framing of an occasional insight, and in the bruising strangeness of two or three scenes along the way, Thomas Pynchon's new novel achieves the manic greatness of his earlier work. And Pynchon's essential sympathies appear unchanged. The author of *V.* (1963) and *Gravity's Rainbow* (1973) once more celebrates marginal figures who fight back against a power-mad conspiracy. As before, the struggle is a quest, and the guerrilla tactics owe as much to Chaplin as to Ho Chi Minh; as before, the most humane element that the good guys find in the enemy organization is a grim sexual need.

This time, however, Pynchon works closer to home than in his three previous novels. The new one sorts through a few singed '60s vets and their broken lives, mostly in contemporary Northern California. In coming down to earth, this way, the rocketman hasn't exactly lost his tailfins. Still, he's not flying anymore. For all its fingertip detail and small-potato heroism, *Vineland* is ordinary in its conception and sentimental in its conclusions. The man behind the book may be a genius, but the work itself brings to light the rawness and intermittence of that genius.

Vineland's situation pulls its author into line with the likes of Tom Robbins and Jim Dodge, the milk-and-cookies iconoclasts.

Vineland begins with Zoyd Wheeler, the warmest and fuzziest of its aging countercultural types. It's 1984, a year so freighted with significance as to break a man's back, and Wheeler in fact suffers a disability. His however is mental, a nuttiness that keeps him on California's payroll, happily at home amid the slackers of the pot country up around Humboldt County. The initial suspense has to do with Zoyd's rummaging around after some crazy public act that will guarantee the checks keep coming. An altogether sane rummaging, to be sure: our hero suffers nothing worse than cynicism and laziness.[1] But the psychotic show he puts on brings both his ex-wife and the man who stole her away crashing back into his life. The wife is the blue-eyed Frenesi Gates, the seducer the black-suited Brock Vond.

If my description emphasizes the couple's surfaces, alas, so does Pynchon's. The superficiality of the ex-wife reflects a more general problem for this author, a problem I'll get to in a moment. As for Brock Vond, he's a cartoon villain—by choice, clearly—and it works. A freelancer for the Department of Justice, Vond can call on regimental levels of ordnance; he sets Zoyd hustling to cover both his own ass and that of his teenage daughter by Frenesi, Prairie. It's a cartoon but it works, as the usual Pynchonian gas keeps the balloons afloat. There's the offhand insight into time and class (these Klamath-Range towns are starting to gentrify), the pleasing dissonance of high rhetoric and gutter talk, the sneaky technical know-how and the sheer head-banging improbability. Then not quite a hundred pages in, teenage Prairie's quest takes over, and the story begins to fail.

With the help of another character out of DC or Marvel, a "floozie with an Uzi," Prairie uncovers her mother's turncoat past. Seems Frenesi snitched on her radical confreres back in the High '60s; she trysted with Brock Vond and set up at least one campus radical for

---

1. *Vineland*'s protagonist found a more engaging incarnation later as The Dude, in the Coen brothers' 1998 movie *The Big Lebowski*. Pynchon seemed almost to return the favor in his 2009 novel, *Inherent Vice*.

murder. Prairie's education keeps the gas flowing, tracing a worm path from the biker hangs of West Texas to a whores' auction in Japan, with locker-room songs and one or two hilarious bits of stage business. Yet while the tale has the right touches of the bizarre, it starts to feel more and more hokey, dependent on chance encounters and smothered in simplistic lefty paranoia.

With these women, God knows Pynchon's trying. He's more than smart enough to recognize how his work has been devoid of developed female character. Even the questress of his second novel, *The Crying of Lot 49* (1966), is a tinker-toy symbol for the decline of the West. In *Vineland* he huffs and puffs to get at sexual predilections, mother-daughter dynamics, the crises of childbearing. But once this story becomes Prairie's, once it starts to require a balance of cartoon and epiphany, scene after scene falls flat. Frenesi's attraction to Brock, the crux of her betrayal, never becomes plausible. In the murder she helps set up, everyone concerned acts on motivations held in place by smudgy Authorial scotch tape.

To his credit, Pynchon summons up a decent ending. The final chapters pull together a lot of earlier sprawl and herd it toward hallucinogenic wonder. So what if the psychology doesn't work? So what if the plot remains nine-tenths coincidence? Pynchon's no realist, surely, no more than his Vineland (its name an echo of an ancient dream America) lies anywhere along the actual route of U.S. 101. The protagonist of *Lot 49* comes apart in our hands, but the book shocks and illuminates nonetheless. Aren't Pynchon's people *supposed* to be mere anagrammatic flotsam? Isn't Frenesi Gates the gates through which we move to frenzy or "free sin," and isn't her inscrutable manipulation precisely the point, suggesting that we're putty in the hands of the state?

Yes, yes…but no. Certainly a number of recent novels have managed to imagine a genuinely suffering humanity within an outlandish aesthetic construct. Outstanding American examples would include Toni Morrison's *Beloved* and Don DeLillo's *Mao II*. Outside our country there are still more freethinking types, Gunter Grass perhaps the oldest, who still manage to harvest something from the over-cultivated terraces of a tortured history. Pynchon is trying the same, when all's said and done. His best effects come out of a dense pastiche of on site specifics, ripe with human avoirdupois; they don't work as mind games alone. He may be no mainstream realist, but he's no Italo Calvino either, spinning stories out of thin air.

Then too, *Vineland* falls well below the standards of the author's own catalog. The shadow that chills this book worst is that of its predecessor, *Gravity's Rainbow,* now seventeen years old. Every bit of business in *Vineland* was worked more profoundly and power-fully in *Rainbow.* Military-industrial nightmare? *Rainbow* offered the birth of the V-2 rocket and the atom bomb, both of them more ter-rifying in presentation and more intrinsic to what's going on than any similar gambit in *Vineland.* The perversion metaphor—the life-force sodomized by the Powers That Be? *Rainbow*'s far, far sicker than *Vineland,* in which the sex is primarily masturbatory and soft-core. And if you're looking for a deliberately ugly approach, an anti-aes-thetic that embraces bad art and tinny talk, look no further than the *Rainbow.* The book squawks, it dribbles, getting sexist and racist whenever it damn well pleases, and it includes a diagram of a lifted middle finger. The novel's a masterpiece of American shapelessness, no less, leaping up beside *Moby-Dick* or *Leaves of Grass* as it leads the whole scary world in its off-key sing-along (the last words are "Now, everybody…").

Poor *Vineland,* having to follow such an act. Nevertheless, Pyn-chon could have accomplished something considerably more modest than the *Rainbow* and still accomplished much. But this novel is only fitfully alive, hippy-dippy when it should be sober, and weak-minded about its own deepest mysteries. Read it for the occasional winning passages and conflagrations, the few grapes that aren't sour.

—*Willamette Week,* 1990

THE MODERNIST UPRISING:
DONALD BARTHELME

"Barthelme has managed to place himself," William Gass once declared, "in the center of modern consciousness." Gass of course meant "modern" in the sense of "up to the minute;" he was praising Donald Barthelme for what always strikes one first about this author's highly imaginative and wickedly ironic fiction, namely, its freewheeling use of contemporary culture in all its kitschy largesse. The majority of his closer critics—Tony Tanner, Wayne B. Stengel, and Larry McCaffery, to name three—have since seconded Gass' judgment, emphasizing what that early reviewer called the author's "need for the new." In general the criticism has stressed how Barthelme revels in the dreck of contemporary culture, how he delights in our brokeback and hopelessly modish contemporary language, using the very elements of a civilization mad for superficial values in order to deride it. Robert A. Morace praises the author's "critique of the reductive linguistic democracy of the contemporary American mass culture" (in *Critique*), and Larry McCaffery adds: "Barthelme's stories...make fictions in an age of literary and linguistic suspicion" (*in The Journal of Aesthetic Education*). By now a number of books have developed the argument at length.[1]

---

1. A more recent example would be the excellent 2009 biography *Hiding Man*, by Tracy Daugherty.

Yet Gass had the original insight a long time ago. His essay, "The Leading Edge of the Trash Phenomenon," was a review of *Unspeakable Practices, Unnatural Acts*—a collection published in 1968. More to the point, what Gass had to say pertained to work in a style that Barthelme later rejected. The complexly written and showily strange prose of that book and the previous two (*Come Back, Dr. Caligari*, 1964, and *Snow White*, 1966) was supplanted by the simpler address and less rococo imaginings of *City Life* (1970) and *Sadness* (1972), a simplification reflected in the differences between the later titles and the earlier. Indeed the directness of the writing and the explosive abruptness of the visions may establish the two early-'70s collections as the peak of Barthelme's career. But the writer moved on again, first to the dialog format originally explored in his novel *The Dead Father* (1975). That book also employs other modes, such as the list and the monologue; such symphonic wholeness makes the text unique for Barthelme. Then in the 1979 collection *Great Days*, the dialog format was dominant. These dialogs, often between nameless protagonists, and never between anything remotely like two developed characters, carry the stories further from the satisfactions of narrative than ever before—indeed, further than in the decade that remained to him. His 1981 career retrospective, *Sixty Stories*, offers occasional revisions of his earlier work, and those revisions, though slight, without exception smooth out the prose and clarify story purpose. The efforts that followed demonstrate an amalgam of previous styles, most effective in the scrupulously arranged *Overnight to Many Distant Cities* (1983), but his 1986 novel *Paradise* was by and large a return to accessibility (to hearty sexuality, for that matter) and to storyline. The same aesthetic held sway in the final novel, *The King* (1990), though the affect was subdued, elegiac, as one might expect of a work that appeared posthumously.

This brief overview of his career and its changes, then, indicates that Barthelme's "modern consciousness" is in fact chameleonic, and by no means limited to the cultural choices or linguistic bricabrac of any one period. On closer examination—in *Sixty Stories*, the authoritative edition—the contemporeana in the texts seems even less reportage, more art.

For instance, in the best of Barthelme's dialogue-stories, "The New Music," the partners in the colloquy start by discussing the question, What did you do today?

— Talked to Happy on the telephone saw the 7 o'clock news did not wash the dishes want to clean up some of this mess?

All nicely late-twentieth-century. But the second speaker replies:

— If one does nothing but listen to the new music, everything else drifts, goes away, frays. Did Odysseus feel this way when he and Diomedes decided to steal Athene's statue from the Trojans, so that they would become dejected and lose the war? I don't think so, but who is to know what effect the new music of that remote time had on its hearers?

The exchange continues likewise contrapuntally:

— Or how it compares to the new music of this time?
— One can only conjecture.

Clearly "The New Music" is concerned with more than just what we did today. Yet it seems a likely "conjecture" that the story refers not only to Homeric poetry, and to all that its ancient music implies of death and renewal in eternal cycles, but also to an artistic movement much closer to our own time. Barthelme refers, that is, to a central work of twentieth-century Modernism, itself inspired in part by the Greek classics. In the 1979 story, the two speakers spend most of their time discussing their mother, who has recently died. They speak of her familiarly but edgily, dwelling on her repressiveness, on all the things "Momma didn't 'low." Yet insofar as two faceless voices can show emotion, these show us something very like guilt. "Yes," admits one of them, "I remember Momma, jerking the old nervous system about with her electric *diktats*." Thus with the early references to Odysscus, and with the characters' ambivalence about hidebound but much-missed Momma, a quiet pattern of allusion emerges. Elsewhere one of the men describes a lit-up theater as "glowing like an ember against the hubris of the city"—a faint but clear echo of Stephen Dedalus, characterizing the moment of catharsis or epiphany (and himself borrowing from Shelley): that moment when "the mind is like a fading coal." Yet another Joycean note is sounded when the two speakers discuss a rather grotesque cemetery, one in which the recorded voices of the dead are played from their graves. Such a boneyard has been imagined before, by Leopold Bloom at Paddy Dignam's funeral. As Bloom puts it, early on in *Ulysses*: "Have a gramaphone at every grave or keep in the house." Talking graves, reinforcing a son's unquiet guilt over a dead mother—we have heard this music before as well.

The references are often this subtle. Yet though he may be quiet about it, Barthelme repeatedly complements his up-to-dateness by similar allusive games, rooted in literary history. The glances backward are not to Joyce exclusively, but nearly always to the great Irish author's peers: to the European Modernist movement of the first third of the century.

Undeniably there's a good deal else going on in his work. As John Barth has suggested, literary conventions may wear out, but the best artists in any mode remain inexhaustible. Yet despite the critical attention given his fiction, Barthelme's reliance on the Modernists—his "modern consciousness" of another sort—remains inadequately understood.[2] Now and again, writers have noted the more

---

2. This essay, like all the work here, has been updated. My original assertion was stronger, claiming that Barthelme's debt to Modernism had all but gone ignored.

obvious references. Even Gore Vidal makes mention of one, in his well-known attack on Barthelme and his peers ("American Plastic," from *Matters of Fact and Fiction*). But too few readers have realized how thoroughly the allusions pervade the fiction. No one has seen that they operate in stories from every stage of his career, or seen, especially, how the Modernist canon provides emotional resonance and internal coherence for "The Indian Uprising," the 1968 story that may still rank as his greatest. Finally, his echoes from the first third of this century inform the larger purposes of his work, and help define his place in contemporary letters.

In one of the earliest stories, "For I'm the Boy," the author refers more or less explicitly to three Modernist masters. The purpose, too, seems clear: given the drama's essential reticence, Barthelme intends to put some teeth in all that's unspoken. Though sportive as ever, he seeks to enhance the intensity each time his main character struggles to put feelings into words. It's a divorce story, after all. The protagonist, Bloomsbury, is getting a ride back from the airport after bidding a final goodbye to his ex-wife, Martha. These names alone call to mind a major author and primary text of the earlier period, specifically, Virginia Woolf and *Ulysses* again; indeed, in Joyce's novel Bloom exchanges dirty letters with a woman named Martha. In Bloomsbury's story, two "friends of the family" have come along for the farewell errand, and one is doing the driving. Over the course of some eight pages these friends grill the protagonist more and more closely about how he's feeling. "I may not know about marriage," one says, "but I know about words." Meanwhile Bloomsbury suffers flashbacks to the growing coldness between his wife and him, and to his adultery. These flashbacks occur in shameless Irish brogue, lightly demonstrating the impoverishment of storytelling. Even a race that once lived by blarney is now subject to withering irony:

Ah Martha coom now to bed there's a darlin' gul. Hump off blatherer I've no yet read me Mallarmé for this evenin'. Ooo Martha dear canna we noo let the dear lad rest this night? when the telly's already shut doon an' th' man o' the hoose 'as a 'ard on?...Martha dear where is yer love for me that we talked about in 19 and 38? in the cemetery by the sea?

Thus murmurs of Valéry—disciple of Mallarmé, author of the signal Modernist poem, "A Cemetery By the Sea"—are added to the echoes of Joyce and Woolf.

Soon after the flashbacks begin, it becomes clear that Bloomsbury's "friends," themselves both separated, expect their companion to share his pain with them. They treat it as their due, they all but demand he open up. "So now..." one friend declares, "give us the feeling." Stranger still, Bloomsbury has actually invited these two along, and not just to armor himself for the leavetaking. More than that, it begins to seem as if he wanted their interrogation, their drawing him out. The friends' avidity about seeing Bloomsbury's bruises is a low emotion but certainly familiar. Bloomsbury's own motives however are more complex, rather like an urge to give penance. At story's end Barthelme delivers just such a ritual cleansing—with an exaggeration at once startling and, for this author, typical. The friends stop the car and work their grieving companion over, "first with the brandy bottle, then with the tire iron, until at length the hidden feeling emerged, in the form of salt from his eyes and black blood from his ears, and from his mouth, all sorts of words."

The Modern canon, for all the author's joviality, functions as part of the characters' emotional blockage. The story's Woolf reference may be of tertiary relevance, but it too makes the protagonist seem stuffy, aloof, on a last-name basis. The wife chooses Mallarmé over making love, and our Irish Rose now lies buried in the cemetery by the sea. So the piece may be said to cut mighty works down to size, as well; the young author struggles gamely, cracking wise, against the tyranny of a previous literary generation. In the story's original version (in *Come Back, Dr. Caligari*), Barthelme indulged more extensive joshing about Joyce and Valéry. The Moderns, like poor Bloomsbury, at times prized intricate games or rules of decorum over "the hidden feeling."

The great period of *City Life* and *Sadness* produced several stories with Modernist underpinnings. Rather than rummage through examples, however, it may be more useful to point out that this author, a former gallery critic, references work of the period in all the arts. The title story from the earlier of these two collections, for instance, features a trombone player named Hector Guimard—not coincidentally, the architect who designed the flowery lamps and Metro stops of fin de siècle Paris. Likewise Barthelme's own work is shoved toward the visual. He has claimed in more than one interview that "Bone Bubbles," from *City Life*, is his own addition to the verbal-plastic experiments of Gertrude Stein. And these two books are the only ones in which his more serious collage stories appear (the picture-pieces in his 1974 omnibus, *Guilty Pleasures*, are intended solely for laughs). These intriguing hybrids feature reproductions of etchings and woodcuts, generally nineteenth century and earlier, alongside whatever drama the author has imagined as a companion. The most provocative was "Brain Damage," also from City Life; one wonders why Barthelme didn't include it among the few collages he selected for *Forty Stories*, in 1987.[3]

But in "Daumier," the last piece in *Sadness*, the references are again literary, again to Valéry, and merit closer examination. The story, as Daumier himself cheerfully admits, "maunders;" our narrator wanders into and out of the surreally cowboyish adventures of his imaginary "surrogate," a creature also named Daumier. The purpose is somehow to "distract," somehow to "slay and bother...

---

3. The story finally saw print again in a '98 compilation, *The Teachings of Don B.*, edited by Kim Herzinger.

the original, authentic self, which is a dirty great villain." Along the way, the twinned Daumier dramas are saturated with French art and literature, from the eponymous cartoonist and painter to the cracked Dumas plot in which the puppet-self frolics. So this heady surrogate, designed to free us from self-consciousness, soon comes to suggest another such stand-in made for the same reason, namely, M. Teste.

One recalls that Valéry (in discussing Mallarmé), claimed that the contemplation of the self was the root of alienation. Moreover, self-absorption and the subsequent loss of contact with others seemed to Valery a vexing and paradoxical offshoot of his love for literature, be-cause any thoughts of self first arise from reading, and yet thereafter leave a reader alienated even from his books, lost in solipsism. This conviction led the author to create his M. Teste, at once a paradigm of pure thought and a proof of thought's helplessness. And Barthelme, replacing Valery's complex and high-flown prose with plain Ameri-canese, has his Daumier create a second surrogate for an interesting reason: "Two are necessary," he explains, "so that no individual surro-gate gets the big head." Indeed. Daumier's second dybbuk, moreover, sounds very much like the original Big Head: "I see him as a quiet, thoughtful chap who leads a contemplative-type life." A single page-long paragraph then gives this surrogate its "trial run"—and provides this maundering tale with its essential declarations: "There are always openings, if you can find them. There is always something to do." The sentences are repeated at the story's close.

Here Valery functions differently, substantially so, than he and his peers did in "For I'm the Boy." The invention of a new Teste-ing device offers escape, discovery, possibility. At one point "Daumier" lightly filches the French poet's most famous opening, "The Marquise went out at five o'clock," and the result is a small festival of city life:

DESCRIPTION OF
THREE O'CLOCK
IN THE AFTERNOON

I left Amelia's place and entered the October afternoon. ... [S] ome amount of sunglow still warmed the cunning-wrought cobbles of the street. Many citizens both male and female were hurrying hither and thither on errands of importance, each *agitato* step compromising slightly the sheen of the gray fine-troweled sidewalk. Immature citizens in several sizes... were engaged in ludic agon with basketballs, the same being hurled against passing vehicles producing an unpredictable rebound.

Here for once the language is toney enough, the insight elaborate enough, to suggest the Gallic. Yet it's Gallic "ludic agon," Gallic play, that Barthelme emphasizes. One recalls too, since in this passage the narrator is leaving the apartment of his lover, that M. Teste had a wife, a woman indispensable to him despite all his ratiocinations. This wife had a humanizing effect on Valery's surrogate, an effect neatly summarized by Edmund Wilson, who explains in *Axel's Castle* that the husband would come to Madame Teste "with relief, appetite, and surprise"—and Madame's first name was Emilie, a close enough approximation of Daumier's Amelia. This woman's amorous ameliorative attentions provide Barthelme's narrator with own his best reliefs and surprises.

Since *Sadness* the Modernist play has continued. *The Dead Father*, a magnificent accomplishment though also the author's grimmest, succeeds best when it snitches a whiskey or two from *Finnegans Wake*. "A Manual for Sons," the book-within-the-book (and reprinted in *Sixty Stories*), slips in and out of colloquial voices, Biblical voices, and essay rhetoric; it equates the Oedipal urge finally with the *Wake*'s central theme, original sin: "There is one jealousy that is useful and important, the original jealousy." Likewise the fictional author of the "Manual" has a name with several working parts, Peter Scatterpatter, and toward the novel's end we enter the mind of the soon-to-be-dead father, where the stream of consciousness is choked by weedy *Wake*-ish punning. Then four years after *Dead Father*, "The New Music" offered its syncopation of Greek mythology and Joycean mother-worship. As for Barthelme's last major work, the excellent novel *Paradise*, the book certainly has Modernist references, but in scope and direction it often escapes those shadows. As such, its consideration may wait till after we are done with "The Indian Uprising."

William Gass, in his '68 review, judged this story Barthelme's best to date, and since then the piece has been the author's most widely anthologized and most widely discussed. Daugherty's recent biography goes on at length about the story, summarizing the criticism (by Klinkowitz, Stengel, and others), and earlier Frederick Karl, in his mammoth *American Fictions: 1940-1980*, devoted as much space to "Uprising" as to many a fat novel. In its density, its speed ("I accelerate," a character explains near the start, "ignoring the time signature"), and its tragic yet open-ended resolution, the piece stands out in this author's madcap but generally looser oeuvre.

At some level at least the story is indeed about an Indian uprising, a Comanche attack on a late twentieth-century city. By means of this comic juxtaposition Barthelme surreally fixes the time setting, the Vietnam era, when the urban chic were fascinated with the primitive and disenfranchised. But from the start he enriches this understanding of the milieu and moment by using the same native assault as a metaphor for a doomed love affair. "The sickness of the quarrel," the narrator confesses, "lay thick in the bed." Our protagonist is older than his beloved, more experienced in romance, but his girlfriend is a willful youngster, an Indian sympathizer. She affects bear-claw necklaces and has an apt name: Sylvia. The uprising in other words both refers to an outbreak in the culture, a time when passionate young women strung themselves in sylvan finery, and also suggests a rise of a more intimate kind, stiff and engorged, in the love-bed. In the process Barthelme, subtly but with accumulative clout, opposes two views of the good life. He sets the romantic, artistic sensibility, forever on the point of battle or breakdown, against the stodgy but more livable quietude that most of us eventually settle for. All this is done in frantic collage. The protagonist expresses now the romantic view, now the domestic, and in the same way he functions at times as the narrator, and at other times as just another benumbed reader of the latest bulletin from the front. Barthelme may change tone or subject in mid-sentence, folding together B-movie clichés ("And I sat there getting drunker and drunker and more in love and more in love") and anguished poetic effects.

With these thematic elements in mind—a diseased and self-devouring social order; an affair between an older man and a freer spirit; and the struggle between dangerous self-expression and un-satisfying sanity—one thinks soon enough of the early T.S. Eliot. And so, the story's opening lines: "We defended the city as best we could. The arrows of the Comanches came in clouds. The war clubs of the Comanches clattered on the soft, yellow pavement." It's Pru-frock's yellow fog, turned deadly. Note too that this time the seepage separates at once into the story's two opposed ideologies: the clouds freeflying yet dangerous, the pavement restful yet cloying.

Prufrock is trapped by the cups, the marmalade, the tea, by "the dooryards and the sprinkled streets." In Barthelme's city the streets are sprinkled more dangerously, hedgehogged with barricades. But these fortifications, described early in the story, contain precisely the sort of thing Eliot's narrator complains about. Here one finds cups and plates, can openers and ashtrays, empty bottles of scotch, wine, cognac, vodka, gin...(though it's not a Modernist reference, one thinks as well of the drinker's slang, "dead soldiers"). In his 1981 *Paris Review* interview, Barthelme described this passage about the barricade as "an archaeological slice," but the digging here is not sim-ply into Vietnam-era arcana. It's a strip of the narrator's own past, the detritus of his own bereft living room perhaps—his own nerves, as Prufrock would have it, thrown in patterns on a screen. And yet the barricade *is* archeology, it takes in the culture at large, and the

story never stops shuttling between private trash and the trashing of
a society. Thus the most explicit echo of Prufrock fuses the narrator's
biological decay with that of his town:

> There was a sort of muck running in the gutters, yellowish
> filthy stream suggesting excrement or nervousness, a city that
> does not know what it has done to deserve baldness, errors,
> infidelity.

It is not only the narrator's hair that is growing thin, but the tissue
of lies by which his city convinces itself that the life it has is worthwhile.
With these mournful catalogues, Barthelme is doing precisely what
most critics say he is: he's calling attention to the stink that our mass
culture prefers to ignore. He's a Jeremiah, brandishing plastic instead
of prophecy. But in this case he lays on the post-Modern chill not by
means of new-and-improved media babble, but rather by acknowledging that another complainant was there first. In the same paragraph,
his desire for the girl quails before still more Prufrockian trash, including some bits and pieces very like the erections of his adversaries:

> But it is you I want now, here in the middle of this Upris-
> ing, with the streets yellow and threatening, short, ugly lances
> with fur at the throat [clearly these invaders have the narrator
> outnumbered] and inexplicable shell money lying in the grass.

"Son of man,/ You cannot say, or guess, for you know only/ A heap
of broken images…" So *The Waste Land* (itself echoing another angry
prophet, Ezekiel) comes to have a place in this Uprising as well, as
a compatibly heartsore investigation of urban diaspora. References to
Eliot's second great work are as lightly handled as those to "Prufrock,"
but they squeeze self and society into still more savage shapes.

Hurt by Sylvia's change of heart, about mid-story the narrator
goes to a "teacher" named Miss R., yet the only help she can give

him is the same reproof as the queenly Chess Player of *Waste Land II:* "You know nothing," Miss R. declares, "you feel nothing, you are locked in a most savage and terrible ignorance." And as love turns to insults, gestures of oppression are confused with those of love. When the people of the city's ghetto join the Comanche attack instead of resisting, the narrator's forces make two wildly disparate defenses. "We sent more heroin into the ghetto," he explains, "and hyacinths, ordering another hundred thousand of the pale, delicate flowers." Here again the political and personal collide. The passage condenses widely held assumptions of late-'60s urban studies—namely, that those in the black ghetto were the natural allies of revolution, and that therefore the white power structure looked the other way when ghetto-ites fell prey to drugs—and in so doing combines those assumptions with the love-gift in *Waste Land*'s "Burial of the Dead:" "You gave me hyacinths first a year ago;/ They called me the hyacinth girl." The lovers' attempt at reconciliation, immediately following, comes off likewise folded and spindled. The narrator points to the section of the battle map held by the Comanches, the enemy with whom his hyacinth girl sympathizes, and he says, "Your parts are green." That is, punning on the color, he acknowledges Sylvia's youth and relative sexual inexperience (his own parts, not insignificantly, are blue). Her reply? "You gave me heroin first a year ago!" In the wasteland of an unbalanced love, even gentle gestures make us think only of power politics.

The Comanches' ultimate triumph combines both poems, adding to the narrator's loss the resonances of those twinned deaths by water. At story's end, the blue player is taken before the Clemency Committee, whose spokesperson is the ambiguous Miss R. It's a triumph of the mermaid, as in "Prufrock," or of the witch, as in *Waste Land*, and facing her, the lover-protagonist also confronts a strange double vision. Outside he sees "rain shattering from a great height the prospects of silence and clear, neat rows of houses in the subdivisions;" inside, he sees only "their savage black eyes, paint, feathers, beads." One recalls of course the apocalyptic rainstorm that ends *The Waste Land*. "Prufrock" however seems here inverted, for Eliot's man drowns in the waters of a repressive society, very like those neat rows of houses visible outside the Committee Room. Barthelme's narrator, on the other hand, glimpses those houses as a "prospect," something to long for when confronted with the painted savagery of his love affair.

Such a domestic yearning is rare in this writer's work, which (like his Daumier) generally strives to create new possibilities. Yet this momentary yen for the hearth is part of what makes "Uprising" a cultural benchmark, and at the same time spiritual kin to early Eliot. Naked before the Clemency Committee, Barthelme's story confronts its essential duality: freedom versus government, passion versus clarity. Miss R. may be Miss Reality, demanding that all lovers face up— though the suggestion of "misery" certainly seems pertinent as well. Understood in this way, the story's close doesn't invert Prufrock's tragedy but rather carries it forward forty years. As in the poem, Barthelme's narrator must balance private desires against public uproar. In both cases, a man's uprising comes to nothing, powerless against what the story describes as the world's "rushing, ribald whole." Or consider the first word Sylvia speaks, in the opening paragraph. The narrator puts the question that underlies Prufrock's meditations, and that drives every wanderer in *The Waste Land*: "Is this a good life?" The girl responds: "No."

So much for smaller samples, a few exemplary instances of allusion at work. What does this detail reveal of the larger picture? How can we apply it to this author and his place?

Barthelme himself explained a crucial aspect of the fascination that the Modernists have for him in his *Paris Review* interview, an exchange that the interviewer (the critic J.D. O'Hara) claims was carefully edited and reworked. Recalling his father's career as an architect, the author says: "I was exposed to an almost religious crusade, the

Modern movement in architecture." And he adds: "We were enveloped in Modernism. The house we lived in, which he'd designed, was Modern and the pictures were Modern and the books were Modern."

Though he goes on to note that the movement didn't amount to much, in his father's arena, the crusade image seems telling. The best art made between, say, 1896 (*La Soirée avec M. Teste*) and 1939 (*Finnegans Wake*) by and large represents a moral reckoning point for this author. Just as he can rarely handle emotion without first wrapping it in deprecatory wit, so his essential ideas are often cloaked in the priestly robes of our century's most demanding literatteurs. That these allusions are often subtle only increases that arcane priestliness. It should be pointed out, for instance, that "The Indian Uprising" also contains two explicit references, each quite serious despite their bizarre placement. The first is to Valery, whom Miss R. names and quotes: "The ardor aroused in men by the beauty of women can only be satisfied by God." The second is made by a Comanche under torture, who adopts the major role from Thomas Mann's *Death In Venice* ("His name, he said, was Gustave Aschenbach..."). Thus the story's twinning of love and war takes on two more suggestions of the search for something better, something beyond the world of compromise and decay. A crusade. Modernism offers Barthelme a bedrock ideological seriousness which, while it may be applied in different ways for different stories, cannot be robbed of its ethical force, not even by his otherwise devastating irony.

This grounding in transatlantic artistic values is in keeping with Frederick Karl's thesis, who argues in *American Fictions* that American literature in general has been "Europeanized" over the last half-century (Philip Rahv suggested the same, previously). Barthelme's particular heroes in that older canon, I can add, help to situate him more precisely in contemporary letters. His commonality with Eliot or Valery or Joyce, that is, helps clarify what he shares not only with experts in the short form, like Robert Coover, but with a lover of excess like William Gaddis; it allows us to see that he has some more unlikely cohorts, names that might not occur to us were it not for the Modernist connection—Cynthia Ozick, for one. Indeed the best theorist of the bunch, William Gass, has claimed: "My view is very old-fashioned, of course; it's just the Symbolist position, really" (Gass was speaking at a 1975 symposium on contemporary fiction, later transcribed in *Shenandoah*). That position unites these authors, more than tics of style or coincidences of close publication. The larger question, then, is whether Barthelme and his peers must forever play second fiddle to their European forerunners. In their defense, I would point out that a century and a half ago a homegrown group of late-arriving Romantics, beginning with Emerson, went on to earn their own considerable place in literary history.

The Modernist connection also provides a better sense of Barthelme himself, as distinct from his contemporaries. Here the key figure is Samuel Beckett, and the most revealing book is the 1986 novel, *Paradise*.

Beckett may or may not be a Modernist; critics are divided and, after *Murphy*, the books are stubbornly *sui generis*. Undeniably however he is essential to Donald Barthelme, mentioned time and again as his single greatest inspiration. Of course the younger author has wanted to take his chosen medium beyond the work of his master, as *Malone Dies* took it beyond *Ulysses*, but Barthelme's means have been in large degree precisely the opposite of Beckett's. The expatriate Irishman attempts to rid his work of cultural flotsam and jetsam; he wants nothing that would interfere with isolating the unnameable. Barthelme on the other hand heaps up barricades of sheer stuff. For all the brevity of his individual pieces, they are far more full of color and circumstance, of names and tastes and tidbits, than the older author's grim parings. Barthelme's bits, as we've seen, include the breakage and shards left behind by Beckett's own forebears, and thus Barthelme may be seen as more the restorer, the preservationist, than he appears at first glance. If he has gone beyond, he has done so in part by digging back. For all his speed and shocking combinations, his "need for the new," this is an artist with respect for artifacts of the old.

Yet that would suggest that Barthelme is some sort of museum keeper, that whatever flash he has is secondhand. His penultimate novel proves otherwise, turning retrospection to rediscovery. *Paradise* also reads like his last finished work, more to the point than *The King*; the posthumous book, rather, impresses one as a mood piece, an elegy for a dream. In the '86 novel, the protagonist is Simon, a fiftyish architect recently divorced, who enjoys what one character calls a "male fantasy." For a few months, Simon shares his apartment and bedroom with three young women he met at a lingerie show. Yet the man's good luck generally causes him to think back on his daughter, his marriage, and his vocation. The architect's introspection under the circumstances is in fact something like his creator's response to the possibilities of fiction after 1945. Faced with the sundering of old narrative promises, he's gone back to where the breakup began. And this book too has its over-the-shoulder glances, mostly to Kafka. The opening dream sequence suggests "In the Penal Colony," the later dream passages other of the Czech master's fictional nightmares, and the overall situation recalls *The Trial*, a similar urban jungle, in which worldly women throw themselves at a protagonist who's trying to figure out where they've all gone wrong. Yet the book is something new for this author. In particular, the sex is like nothing he's done, the scenes briefly scorching, full of flesh and unabashedly perverse. The novel begins by presenting the menage as something Simon has already outgrown ("After the women had gone...") and it ends with the laissez-faire spirit of the weekend ("It does feel a bit like Saturday..."). Exploring their complex new freedoms, both Simon and one of the women have outside affairs, which he refers to as "frolic and detour," and repeatedly his lovers admit, in one way or another, that their situation doesn't "fit the pattern" of "suppression and domination of female-kind."

It would be a misrepresentation, a bad one, to suggest that the book is a mere soulless romp. Simon starts from heartbreak and his story generates enormous sympathy for the women, powerless and uneducated "pure skin," as one of them says. Yet just as the architect emerges reborn from his brief burial in flesh and economic constraints, so in this novel Barthelme himself may have at last gotten that demanding Modernist monkey off his back. The title recalls a far older master, namely Dante, and so does the situation of being guided by women at once more innocent and more knowing, like Dante's Beatrice. Then too, the women abandon the exile, after revealing their mystery. So the text challenges us to find the harm in sabbatical pleasures: "Everybody always want somebody to be sorry. Fuck that." Its *Trial* is paradise.

"You're not a father-figure," one of Simon's lovers tells him, defiantly. "That surprise you?" Not at all: bright youth has always had to deny its forebears. For the upstart Barthelme as well, the father remained a stubborn image, in spite of all the times the author denied the old man or left him in fragments. Likewise the intractable seriousness of Modernism, as it lurks in the novels and stories, is to some extent the ineradicable whisper of Dad. That is, there are personal implications in my analysis, considering what Barthelme has said about his own father's career.[4] But *Paradise* makes clear that this author wanted no part of surrendering, all Oedipally, to fate. His art exists not to prove us the pawns of Freudian theory, nor of any other uprising put down long before we were born, but rather to sift and reshape the debris of those earlier struggles, scotching this piece of law to that emblem of freedom, this nose off the Emperor's bust to that foldout from the latest issue. Any bedrock moral seriousness, after all, is only so much dirt if lacks application to contemporary surfaces. John Barth has called his brand of Post-modernism "the literature of replenishment"—an attempt to reinvigorate narrative fic-

---

4. Daugherty's biography explores the Oedipal implication thoroughly.

tion despite the exhaustion of certain conventions and approaches. Donald Barthelme should be understood as, among other things, our replenisher of Modernism. Whatever he has achieved, he's done it not merely by reference and mimicry but by a more vital connection, by his passion for the new in the old, by his insistence that Stephen Dedalus wasn't the last to have an epiphany at seeing a woman's bared thighs. Barthelme by no means stands with the "old artificer" of Dedalus, but he has the genius to recognize the ancient figure, and he has the courage to stay with our resurgent contradictions at every unexpected glimpse.

—*Southwest Review*, 1990

SECOND TIDE

INVERTED INFERNO:
TONI MORRISON'S SULA

In interview, and in her rare writings on her craft, Toni Morrison prefers the role of Black Woman novelist. That's capital B, capital W, and a small, tertiary n. Her lone work of literary criticism, her collected Massey lectures from 1992, bears a title that insists on the same priorities: *Playing in the Dark*. Her book-length fiction always demonstrates considerable imaginative freedom, but when asked, the author herself speaks primarily of social freedoms. She claims to be concerned above all with the idea of "a black community"—what such a community once meant, how it has changed, and how despite those changes its opposition to the white power structure must be maintained. Morrison alters the argument according to the occasion, for instance in the essays of *What Moves at the Margin* or the lengthy interview with Robert Stepto. Nonetheless her allegiance remains with that outsider community, one she perceives as renegade. At the International PEN Congress of January, 1986, Morrison announced she'd never felt like an American. She defined herself as a voice for those outside our culture's mainstream, not just black and female, but also Third-World, Carribean.

Critics have followed the artist's lead. Frederick Karl, in his mammoth *American Fictions 1940-1980* (1983), categorized the author as one whose whole purpose is social responsibility: "Morrison is attempting to gather in...politics, caste, class, sexism, [and] genealogy."

Barbara Christian offers a more thorough overview, in *Black Feminist Criticism: Perspectives on Black Women Writers* (1985); but she too emphasizes Morrison's "tension between the natural order and the unnatural points of [social] discrimination—race, sex, money, class."

Such readings have their merits. Morrison's novels certainly demonstrate the damage that racial and social discrimination has done. Yet what refined, even exotic demonstrations she chooses! The opening page of her first, *The Bluest Eye* (1970), actually embodies the torment of living as an outsider typographically. The page contains three reprints of a passage from what is obviously a mainstream child's reader:

> Here is the house. It is green and white. It has a red door. It is very pretty. Here is the family. Mother, Father, Dick, and Jane live in the green-and-white house. They are very happy…

Each time these lines are repeated, they look more tortured: first the punctuation disappears, then the spaces between the words. Likewise the third novel, the award-winning *Song of Solomon* (1977), makes its points about African American identity and the struggle between the sexes by fantastic means, by rediscovering the myth that "the people could fly," and finding disturbing, ambivalent truths in that myth. In other words, one of Morrison's significant subjects for her longer stories is always storytelling itself. The shape that gossip, superstition, and telling tales give to experience matters enormously Morrison's most famous and honored novel, *Beloved* (1987). Late-twentieth-century readers must track a few obscure and widely scattered clues in order to understand that the "ghost" in *Beloved* is only an abused African girl, driven mad by her recent abduction into slavery. In the minds of the novel's mid-nineteenth-century characters, the young woman exists first and last as a long-rumored spirit at last come to life; it is as a ghost, a community fiction, that the poor girl engineers the major actions of the plot.

Morrison's novels, in fact, depend on highly sophisticated literary techniques, structural and intertextual devices generally associated with Modernism and whatever has come since. An author more ordinarily concerned with "race, sex, money, class" would proceed by more ordinary means. An exemplary case is *Sula,* the second novel, published in 1974. Yet while I do wish to illuminate some of this writer's more cunning aesthetic niceties—while I do think they've been overlooked—I want also to bring such niceties together with the author's avowed commitment to social or historical responsibility. I believe Morrison knows what she's about. I believe such commitment is in fact at the core of her work.

Sula covers fifty years, yet it has the brevity of a nightmare. It achieves microcosm: Morrison never leaves her imaginary Ohio community, "the Bottom," for more than the occasional few pages, yet she overlooks none of the changes in black experience that occurred between the First World War and the mid-1960s. Part of this success is due to a striking hiatus in the novel's plot. Between Parts 1 and 2, the book jumps some ten years, from 1927 to 1937. Of course the prologue (set, like the epilogue, in 1965) has established that the book will cover a lot of ground, and there are a number of plot concerns connecting the two Parts, in particular the twinned lives of Sula Peace and Nel Wright, the protagonists. The two women spend most of the first half as best friends, most of the second as worst enemies. Each eventually returns to spiritual sisterhood: Sula on her deathbed in 1940, Nel (an emotional circle, matching the chronological) in the 1965 epilogue.

But this thumbnail outline itself makes clear that the connections between the novel's two sections are often subtle, in some cases detectable only after the book has been completed. Morrison's plotting constitutes a considerable aesthetic risk. The interruption raises ideas over narrative—and not just ideas, but also more rarified unifying principles, such as metaphoric structure.

What ideas? First things first: Morrison is indeed examining a lost community. The issue comes up at once; the opening is straight-forward, though seductive:

> In that place, where they tore the nightshade and blackberry patches from their roots to make room for the Medallion City Golf Course, there was once a neighborhood. It stood in the hills above the valley town of Medallion and spread all the way to the river. It is called the suburbs now, but when black people lived there it was called the Bottom.

The omniscient point of view is obvious; so too is an essential fondness. The authorial voice in Morrison is forever celebrational. Her omniscience is not that of a distant recording angel, but of a community spirit, and she comes to each character "in that place" with sympathy. Morrison's first book gave us one of the most ex-traordinary examples of that sympathy, a compassionate portrait of a man who rapes his own daughter; her latest novel, like *Sula,* brings to life an entire black Ohio community. In *Sula,* as the many players take their turns—each in some way bent to extremity by poverty, op-pression, or loneliness—this all-knowing, all-forgiving point of view allows for some complicated effects, as we shall see. But the immedi-ate impression is trustworthy and humane: precisely the sort of thing that would make her purposes seem simple. The closest parallel to Morrison's familiar omniscience occurs in the deceptively simple *One Hundred Years of Solitude;* Garcia Marquez is very nearly the only contemporary Morrison will mention when asked to name authors she admires.

She first tells the story of another sort of local spirit, poor Shadrack, so traumatized by combat in 1917 that he institutes the mad celebration called National Suicide Day. Comic yet gloomy, the date becomes a landmark at the beginning of each new year in the Bottom. Only after that ambiguity in the community self-definition is established does the principal storyline begin, and only then to digress again at once. Morrison makes her single extended excursion outside the Bottom, a 1920 visit to New Orleans by Helene and Nel Wright. On this African American home ground Nel at last meets her grandmother, a prostitute of impressive standing and self-possession, and so by the time she returns to Ohio the girl has gained "a new-found me-ness;" she has "the strength to cultivate a friend in spite of her mother," and that friend is Sula. In short, Nel undergoes an ambiguous self-definition to match that of Suicide Day. Seeming digressions come together; the changes in particular people fit changes in the general fabric of life.

There are other devices set in place, in the thirty pages before Sula arrives on stage. Shadrack comes to function outside the rule of church and family, immune even to white control: in his madness he can insult the occasional visitors from Medallion. Helene is presented as just the opposite; her whorehouse raising has driven her to become a pillar of the community in the conventional sense, "a woman who won all social battles with presence and a conviction of the legitimacy of her authority." The mad veteran's single name recalls both the Old Testament believer who risked destruction in the fiery furnace and a common river fish known for living in dirty waters; Nel's mother last name suggests both a maker and moral uprightness itself. Between them, the Bottom takes on definition. But more than that, another of the novel's core structures is established, strongly enough to carry it through those places where simple narrative breaks down, namely, an intricate and continuous reliance on duality.

There's hardly a character in the book that doesn't need some other in order to feel complete, or an incident that isn't eventually paired with some other in order to enhance the meaning of both. The essential twins are Nel and Sula. Just before the central event, the girls' accidental drowning of a boy named Chicken Little, the two are presented in a description that exemplifies their complementary nature: "They lay in the grass, their foreheads almost touching, their bodies stretched away from each other at a 180-degree angle." Sula Peace is one radius, Nel Wright the other; their two arcs encompass a book of wheels within wheels.

Their families and houses appear like mirror reversals of each other. Helene Wright has renounced her forebears' whoring and has become instead the conservative backbone of the Bottom, creating a home in which a daughter's wedding is "the culmination of all she had been, done or thought in this world." This element of the community is run by the women, and sooner or later abandoned by their husbands. On the other hand, there's Eva Peace, Sula's grandmother, who literally bartered her flesh, sacrificing a leg in order to collect railroad insurance. Thanks to that inheritance, the Peace family lives in "a house of many rooms" where "manlove" is the rule—a whorehouse without prices or pimps, where Sula's mother Hannah will "fuck practically anything" simply because she enjoys it.

These motifs recur and ramify. Sula goes to college on the insurance money from her dead uncle and mother, more flesh-peddling, and when she returns to the Bottom she rules her house and her life, as Nel points out, "like a man." After her return she becomes the Bottom's pariah, a "roach" who sleeps with white men. In the meantime, Nel defines herself ever more firmly as a woman, a pillar in the same sense as her mother. When Sula seduces Nel's husband, Jude, Nel reprises her mother's holier-than-thou manipulations, lapsing into a silence that drives Jude away. Indeed, in the pages after Nel discovers Sula and Jude, hand-me-down roleplaying proves stronger than any love between husband and wife. This part of the narrative is from the point of view of the betrayed wife and friend and brilliantly evokes a spirit in the grip of unconscious promptings. Nel is silenced as much by memories of her mother as by what is taking place before her eyes; she manipulates unintentionally. Thereafter, Nel retreats into the smarmy embrace of general opinion. Falling back on her position as the injured party, she joins the rest of the women in the Bottom in adopting an increased moral strictness, defined specifically against Sula.

Nel adopts the role of Good Woman, in other words; Sula's function is Bad Man. So at least their fellow townswomen see them, and the authorial familiarity keeps the reader with the public perception. But each of the novel's central twins is also representative of another rich symbol system, a system known to author and reader but not to the uneducated inhabitants of the Bottom. Each woman embodies one of the four elements. Sula's identification is easier to trace. Her uncle and mother both burn to death, and she herself suffers, in her last illness, "a kind of burning." She and Shadrack are described as "two devils," and her death plunges the Bottom into a terrible cold snap. Nel's element however must be deduced from her contrast to Sula—yet another way in which the novel depends on duality. At the story's end Nel recalls for the first time in years Chicken Little's drowning, the secret which began the inevitable separation from her soulmate. Sula had been whirling the boy around at arm's length, and he'd slipped and flown into the river. Nel, standing beside them, did nothing either to save the boy at the time or to reveal the truth of what happened later. In her stunted perception, the guilt was entirely Sula's. Now however, in the novel's epilogue, she meditates:

> All these years she had been secretly proud of her calm, controlled behavior when Sula was uncontrollable.... Now it seemed that what she had thought was maturity, serenity and compassion was only the tranquillity that follows a joyful stimulation. Just as the water closed peacefully over the turbulence of Chicken Little's body, so had contentment washed over her enjoyment.

Moreover, the circle of elemental symbolism is rounded out by the two most important men in Nel and Sula's lives. Nel's husband Jude Green is driven to marry her out of a feeling that "the two of them together would make one Jude;" the whites of Medallion won't let him do the roadwork he loves, and so he feels cut off from his true self. "He wanted to swing the pick or…shovel the gravel." Jude is of the earth, his very name is Green, and he marries in order to find something like the satisfactions of earthwork. As for Ajax, the man Sula falls in love with, his dream is of flying, airplanes, the air itself. Sula's crucial mistake concerning him is that, in the beautiful passage on their lovemaking, she mistakes him for earth. She imagines rubbing away his color to discover "gold leaf," then scraping away the gold to find "alabaster," then at last cracking the alabaster to "see the loam, fertile, free of pebbles and twigs." This mistaken identity is underscored after he leaves for an "air show in Dayton," when she discovers his driver's license bears the name Albert Jacks. What Sula took for a Greek demigod in alabaster proves instead something brief and flighty as cards or a child's game.

That ambiguity about a person's essential self suggests something still more aesthetically complex, still another way Morrison manages the interplay of elements and dualities. Sula may generally function as Fire, but in her childhood intimacy with Nel and in the adult act of love she finds "my water:…the postcoital privateness in which she met herself, welcomed herself, and joined herself in matchless harmony." Likewise at her death she finds joy, joy she wants most to share with Nel, in "the sleep of water." As for Nel, Sula of course is the one who provides her joyful stimulation, releasing otherwise dammed-up elements. "[Nel's] parents had succeeded in rubbing down to a dull glow any sparkle or splutter she had. Only with Sula did that quality have free rein." As each woman finds herself briefly in a male lover, so each was always and truly completed by the more perfect, Platonic opposite of her childhood friend. Nel and Sula initially meet in their dreams; their first conversation occurs while "facing each other through the ropes of the one vacant swing." There, each tells the other to go on: mirror-creatures unwilling to rupture the unearthly balance they share.

Now what has all this to do with community? Perpetual cycles, pairs of emotions and elements—such stuff sounds like art for art's sake. The formal rigor recalls the devices of Vladimir Nabokov. What of Morrison's avowed commitment to the renegade, to serving as a voice for the voiceless?

Part of the answer is that this book is a remembrance, an elegy. "We was girls together," Nel cries to her dead friend at novel's end. With that, too, she finally acknowledges her complicity in the death of Chicken Little, the original sin of separation from her other half. The Bottom is gone, we know from the novel's first line, and with it the perfect symmetries of our childhoods. Isn't the whole notion of community an attempt to provide again the security of Mamma at crib side? Eva Peace here sets fire to her son Plum, not simply because the War has made him a junkie, but because she understands his addiction is the first step in becoming a baby again: "He wanted to crawl back in my womb." Eva's reasoning of course also implies a familiar criticism of the modern black male (expressed more directly by authors as different as W.E.B. DuBois and Malcolm X), namely, that beneath a young black's cock-of-the-walk act lies a ruinous immaturity. Many of *Sula*'s poetic flourishes bear a similar specific pertinence to, as the author puts it in her later title, what moves at the American margins. Yet the point about seeking childhood comfort in neighbors and a way of life resonates beyond specifics of place and race. Seen this way, community is always elsewhere. The idea is an ancient one, and some of its most famous expressions seem to apply: the prophet's glimpse from the mountaintop, the Wonderland beyond the looking-glass. At *Sula*'s end, Nel meditates on how her former brothers and sisters are fleeing the Bottom:

> The black people, for all their new look, seemed awfully anxious to get to the valley, or leave town. It was sad, because the Bottom had been a real place. These young ones kept talking about the community, but they left the hills to the poor, the old, the stubborn—and the rich white folks. Maybe it hadn't been a community, but it had been a place.

But there is another way in which the subtle dualistic play of *Sula's* characters and events fit this author's social commitment, her desire to forge a conscience for her race. One must understand that, above all, the drama here is one of *misperception*. The events aren't caused by trespassing beyond some moral absolute dictated by the author, but by how the people of the Bottom wrongly perceive some things as absolute, and how they then act on this misapprehension. Other critics have noted the importance of such wrongheaded perception, in particular Barbara Lounsberry and Grace Ann Hovet in an essay for *Black American Literature Forum*, but they too don't connect the social issue of community consensus to the literary strategies of symbolism and structure. Morrison herself says something about those strategies in *The Dictionary of Literary Biography*, back in 1980: "I was writing [in *Sula*] about good and evil and the purposes to which they are frequently put, *the way in which the community uses them* [my italics]."

The great tool for manipulating perception is of course Morrison's familiar omniscience, her fond angel's point of view. That manipulation, it must be said, is enhanced at every juncture by the boldness and intimacy of her style. *Sula* manages repetitions that are intricate and yet incantatory; each scene has the effect of tour de force, whether the subject be joshing, muscular sexuality or austere, self-sacrificial posing. Even sorrow can be celebrated, like a funeral march in New Orleans. The best contemporary analogy would be, again, the Garcia Marquez of *One Hundred Years*. Still, the rhetoric never rises simply for its own sake. It serves to create a drama where any viciousness may be viewed sympathetically (even doing nothing to save a drowning child), and any innocence may be taken as malicious (even the simple horseplay that precedes a child's drowning). So every character sees some different animal or weed in the distinctive birthmark over Sula's eye: everyone has their own reading. There is tragedy in such misperception, but the author never corrects it. About as close as she will come to making judgments occurs in her discussion of the gossip about Sula's sleeping with white men:

There was nothing lower she could do, nothing filthier. The
fact that their own skin color was proof that it had happened
in their own families was no deterrent to their bile. Nor was
the willingness of black men to lie in the beds of white women
a consideration that might lead them toward tolerance. They
insisted that all unions between white men and black women
be rape; for a black woman to be willing was literally unthink-
able. In that way, they regarded integration with precisely the
same venom that white people did.

And if it seems unlikely that a capital B, capital W writer would
take her own people to task for their racism, consider that when Sula
makes love with Ajax she is trying to dig under his skin to the "loam."
The writing is so lovely that at first we may not notice it is an image
for getting past differences of surface color.

The community pariah is in fact a greater subversive than anyone
else in the Bottom, because she challenges comfortable perceptions,
particularly those of white oppression. Just before seducing Nel's
Jude, Sula laughs at the husband's easy, "whiney" declaration that
"a Negro man had a hard row to hoe in the world." When she dies,
too, the community is robbed of the "devil" which made their placid
acceptance of white control appear heroic. "[M]others who had defended their children from Sula's malevolence (or who had defended
their positions as mothers from Sula's scorn for the role) now had
nothing to rub up against."

Years before, when Hannah Peace had asked her mother if she'd
loved her children, Eva could hardly understand the question: "What
you talkin' about did I love you girl I stayed alive for you." But Hannah's daughter went to the big city; she came back with all "those
lovely college words like *aesthetic* or *rapport*." In short Sula was a
one-woman urban migration, and she returned with a new means
of regarding the world. To her, loving can no longer be defined simply as staying alive. It has to do instead with living to full human

capacity, with "craving the other half" of one's personal "equation," and with "the creation of a special kind of joy." Sula upsets the others in town not because she's vicious, but because she's visionary. The book's epigraph is from Tennessee Williams (not just a white Southerner, it's worth noting, but one inextricably linked to New Orleans). The Williams title that Morrison selects from, *The Rose Tattoo*, recalls Sula's birthmark, and the words could easily be hers too: "I had too much glory. They don't want glory like *that* in nobody's heart."

Thus, without Sula, without her glory misperceived as evil, the other families no longer can justify how they scrape along. "A rain fell and froze;…Christmas…haggled everybody's nerves like a dull axe." On the next National Suicide Day the inhabitants of the Bottom erupt in their first genuine act of revolt.

This eruption is pitiable, a mass panic at the river's edge. It anticipates the cataclysm at the end of *Beloved*, another sorry mix of the seditious and the self-destructive. *Sula*'s riot, in a piercing irony, takes place on the first Suicide Day when old Shadrack no longer cares. Ever the town's dark mirror, the madman lost his faith when he heard of Sula's death. Yet even the drownings recall Sula's last visions: "They found themselves in a chamber of water…[Y]oung boys strangled when the oxygen left them to join the water." In this apocalyptic "sleep of water," the pariah's deathbed prophecy perversely comes true. Sula had claimed that one day people would love her: "After all the old women have lain with the teenagers; when all the young girls have slept with all their drunken uncles…" In the collapsed river tunnel, just such an orgy takes place. So at great cost—without sacrificing the ambiguity inherent in "lovely college words like *aesthetic*"—the people of the Bottom are rid of their pious and largely pointless abnegations. Turn the page, and it's 1965.

Finally, Morrison underscores her drama of misperception by a series of literary or Biblical allusions, evident especially in her choice of names. Like Sula, she isn't so concerned with surface; our entire culture is her loam.

Biblical references abound, to be sure. They don't follow the chronology of the Scriptures strictly (one point on which *Sula* and *One Hundred Years* differ), but in general the movement is Old Testament to New. Shadrack figures mostly in Book I, and the apocalypse ends Book II. Eva the first mother in Book I, Jude the Judas in Book II. And just before she throws Chicken Little in the river, Sula leads him up a tree that allows him to see farther than ever before: a Tree of Knowledge to presage the book's original sin. Indeed, isn't Sula's very name a feminine reconstruction of Lucifer, whose province has always called right and wrong into ambiguity? The community's name derives after all from a "nigger joke" about "the Bottom of Heaven." The Queen of this Inferno, however, lives at an address recalling the Prince of Paradise: number 7, Carpenter Lane. The contradiction in the address perhaps mirrors the way "Sula" is actually an *inversion* of "Lucifer." If only the community could perceive her rightly, she might prove just the opposite of a devil, she might serve instead as their avenging angel. After all, her name and those of her forebears (Eva, Hannah, Sula) contains the joyful "ah" of real living, of better than mere staying alive. If anyone's name suggests death and damnation, it is Nel's, Nel's and Helene's and even the grandmother Rochelle's. The knell tolls down the generations of the Wrights, and it tolls for the Bottom. No community that prefers one-dimensional right-ness over living at peace with all the divergent elements of its nature deserves to last forever. Its children must look elsewhere.

In the book's closing sentences, Nel comes at last to this complex and humbling perception. The truth provokes a howl: "It was a fine cry—loud and long—but it had no bottom and no top, just circles and circles of sorrow." A reader may see Dante in that description, and see as well the ever-turning, ever-renewing wheel of the elements. He or she may see Heaven and Hell, and the whole question of top and bottom, pillars and pariahs. Yet it would be terrible narrow-mindedness to think such metaphoric reinforcement in any way betrays the essential impulses of the book: toward a greater humanity, and toward a braver sense of community purpose. Morrison's sympathies for the renegade are perfectly appropriate. A renegade wants nothing better than to break out of those sorrowful circles. Or at least, a renegade will erupt in a "fine cry" like *Sula,* imposing its genius on a devious and discouraging world.

—High Plains Literary Review, 1988

NARROWING IN ON TRAGEDY:
RUSSELL BANKS & SUCCESS STORIES

Russell Banks is the square peg that won't be fit into the ever-narrowing categories of American fiction. Thus far the apogee of his quirky career has been the 1985 novel *Continental Drift*. That nightmare of worlds in collision (declining white-collar New England, rising no-collar Jamaica) was a terrific accomplishment, and with *Drift* looming so large in the background, *Success Stories* might be mistaken for a publisher's holding action—keeping the author's name before the public while he prepares his next big event. Happily, the book outfoxes such thinking. Bank's fourth collection of stories proves an idiosyncratic triumph, strictly arranged and narrowing in on an essential tragedy. Indeed. *Success Stories* offers insight into the writer's entire body of work.[1]

The book contains two different sorts of stories, and the mix would seem unlikely. One grouping is realistic, full of sympathy, richly meditative about its characters' political and economic circumstances. These stories are contiguous; each concerns Earl, who grows up poor in New Hampshire after his father abandons the family, and who subsequently runs away himself, to the Gold Coast of Florida. There Earl achieves a tentative adulthood, though

---

1. What I have to say about the career is as of 1987, obviously. The elements I discuss in *Success Stories*, however, are the same ones that Banks went on to explore so rewardingly in *Affliction* (1989), *Rule of the Bone* (1994), and later fiction.

the last two stories see him back in New Hampshire and still prey to the dislocations of his impoverished youth. Alternating with the chapters of this *Bildungsroman,* however, are five tales that border on the surreal. Their settings are stylized—a hoodoo-haunted military regime, a suburb frightened of it own children. Some attempt parable, others offer formal experiment. All avoid the sympathy which distinguishes Earl's initiations.

Banks has worked this mixture since the beginning. His *Searching for Survivors,* appearing in 1975, clearly owed a debt to American Postmodernism as it was practiced in the preceding eight or ten years, yet the best piece in the book was "The Defenseman," the long closing elegy to a shattered New Hampshire family. And his 1981 collection, *Trailerpark,* though grounded in the sort of blue-collar realism its title suggests, made room for "The Child Screams and Looks Back at You," a fable about a youngster's death no less chilling for its counterpoint of third and second-person. What allows Banks such freedom?

His unusual narrative voice provides part of the answer. Banks is neither heartlessly flashy like the most vapid of the Postmodern experiments, nor tamped down and minimalist in keeping with the current tulip craze. In "Adultery," here, he provides a glimpse of the affect he strives for while describing the difference between Earl's New Hampshire flatness and his girlfriend's Florida drawl:

> My talk was merely that, talk, or so it seemed to me—ideas made over into sounds, feelings translated into symbols and emblems. Hers, though, was the thing itself—feelings and sunlight and rest.

Banks refuses to hurry. His declarations troll the waters with commas and dashes and conversational fill like "or so it seemed to me," and with lists, like the magnificent tabulation of how the day's first vodka goes down in "Firewood." Such methods of modulation allow him enormous flexibility. His lines are both stretched with "feelings translated into symbols" and weighted with "the thing itself." His more surreal pieces work the same combination—though it must be said that their terrors can't match those of Earl, his heart steeped in American poverty and the guilt that comes with it.

What finally sets Banks apart, though, isn't voice; his omnivorousness can be sloppy. Rather, his great gift is his insistence on naming sources, reasons, first causes. The world here is one that too few writers ever consider, granted. But sympathy for the downtrodden can lead to blindness; and that *Success Stories* never allows. Earl proves as much of a manipulator as any of the better-born, and he shares many of their desires and fears. Banks identifies differences of class not just to shame us with them, but because it is only once those difference are tagged and out of the way that we can understand what the true "thing itself" consists of—what humanity itself consists of. The masterpiece here, "Sarah Coles: A Type of Love Story," climaxes with just such a stripping-down. The point of view is another strange one, retrospective first and third-person, and yet the protagonist/narrator is clearly Earl. By now he's a professional man, good-looking and single, a success. But he falls for a woman far beneath his newly achieved station, the ugly divorcee Sarah. And when at last the clothes come off, in spite of their differences these two rise to something near the level of the Ideal:

> Two naked members of the same species, a male and a female... both individuals standing slackly, as if a great, protracted tension between them had at last been released.

—*Boston Review*, 1987

BLUE WITHOUT BLUES: GILBERT SORRENTINO, BLUE PASTORAL, & THE SUBVERSION OF THE NOVEL

No literary genre lasts forever. The epic, for example, is extinct, and one that would seem to have gone for good is the pastoral. With its praise of rustic living, utopian leanings, and occasional earthiness, the genre had a long and rich existence. Created by the Greeks, refined by Virgil, the pastoral later served our own literature superbly at the hands of Spenser, Shakespeare, and Andrew Marvell. Then however came rise of industrialization, and anyone with a couple of semesters of English Lit can tell you what that meant for the pastoral. Altered vistas call for altered voices. Yet now—out of the blue, as it were—there comes a pastoral clumsily disguised as our current dominant literary form, the "novel." In quotes, yes. Gilbert Sorrentino's *Blue Pastoral* is just the sort of book to turn a form fuzzy.

Blue Pastoral claims to offer a panorama of America ("It was a slice of America, this great land that has dreamed its great dream of democracy for ages and ages, or, in any event, for seventy-two years longer than CCNY"), yet it neither renders a lifelike American landscape nor develops a plausible American character. Nor any kind of character, really. It gives us a portrait of a marriage ("I've been a good wife, interested and boned-up on everything you do, asking intelligent questions"), but one in which praise and insult converge loonily ("Just to hear you once again spout forth your dizzy horseshit perks my spirits up like seltzer!"). It pretends a meditation on Time ("great sacrosanct and bulging Time, that again, at this turn of the year, comes round once again") and of course Nature ("that potency that men call Nature, in all its warps and woofs"), but it never puts together two serious sentences in a row. It's a quest ("For it is somewhere past the glimmering horizon that we shall find…perhaps, the answer to our quest") that achieves a highly suspect Grail.

No label will stay put on this text. As the above string of quips demonstrates, anything that strays into the author's sights is mocked with equal verve and panache. As the protagonist puts it at one point, "Vigour gives equal title." Indeed, this idea, this up-and-at-'em energy which brings any purpose to life, might be the best way to start an assessment of Gilbert Sorrentino's highly various but steadily lengthening shelf of books. *Blue Pastoral* is his eighteenth published work in the last twenty-four years, his ninth work of fiction. Moreover he has maintained this pace despite never writing a book remotely near a best-seller. On top of that, as a product of Brooklyn public schools who never completed a BA, he spent many years punching the clock at real jobs: "at least 25 jobs of all sorts" in and around New York, as he told *Contemporary Literature* in 1977 (he has also received most of the good grants and fellowships, from the National Endowment for the Arts and the Guggenheim Foundation). Still, he's published often and nearly all of his work remains available. Just this past year, too, he landed a university appointment worthy of his accomplishment, at Stanford. It does appear that, in his mid-fifties, Gilbert Sorrentino has started to see his "vigour" rewarded.[1]

---

1. Remarkably, these claims from 1983 still hold true, even beyond the author's death in 2006. Everything he wrote remains in print, a rare thing for so unconventional a sensibility. The aesthetic shifts are so radical that, here in *Sea-God's Herb*, I've separated my two Sorrentino pieces.

He belongs with the iconoclasts of contemporary American fiction. Energy and imagination drive him to set up complex and unusual literary edifices, as structurally daring as Thomas Pynchon's. Even his earliest and most conventional novels tinkered with point of view and chronology, and the ones since then have taken on more and more of the linguistic games that distinguish his poetry. In these games, as in *Pastoral*'s parodies, Sorrentino frequently achieves a wicked irony and verbal zest that recalls Donald Barthelme. Above all, college degree or no, he has a mind that can burn through the very constructs it puts up. "Vigour gives equal title" is followed by "[a] wondrous phrase, yet all methinks devoid of meaning." Sorrentino is especially quick to rip down those all-too-human constructs we call pretensions; few Americans now writing can prick our bubbles with a meaner joy. In his art, this impulse leads to an adamant denial of all abstraction, since symbol making or turning people into ideas is only more pretense. The upshot is that he's become our poet of bitterness. At Sorrentino's best, that bitterness can be uproarious, though rooted in regret at how we so often prove ourselves "all devoid of meaning." Still, his refusal to sugarcoat his concerns—ideals gone perverse, communities splintered to bits—undoubtedly has more than a little to do with his lack of commercial publishing support.

Blue Pastoral, however, is his happiest work. Nothing if not an untrammeled expression of his trapeze-artist's imagination, the book somersaults overhead with breezy *sprezzatura.* In this way it helps illuminate not only his purposes but also those of the dozen or so Americans like him. Sorrentino and his peers, it should be understood, are not only iconoclasts but also renovators. They don't merely smash the conventional novel and short story, they reshape the forms. In order finally to appreciate this reshaping, it should be understood that Sorrentino represents a tradition new to this country (and not yet very old elsewhere) that has begun to change American fiction.

He began as a poet. In 1960, the year of his first collection *The Darkness Surrounds Us,* he wrote in a biographical note for *The New*

American Poets that his foremost "literary markers" were Ezra Pound and William Carlos Williams, a Modernist heritage that helps clarify his own ideals. Ever since, his poems have been notable for an attention to rhythm and shape that's consistent enough to intrigue but never so severe as to bore, and for a linguistic control so mature it can sustain even deliberate clichés (borrowed from love songs, especially) and obscenity. He's erudite, high-minded, but not fussy. Indeed, Sorrentino's work in both poetry and prose, in keeping with his excoriating intelligence, is as dirty-mouthed as anyone this side of Charles Bukowski. One of his earliest pieces of criticism was a fiery defense of Hubert Selby, Jr. and the then-unpublished *Last Exit to Brooklyn;* Selby eventually dedicated the novel to Sorrentino. Indeed, it's a Selby-like despair that howls through the poetry's formal control. Sorrentino's verse can fail out of too strident a bitterness, self-pitying as in *Black and White* (1964), as well as from conceits too strictly maintained. *The Perfect Fiction* (1968) almost suffocates under its structure, with a poem for each of the fifty-two weeks in a year and every stanza three brief lines (the Williams stanza, in other words).

But *The Orangery* (1978) balances shape and sadness. Its loose sonnets all work some variation on that notoriously unrhymable word "orange"—and in this provide a means, one comes to learn, for getting at the death of the poet's mother. Nothing so expresses a grief beyond words as the impossible aesthetic task: "Nothing is the thing that rhymes with orange." As for *Corrosive Sublimate* (1971), that speaks still more eloquently. Again this is poetry impelled by death, the death of old friends; again all sentimental visions are refused. The speaker ignores neither the ruin of his present state nor the bitter taste now given remembrance: "What/ quality of American light/ that is not bitter/ is departed" ("Rose Room"). As usual the poems tend to be short, each internally consistent about stanza and line length; but here the sharply focused particulars move from private sorrows to public ones. These friends gone down are placed in the context of history's mass deaths; Stalinist work camps and Nazi rallies figure in

"Give Them Blood," our own Civil War and a "gook hamlet" in "Veterans of Foreign Wars." In the end the expanding vision, corrosive yet seeking the sublime, produces something few poets have brought off, an elegiac celebration. Even in Sorrentino's *Collected Poems* (1981), the excerpts from *Corrosive Sublimate* stand out.

The year 1971 was in fact a good one for him, since it saw the publication not only of those poems but also of *Imaginative Qualities of Actual Things*, which may be his most satisfying novel. This juicy and hilariously sour meringue is cooked up from bits and pieces of the New York literary and artistic scene. Visiting with rejects from both big presses and better galleries, the novel exposes not the rich but the poor; each of the eight chapters sketches another loser who whores after bucks while nobly mouthing off about Art, and only one of them has the talent worth a drink. But the main characters of *Imaginative Qualities* (the remarkable title is another homage to Williams) are the sorrowfully cynical narrator and the '60s New York in which these schmucks go down. Voice and place are the actual things. Any attempt to gloss over either would rob the world of its living, imaginative quality: "We are measured…by the graph of specific losses and individual disintegration."

Sorrentino's novels come in two modes, which could be termed "realistic" and "experimental"—except those terms also gloss over too much. Perhaps we could call them "familiar tunes" and "unchained melodies," considering how the author has relied on popular music to help define his milieu. There are the snippets of song in his poems, in *Imaginative Qualities* people are forever dancing to the Beatles or the Stones, and big-band trivia sneaks into every book. The music functions as another weapon against abstraction, like the obscenity but more insinuating.

The "familiar tunes" all detail some breakdown: specific losses and individual disintegration. As such they risk mere glumness, and indeed Sorrentino's first, *The Sky Changes*, did whine unnecessarily. The novel anticipates *Blue Pastoral* in that it too takes a husband and wife (on the verge of divorce, in the earlier book) to the deserts of the Southwest, but the difference is that between a writer who doesn't have a handle on his bitterness yet and a finished artist. *Steelwork* (1970) and *Imaginative Qualities* evinced that control in increasing measure, as did *Aberration of Starlight* (1980, and a finalist for the PEN/Faulkner Award). At the same time, the tinkering with point of view and chronology continued. *Steelwork's* chapters are dated but arranged out of order; *Aberration* triumphantly orchestrates four different characters' perspectives on a botched seduction during a vacation weekend in 1939. Only in *Crystal Vision* (1981) does Sorrentino combine street life and aesthetic fancy in something like Latin-American magical realism. We recognize the layabouts of *Crystal Vision* and the bebop-era watering holes where they gather, but everything's exaggerated. That's what drinking in dark places will do to you, and yet another of this author's motifs is the old-style corner bar. Some of his best moments occur in these dives, where music and obscenity converge and where we can spot the ravages of our lives even as we drink to forget them.

The two "unchained melodies" before *Blue Pastoral* offer brilliant music, if only intermittently affecting. *Splendide-Hotel* (1973) is short and unfairly neglected, *Mulligan Stew* (1979) massively thick and rather too highly thought of (Hugh Kenner praised the novel in *Harper's*, for example). In the first, Sorrentino's imagination makes use of a springboard that has nothing to do with narrative: *Splendide-Hotel* follows the alphabet rather than a storyline. The result is a surprising meditation, all about loss and memory, an airier *Corrosive Sublimate*. *Mulligan Stew* draws its reader through far thicker gruel. It's a brave novel, years in the writing and years more in finding a publisher, but more will than inspiration. The protagonist is an avant-garde writer who's losing his mind, and his compulsive list-making, his now-awful, now-decent prose, overwhelm even Sorrentino's most berserk imaginative leaps. *Mulligan Stew* is finally inert.

Blue Pastoral appears to have learned a lesson from these two. Although as surreally various, as superficially arbitrary, as *Splendide-Hotel,* the new novel maintains basic story elements. It's about a journey, a search, and the give and take between husband and wife. And though as riddled with lists and as literary as *Mulligan Stew,* it's playful and invigoratingly speedy. No list goes on for six pages, as in the earlier book; indeed few chapters last longer than two or three.

The plot itself concerns coming unchained. *Blue*'s questers are Serge Cavotte ("Blue Serge" to his friends), his hag of a wife, Helene, and their little boy, Zimmerman. A dancing coat, a mythological beauty now losing her hair, and a pop singer turned back into a thumbsucker? These people are cartoons. But then again, since when can't we root for the folks in cartoons? On the verge of middle age, Blue Serge has experienced an artistic calling: he wishes to play the piano. A sinister doctor urges the late-blooming artiste to go west, to seek out the Perfect Musical Phrase, and Serge the Sucker hauls the family off in a pushcart. With that, what passes for plot goes wilder still. One of the liveliest lists comes near the end, in a chapter that ticks off some seventy-seven possible dramatic climaxes, should anybody want one.

It's folly from the first. Literally: Sorrentino introduces Serge with a parody of that five-century-old joke of Erasmus, *In Praise of Folly.* Thereafter each new place has its appropriate parody. In Washington there's a brutal demolition of Congresstalk, and outside New Orleans comes an outpouring of vituperative black jive. Both are ear-perfect, and there's all manner of verse as well, from rhyming couplets to the French *ballade.* Likewise the great sloppy helpings of sex—it's a *very* blue pastoral—get parodic treatment. People screw in iambic pentameter and in fractured translations from the French, as well as in the book's "standard" language, a pastiche of late-Renaissance locutions and contemporary slang: "What think you of this other posture? 'Tis loved by those who favor knocking off a quick one in the kitchen while the tuna glops and nicely browns."

Sex seems central, actually, to the more serious purposes lurking here. Not that *B.P.* isn't batting practice, to a large extent: part exercise and part game. It's a device for refreshing our own language with that of the early English pastorals, and its bright zip makes a lovely contrast to the grainy mood shots in *Aberration of Starlight*. Nonetheless the parody always has a grim side. All are rooted in prejudice: academicians sneer at women, Hoosiers at kikes and jigs, and the jive talker says of whites, "Them muthafuckas all the same anyways." And what are we to make of those two big issues Blue can't stop talking about, namely, Nature and Time? To be sure, those were the common themes of the original pastorals, and their treatment here is nonsensical. On foot and shoving along a pushcart, Blue and family cross Missouri in minutes flat; elsewhere sheep eat wild scones and crumpets, couple with newts and snakes, and excrete "tons of…wondrous mozzorone cheese." Anything you say. Yet this phantasmagoria includes the beasts' sex life—a lot like the fantasy we're reading, in which Blue and Helene are always quick to make "the beast with two backs." All this hot air about Nature and Time, that is, never changes the temperature of the marriage. The politics between husband and wife remain consistent and recognizable. We know these cartoons: he's got his head in the clouds, and she's unfaithful.

Still, what we're watching here is an athlete at play, his movements fundamentally abstract. We steer by stylized patterns in prose, plot, and character. Even the portrait of a squabbling America emerges only as a leitmotif of exaggeration and fear. Thus for all the low humor and loony tunes, all the nasty cracks about academics, this novel demands the sort of well-prepared readership that's unheard of outside the university. One of the book's subtlest pleasures, for instance, is its play on the canonical works of Modernist literature. Baudelaire had his *fleurs du mal,* and Sorrentino here gives us *les mauvaises herbes.* Such in-jokes can never be redeemed, for most readers, by lascivious potshots at contemporary society. An artificial *Pastoral*, this one stays true to heroes of artifice. Samuel Beckett has claimed that any word mars the silence of nature, and thus his art continually shrinks to murmurs and motionlessness. Sorrentino perceives that same silence, the emptiness of abstraction, but his response is the opposite: madcap energy that brings into being a madcap, surrogate world. His seems a highly American solution, a can-do Marshall Plan for replenishing an exhausted literature. Blue and Helene's moment of epiphany comes not on the shore of the Pacific but in Arizona's Painted Desert; there, at sunset, they talk over the colors they see around them. Their conversation starts to smack of desperation, as night comes on and everything turns black, but it never drains of comedy.

This has happened before. Between the turn of the century and the Second World War, in Europe, there bloomed a generation of literature that insisted its own reality was greater than any other. Valery and Proust in France, Virginia Woolf in England, James Joyce all over—these and others founded a rigorous and anti-populist aesthetic. As for Americans who sought to embrace the Modernist movement, like Pound or Gertrude Stein, they went abroad. William Carlos Williams was pretty much alone, on this side of the Atlantic, in trying to carve out a career based on such a notion of the art. He paid the price, too, suffering near-universal neglect till the last years of his life. Thus what we may have seen in the last twenty-five years in this country, with the rise of authors like Sorrentino, is the first homegrown Modernist movement. By now the dozen or so authors who define the mode are easily listed: Barth, Barthelme, DeLillo, Gaddis, Gass... Certainly critics have been trying to come up with a name for them; the most common stab is "Postmodernists." But it may be more useful to think of them as American Modernists, applying the methods of an earlier movement to a country that's at last grown complex enough—decadent enough, if you prefer—to warrant such treatment. Whether our '60s and '70s Modernists will eventually earn their own place in literature, the way the American Romantics of the 1840s and '50s carved their Transcendental niche remains to be seen.[2] But certainly Gilbert Sorrentino ranks among the boldest working in the field. *Blue Pastoral* is an investigation of reality perversely true to itself, his best in that regard, if lacking the emotional satisfactions of one or two earlier novels.

—*Boston Phoenix*, 1983

---

2. Sorrentino read this piece and sent a gratifying letter. He disagreed, however, with what he called my "interesting" final observation. He argued that the problem with American criticism was its failure to understand the *subsequent* literary movement, the novel since 1945. Fair enough. I'll stand by the concluding argument of this '83 piece, but in other work for *Sea-God's Herb*—in particular the later Sorrentino essay—I made it a point to address the man's concern.

DAY TO DAYNESS:
STEPHEN DIXON & TIME TO GO

According to the biographical sketch in *Time to Go*, Stephen Dixon has published stories in some 175 journals and magazines. This is his sixth book and his fourth collection of stories in less than ten years.[1] Prolificacy like that generally requires that an author reach for materials close at hand, and sure enough, Dixon's imagination remains on a short leash in nearly all these pieces. His principal subject is the clash of the mundane and the aberrant, those unsettling run-ins with wackos or former lovers all too familiar to anyone who's ever lived in a city. The city in *Time to Go* tends to be New York, where Dixon has spent most of his life, and the protagonist is at first an unmarried male writer in early middle age, then later on recently married, then finally a new father. On top of that, more than half the stories are about the same writer, Will Taub, who teaches in a university very much like Johns Hopkins University, where Dixon teaches.

The collection, to be fair, has its touches of exotica. The title story features a running conversation between Taub and his dead father (the ghost proves one of the liveliest talkers in the book), while other stories disrupt chronology or, metafictionally, reflect on the story in process. But only one piece genuinely breaks away from the metropolitan settings and writerly circumstances. Breaks away

---

1. I've let these 1984 figures stand, in light of the Dixon review which follows.

and, alas, breaks down. The surreal "Come on a Coming" proves grounded in obvious symbolism, and patly predictable besides, so much as to suggest this author is better off with his more down-to-earth urban encounters.

In these stories, everyone arrives eventually at the same conclusion, everyone winds up preferring the day-to-day to the outlandish, and the logic they use in getting there provides the best moments. Dixon allows every character a monologue in their own defense, enjoyably lunatic. For instance there's a prolonged analysis, rich with cranky charm, of how best to catch the eye of a woman you once lived with.

Outside of such moments, however, *Time to Go* feels awfully underdone. The opening story, "The Bench," concerns some subdued and pointless gossip about an unnamed father and his baby girl, and the last story, "Reversal," offers nothing more than the depressing thoughts of a character diapering his child. When some excitement does occur—even the robbery of a wedding ring—it too is handled with a stick-figure soullessness:

> I yell upstairs, 'Police, police, catch that kid with my satchel— a canvas one,' as I chase after him. On the sidewalk I say to [a] woman, 'Did you see a boy running past?' and she says, 'Who?' but he's nowhere around.

The vast majority of these encounters lack any but the most general physicality. Even quieter moments, which a writer interested in day-to-dayness would be expected to savor, rely on the same abstraction. The changing of diapers in "Reversal" includes an intimation of threat, but this is smothered in a presentation that recalls a how-to manual:

> He raises her bottom by holding her feet up in one hand, slips the double diapers out from under her, sets her down, keeps

one hand on her chest so she won't roll off the changing board to the floor, drops the wet diapers into the diaper pail and closes it.

American short-story writers, just now, tend to take Raymond Carver as their model for the form. The repression of rhetoric and an emphasis on the trivial have become hallmarks of the form. But Stephen Dixon is so unrelenting in both regards that, at his worst, he compounds a lack of imagination with a near absence of passion (another reason why the title story, the most full of feeling, stands out here). His characters' theorizing all starts to sound the same after a while. His endings, deprived of even the least bubble of poetic effect, suffocate. Despite its sensitivity to bad moments and its pleasing attention to structure, *Time to Go* amounts to less than its predecessor, *14 Stories*. Its failures point up the dangers in the fashion for the understated.

—*New York Times Book Review*, 1984

ALL EXITS LEAD TO SORROW: STEPHEN DIXON & INTERSTATE

Stephen Dixon's latest novel, *Interstate*, sets itself the sort of challenge that distinguishes a work of rare imagination. In the opening pages, the protagonist's younger daughter, six years old, dies in a random shooting on the road. Nathan Frey (caught in the fray, then fraying) is out on the interstate with his girls, Margo and Julie. The family seems happy; the mother, Lee, simply wants to stay with her folks in New York a couple of days longer. But on an empty stretch of highway, first a van begins to shadow Nathan, then one of the men inside pulls a gun. Just when the father seems to be safe on the highway shoulder, "bullets go through the windshield." Julie's gone before he can lift her small body from the back seat.

What's a novelist's best move after that? Dixon's answer is yet another challenge: Why move at all? First and foremost, *Interstate* bares the scars and stains that such a bloody trauma incurs, exposing its messes more nakedly than most authors would risk. Yet despite the book's raw emotionality, in time *Interstate* also reveals itself to be an exercise in style.

Each of the book's eight chapters returns to the initial tragedy. Most sections begin with that same first glimpse of the killers' van. Each retelling uncovers some new hurt; the most disturbing suggests that the father shares the culpability for what happened. But each also brings to light, though the visibility may be murky, moments of strength or renewal. Still, it's the first of the chapters—perspectives?—that moves the story the furthest along. Dixon's swift opening slows to dramatize Nathan's obsession with his daughter's murderers and the killing's results: divorce, manslaughter, lonesome old age, and finally a kind of ghost's redemption. If this haunted book has a good spirit, amid the nightmare reiterations, it's the surviving daughter, Margo. In the novel's first run-through, Margo, a grown-up good mother, brings a modicum of grace to her father's last years.

In later chapters, Nathan Frey generally doesn't get past the terrible drive home. Two of these takes on the tragedy end in the hospital to which the father rushed after the shooting, and another works in retrospect, so that its closing scene occurs before the journey begins. In these too, however, the nine-year-old Margo occasionally eases Nathan's murmuring grief, his gathering guilt. The conventional metaphor, given the novel's pervading gloomy weather, would be that the surviving girl reaches him like sun through fog—but this author has little to do with convention, and you could even say he eschews metaphor.

In the late '70s or early '80s, Dixon's style might have been called "Carveresque." But the first of his many works of fiction[1] appeared in 1976, and the first of more than four hundred published stories years earlier. Thus Dixon long ago established his own voice, one which may harmonize now and again with Raymond Carver's minimalism, with that sort of Americanese, but which also groans more openly and rambles more furiously. In *Interstate*, sadness pours out with natural force, more about honest disorientation than manipulative drama. In one later chapter, the father prepares to enter the hospital room where the doctors have finished with Julie:

How do you see her without cracking up? Going mad and getting as sad as anybody can get—complete grief, that kind

---

1. As of 2013, the number's up past thirty.

of cracking up. Both, all. They no doubt have her all cleaned up and everything like that by now, presentable, and she'll be looking—oh, stop it, but you're only trying to give yourself reasons—not 'reasons' but some word that means you'll be able to face going in to see her.

To find that "word," and the others like it that sustain the bereaved, Dixon veers into many a fumbling digression. Characters talk themselves through backwaters of memory (sometimes creating comic relief) or sail into dreamy what-ifs, all in order to put off some looming and drear inevitability. In conversation, one may mention an important insight that he or she has to share, then spiral away through a half-dozen distractions before revealing what matters. The format feels like a natural fit to the shuttered claustrophobia of worry and loss. So do the jam-packed paragraphs, sometimes running several pages without a break. Better still, these blocks of talky phrasing flicker with light, even (every now and again) with happier possibilities. The final two chapters offer alternatives to the bad news, one perhaps more horrifying, the other very much less.

All in all, *Interstate* builds on the successes of its 1991 predecessor, *Frog*, a finalist for the National Book Award and the PEN/Faulkner. The new novel presents a tough-necked American hybrid of the imaginative and the mundane: nugget-like, darkly perfect, impossible to shake. Indeed, the book proves how a writer's talent should never be counted out. More than a decade ago, reviewing one of Dixon's earlier collections for the *New York Times*, I wasn't particularly impressed. This time around, I find myself feeling just the opposite.

—Portland Oregonian, 1995

UNLEASHED, LIKE ISAIAH: ISHMAEL REED & JUICE!

When Ishmael Reed gets celebrated these days, now that he's well past age seventy, it's usually for the work he did decades ago.[1] The novels that enjoy broadest critical approval are *Yellow Back Radio Broke-Down* (1969) and *Mumbo Jumbo* (1972), two comic and surreal historical revisions. Reed was hailed as the great African American among our homegrown postmodernists (Thomas Pynchon gave him a tip of the cap in *Gravity's Rainbow*), if not our foremost black novelist. Esteem like that no longer flutters around his name, but the author himself was the first to shoo it away. He derided such praise as racist.

Racism, for Reed, remains a sickness badly diagnosed. A 1988 selection of essays bore the title *Writin' Is Fightin'*, and the opponent in many cases was some crude misrepresentation of African Americans or other minorities. His argument lies primarily with the media—literary tastemakers, the white conquerors who wrote the history books, and the kingpins of TV and the movies who think they know the black experience (recently he lashed out at both *The Wire* and *Precious* for their ghetto stereotypes). So he edited the anthology *MultiAmerica: Essays on Culture Wars and Cultural Peace* (1996), intended as a corrective. So too, with greater energy and less interest in

---

1. This piece, as noted at the end, appeared in 2011.

healing, he's brought out a brilliantly sustained rant of a new novel, *JUICE!*

The eponymous figure, to be sure, is based on the former running back, currently serving time in Nevada. Note the title's exclamation point and its all-capital-letter format: What Reed calls O.J.'s "public lynching" provides the novel itself with much of its fuel, or juice. Here, the media frenzy has gone on years past the man's acquittal for murder, and on almost every page, Reed excoriates the way constitutional protections were trampled as O.J. became the country's "dancing monkey" (a quip from O.J. himself, used as the epigraph).

Novelistic subtlety, in other words, has little place. *JUICE!* is concerned primarily with public life, and its insights are put across with the broad, jagged strokes of a political cartoon. Indeed, the novel's protagonist draws cartoons for a living, and many passages here are punctuated by his drawings (actually the work of Reed himself, who's published cartoons since the '60s). The artist's name is Paul Blessings, and he has no connection to Simpson—other than that he's another successful black American at risk of becoming a "dancing monkey." His cartoons used to have an edge, a firebrand central character, but now he has chosen to count his small blessings. As the book opens, O.J.'s arrest has set off "the Jim Crow media jury," and much as this galls the cartoonist, he uses the media as sanctuary. He agrees to produce a toothless weekly piece, featuring the "charming curmudgeonly…Koots Badger," for the TV ratings king KCAK. Like its name, the network's politics smack of the KKK.

The characters' names themselves capture the satire that *JUICE!* offers—the pun's too right-on to resist—liberally. The racist who runs KCAK isn't Rupert Murdoch, or not exactly. He's B.S. Rathswheeler, and he keeps all the rats running in his bullshit wheel. When Blessings and the token Latina Princessa Bimbette scream at each other about O.J., the racial tensions reverberate hauntingly, wittily, but in the office both remain mere pets.

Now and again, the narrative does enter the domestic arena, and there confronts issues that would seem to invite psychological development. Blessing's wife is a light-skinned Hispanic, his daughter is experimenting sexually, and he suffers from diabetes. These opportunities for emotional engagement, however, serve Reed only as the chord changes on which he can riff. He rejects conventional character identification; at a moment of family reconciliation, Blessings himself pokes fun at acting "like a protagonist in one of those novels which have been written fiftymillioneleven times." Similarily, the cartoonist's longtime friends, all fellow artists and thinkers, function not as individuals so much as a chorus. They echo the general indignation, sometimes delivering the bad news straight: "As long as African Americans are blamed collectively for the actions of an individual or a few, they aren't free."

In the same way, the scenes between friends reveal a defining tic in the point of view, a switch from first person to third. Without warning, Reed confounds the impulse to empathize. He even ruptures the easy connection between main character and author. Toward the story's end, as Blessings stands at the podium to receive some bogus award, he knows enough to give the white folks in their tuxedos what they want, and he lashes out at Reed by name.

The result is a genuinely inventive novel, which depends not on people in catharsis but on the pleasures of the riffing itself, which allows Reed to address, with savvy variety, all the foibles of a country kidding itself about "the world of post-race harmony and sunlight." Consider, for instance, what one of Blessing's friends has to say about "mass media magazines:"

[They're] always putting black gangsters on the cover, but… they'll have long articles about depression, which must be a big problem among their white subscribers. Half their ads are from pharmaceutical companies. I think the two are connected. The showing of black people as the nation's uglies and the depression of white people. Dissing blacks is like a kind of stimulant for the pleasure centers of their brains. White supremacy is social morphine.

The novel is Reed's longest, and its heft recalls Isaiah unleashing his visions. It reiterates core elements of its predecessor *Japanese By Spring* (1993), such as a black sellout, although it's less contained, a quality that strengthens the book's effects even as it undermines its character development. Together, in any case, Reed's late novels strike me as the richest distillation of what he's about. His critique has gone beyond correcting history, and *JUICE!* raises his most pertinent warning: even under a black president, America suffers "untreated racism…destroying the country."

—Bookforum, 2011

BEYOND THE HIGH-TONED WILLIES: PATRICK McGRATH & THE GROTESQUE

Of all the narrators a novelist might choose, none may be so difficult to bring off as the old curmudgeon. The aging crank must be at once monstrous and charming; even smart-mouths like Thomas Berger *(Little Big Man)* and Stanley Elkin ("The Bail Bondsman") can't seem to generate the necessary brio for more than a few chapters. So perhaps the fundamental success of Patrick McGrath's brilliant and swift first novel, *The Grotesque,* is that it gives us a crab for all seasons. Sir Hugo Coal, the book's black-hearted visionary, never lets down his cantankerous attack. This sixty-ish landowner details a nightmarish six months in which more and more of what happens follows a nightmare logic. Yet though Sir Hugo loses control of his estate, though his family goes mad and he himself winds up a mute paralytic, he never loses his bile, his freshly stropped sharpness.

For all its brevity, *The Grotesque* offers a terrific range. Ostensibly a murder mystery pervaded by Gothic threats and heated by an appalled sexuality, McGrath's story nonetheless proceeds from a cunning infrastructure of image and idea. It's a novel of ideas, no less, though it reaches the brain via chills up the spine. But it's a triumph of style first, of smart curmudgeonly swagger:

> Butlers, I think, are born, not made; the qualities of a good
> butler—deference, capability, a sort of dignified servility—are

qualities of character that arise in cultures where a stable social hierarchy has existed, essentially undisturbed, for centuries. One rarely encounters a good butler in France, for instance, and a good American butler is a contradiction in terms.

The nature of servants is much on Sir Hugo's mind as the novel opens. His wife, Harriet, has just engaged a new butler, named Fledge. But the lord of Crook Manor has detected an "immediate and intense antipathy" in his retainer. Sir Hugo can only infer Fledge's hatred, his sole bits of evidence being sidelong glances and muffled noises in the throat—yet the old man never wavers. Fledge, Sir Hugo decides, is a "ghoul," out to cuckold him and usurp his place at the head of the table. It is the winter of 1949, and the Coals have been at Crook for three hundred years. Sir Hugo strides the grounds like a tyrannosaur:

> I permitted myself to become absorbed in a familiar fantasy, in which the civilization that encroached with increasing shrillness upon these quiet natural places simply vanished into thin air, and I moved upon a planet that knew nothing of humanity.

He perceives no such encroaching shrillness in Fledge's wife, Doris, or in their cook and maid. "Doris," he says, "is unmistakably a servant." The woman also reawakens the old complainer's libido, prompting an unusual wet dream, one that fairly reeks of fungus. Doris is shapeless and middle-aged, an overworked drunk. Indeed, the novel's major characters are all past their prime, and *The Grotesque* revels in the exotic insecurities of an unreliable narrator. Each time Sir Hugo declares that the butler did it, his bilious wit carries far more weight than any of his doddering deductions. Upstairs, downstairs: this is social comedy with a filigree of malice. About a third of the way along, Sir Hugo's daughter's fiancé disappears in the nearby marsh and, to her father, it seems a secondary irritation. First he's got to get the best of his uppity manservant; then he'll bother about the murdered boy.

The novel is dreary yet exotic, chilled and boggy yet full of high fever—in a word, Gothic. Crook is a gabled ruin in which "the windows peer through the foliage like the eyes of some stunted and shaggy beast," and his lordship likes to spend his days, literally, with a monster. He's a gentleman paleontologist, and out in the barn he's slowly reconstructing the skeleton of his discovery, *Phlegmosaurus carbonensis*. Gothic, Gothic, Gothic. Plus there's a pig farm down in one corner of the estate, where Sir Hugo can hang out with his gardener, and with other lowborn, half-pagan celebrants of manly cheer:

> [T]hey sat there like feasting gods, like woodland deities, those satyrs of Ceck, and their talk was brusque and clipped and jocular. The candles flickered, the lamps glowed, and I could feel the spirits of deep winter drifting over the cold, snow-covered, moon-silvered country outside.

McGrath has recorded such haunted scenes before, in his recent and highly praised collection of stories, *Blood and Water and Other Tales*. The genres of horror and Gothic liberate McGrath, allowing him outrageous postures and vocabulary. In part, of course, he's responding to the timeless call for madder music and stronger wine. But McGrath also belongs to a movement of the moment. He's one of several more or less younger fictioneers currently in revolt against understated '70s realism, among them Kafkaesque imaginations like Paul Auster (*In the Country of Last Things*), and even the occasional popular success like T.C. Boyle. These authors take their inspiration at least in part from a previous generation of American experimentalists, writers as yet only fitfully understood, from John Hawkes and Thomas Pynchon and Donald Barthelme (McGrath is English, but he's spent the last decade living in New York). In other words, Mc-

Grath has a serious aesthetic stake in his novel, a commitment to more than the high-toned willies.

Well then, what can he show us? To begin with, being a bit of a dinosaur himself, Sir Hugo proves more prescient than senile when it comes to those ancient reptiles. Indeed, *were* they reptiles? The narrator thinks otherwise. Using *Phlegmosaurus carbonensis* as an example, he intends to prove that the dinosaurs had more in common with birds than with lizards (a thesis that, since 1949, has been shown to be precisely the case). Indeed, every heightening of Sir Hugo's unspoken war with his butler may be rooted in some blow to his paleontological ambitions. His fear deepens as his career founders, although the connection can only be perceived indirectly, the more so because Sir Hugo is deliciously snide about the deskbound academics who fear his freethinking ways. The point of view thus creates a suspense unavailable to the less ambitious novelist, and ironies that smack of Nabokov's *Pale Fire*: as the narrator self-destructs, so does the plot.

"How hard it is to lose the self!" Sir Hugo laments, "…to ditch that gibbering little monkey and merge for a moment with the Nature of which we are a part, yet from which we have so effectively alienated ourselves." Yet while he rails against his socialization, the man is in fact enjoying its fruits: he has a carnivore's exultant sense of domain (even cannibalism becomes a part of his experience, in a moment of fine Senecan grue). But it is as an aristocrat that this occasionally horrific, ultimately pathetic old man is alienated from his own best self: from the creative thinker, and from the father who, almost ashamed of the emotion, wants what's best for his daughter. Sir Hugo's tragedy is that he perceives his servant as a monster—the name Fledge echoes that of the dinosaur—and, until it's too late, he never sees the flesh-eating grotesque in himself.

Now, the layered silt of metaphor won't always yield up a satisfying story, and some readers may feel they're leaving *The Grotesque* empty-handed. At the conclusion, Sir Hugo is confined to his wheelchair, miles from either the courtroom or the prison where the mystery of the boy's disappearance is being hammered out. Yet the narrative has promised a solution. McGrath provides one, but it comes from so deep within Sir Hugo's paranoia that it lacks the necessary external corroboration.

Nonetheless, the most liberating sex scenes also come at the end, and the most arresting dream sequences. Harriet and Fledge fox trot off to the bedroom; the working poor from around Crook put forth wings and soar over the gables. All the while the old man sits wheelchair-bound, "a living fossil." Reversal within reversal: the master enslaved, the scientist turned into the thing under study. This accumulative tightness of image may be what McGrath has to contribute to the new formalist movement in fiction, a succulent density like classic British butterscotch.

—*LA Weekly*, 1989

DISTANT MOONS

NIGHTMARE CIRCLING OVERHEAD:
CAN XUE & OLD FLOATING CLOUD

Can Xue's disorderly, brilliant visions of contemporary mainland China first appeared in English in the 1989 short-story collection *Dialogues in Paradise*. This new volume, *Old Floating Cloud*, comprises two novellas that were written in the mid-1980s: "Yellow Mud Street," a harrowing and hilarious urban portrait, and the title piece, part psychotic romance and part office burlesque. Like Can Xue's stories, these longer works offer nightmare images of life under a punishing regime. To Western eyes at least, this still-young writer (the woman was born in 1953) presents what must be considered a critique of her homeland.

Yet for the past decade Beijing has allowed Can Xue to publish, if in bowdlerized form; the present volume includes the only complete version of "Yellow Mud Street" available in any language. It would seem that the censors can't figure her out. Can Xue's sarcasm may be rabid and delicious, but it's always couched in situations funnier still for their sheer strangeness. Her descriptions have a physicality that's nothing short of disgusting—few writers spend so much time depicting excrement, infection, and insects—yet they concern characters who seem all but disembodied. Her surreal scatology often provokes startled laughter, and her dialogue can dispense with any sense of who's speaking while retaining entirely familiar qualities of resentment, gossip, envy, and whining.

"Yellow Mud Street" takes up some two-thirds of the book. Set on a hallucinatory fringe where urban politics meets agrarian superstition, it presents convoluted episodes of communal failure in which the neighborhood around Yellow Mud Street fails to solve or even fully clarify any of the "more than thirteen major problems" festering among its people. There's sabotage and murder, for instance, and the novella's overlapping stories can generate a dreamlike suspense. The author also has feminist and political purposes; at times, her work mimics propaganda from the Cultural Revolution of the late '60s and early '70s. But ordinary fictional devices repeatedly give way to rawer stuff, breathtaking and gut-wrenching: a hen pecks its dinner from a man's fever sore; a husband imprisons his wife in a cage with legs shaped like buffalo feet.

The second novella, "Old Floating Cloud," has a more conventional subject: an affair between neighbors and the man's concomitant degradation at work. The adulterer and others have more recognizable psychologies, including family concerns, than anyone in the first piece. But Can Xue carries these elements toward the animalistic, the fabulous. When, for example, one of the female characters wants to say "something nice, something intimate," she begins: "In the corner grows an odd mushroom as big as a human head. Often a leg unexpectedly stretches down from the ceiling, a leg with spiders crawling on it."

In both stories, the language (serviceably translated by Ronald R. Janssen and Jian Zhang) is capable of swift, telegrammatic force: "Her mind was as small as a soup spoon;" "A nightmare circled in the starlight, a black, empty overcoat." Can Xue also has a marvelous facility for iterative, unfolding metaphors: peepholes in the walls, dead flies in the rice bowl. At times she calls to mind a painter at once untrained and visionary, sketching twisted figures against a disturbing landscape. Other passages invite comparison to the century's masters of decay made meaningful, to Kafka especially, in that she's coined a fresh language of images out of a world that seems terminally sick.

The journalist's cliché for art that emerges from harsh circumstances would be "a miracle." In Can Xue's case, the expression is appropriate as much for the work itself as for how it's happened into print.

—*New York Times Book Review*, 1991

CULTURES BLASTED AND RESTITCHED: MICHAEL ONDAATJE & THE ENGLISH PATIENT

A novel of war and regeneration, of fragile growth and brute blasting away, Michael Ondaatje's *The English Patient* has the impact of a masterpiece: it strives to redeem an entire bomb-shocked century. The novel—the fourth by this Indian-born Canadian, and the winner of England's Man Booker Prize—works within tight constraints. It concerns four dropouts from the Allied effort, in the summer of 1945, in a villa outside Florence. Yet the memories and yearnings of these four bring meaning to a devastation that reaches around the world. The narrative veers from the desert silence outside El Alamein to the atomic flash over Hiroshima, in linked nightmares from which everyone struggles to wake.[1]

The center of this struggle is "the English patient," a man brought out of the Sahara two years earlier, burned beyond recognition. A former desert explorer, a brilliant pan-European scholar, his identity remains a mystery for most of the book. His recollections take up most of the flashback material and generate remarkable suspense. More than that, the English patient's story provides a focus for the rest, the archetype in these nightmares. The patient's love for a colleague's wife—the novel's central tragedy—holds a dark mirror up

---

1. Bizarrely, the Oscar-winning movie of Ondaatje's novel omitted all references Hiroshima. One wonders what damage this did to the book's standing as literature.

to the affair which blossoms between a Canadian nurse and a Sikh sapper. The man's harrowing adventures in the Sahara reveal much in common with the espionage work of the fourth character, a former thief mutilated under torture.

The tunneling between broken hearts often burrows further still, toward the great escape artists of myth and religion. Ondaatje nods to Odysseus and Christ, in particular, and to the Vedic hymns of his Sikh sapper. Staking a claim in exalted territory requires exalted style, more so than the usual Postmodern appropriation, but the author's demonstrates the advantages of an apprenticeship in poetry (Ondaatje has three highly regarded collections). One sequence of sentences erupts like a string of landmines, while the next wheels round as agile and arresting as doves over a battlefield. The descriptions of lovemaking come up with much-needed new vocabulary.

"We are communal histories," the English patient muses toward the end, "communal books." In this new novel Michael Ondaatje becomes nothing less than integral to the communal tale of his hybrid Anglo-Asian culture, and to a time much-tattered, much-restitched, and still in need of repairs.

—Harvard Review, 1993

HOMICIDE AS HAUNTED BURLESQUE: ALAIN MABANCKOU & AFRICAN PSYCHO

The man who can murder as an act of vanity! As self-expression! The narrator of *African Psycho* expresses the pathology this way: "To kill at last, crush…I was going to exist at last, that's it, exist…I was going to be somebody." Such a lunatic yearning is familiar in fiction, a trick that goes back at least to Dostoevsky. The drama's in the waffling: will he or won't he? Alain Mabanckou's novel, the first of three of his books to appear in English in 2007 (the Congolese author has won a number of prizes in France), discovers a fascinating new way to hang readers on those tenterhooks. *Psycho* presents no gloomy Raskolnikov, nor the fixed sneer of Patrick Bateman, but a haunted burlesque.

The narrator's name, Gregoire Nakobomayo, may contain a clash of cultures, colonizer and indigenous, but the man proves good company. An orphan raised largely in the streets of his African metropolis, Gregoire achieved most of his education via a mashup of comic books and "the prestigious titles of the Pleiade collection." The result is a voluble palooka, likeable, with a knack for car repair and a loyalty not to his city or country, which both go unnamed, but to his shanty neighborhood, very much named, in one of the cleverest of the novel's frequent onomastics: He-Who-Drinks-Water-Is-An-Idiot.

But lately Gregoire's thinking has turned from the comic to the noir. He dwells on murder and on one murderer in particular: the legendary Angoualima. This name's another shotgun marriage, part French royal family and part Congo River tributary, and so Angoualima holds up a shadowy mirror to Gregoire. The "Great Master" of killing had magical gifts: "He lived underground because the worm was his totem;…he lived at the bottom of the sea because the shark was his totem;…he lived in freight trains because…he was able to turn himself into a package."

The translation, by Christine Hartley, locates an effective balance between the mythic "totem" and the mundane "package;" the dilemma for the story is whether its mayhem-minded narrator can achieve the same. Gregoire talks a violent game, and he takes instruction from the ghost of his Master, yet he can't stop asking a very different question: "Where are we going?" His destination may not turn out to be steeped in blood. His delusions of *Scarface* grandeur (the film's a hit with Gregoire's old gang) are belied by the humble and comfortable home he's made with his intended victim, the prostitute Germaine. And in those few passages depicting actual rather than imagined violence, *Psycho* generates a chilling verisimilitude as powerful for its hesitations as for its blows and cries.

Mabanckou's sprightly negotiations of extremes and opposites demonstrates anew how the novel form is nothing if not flexible— a significant demonstration given the book's provenance. The author breaks with the norm for novels out of Africa, these days. Celebrated cases like Iweala's *Beasts of No Nation* and Forna's *Ancestor Stones* have been documentary at bottom; what matters most is getting the pain right. But this splendid freak show reminds us that no novelistic record of sensibility (especially an entire continent's sensibility) can be complete without its Dionysiac yawp.

—The Believer, 2007

RINGS, PLANETS, POLES, INFERNO, PARADISE: A POETICS FOR W.G. SEBALD

Our pilgrim storyteller, once again, is letting someone else do the talking. His old friend Michael Hamburger, whose family fled Berlin for Edinburgh in 1933, speaks of a postwar return to the building in which he'd lived as a child. For Hamburger, the details of place have an immanence, on the verge of miracle: "Like pictures in a rebus that I simply had to puzzle out correctly in order to cancel the monstrous events that had happened since we emigrated."

Now, no fiction can equal the fact of Holocaust—we need no Cynthia Ozick to tell us that—but few texts imaginary or otherwise pose quite the riddle, rebus-like indeed in its combined transparency and opacity, as the late W.G. Sebald's *The Rings of Saturn*. Published in German in 1995, in English in '98, the very genre of the text can seem a puzzle. It's been designated a novel, a determination that must've begun with Sebald himself, but no attempt to understand the book's power can overlook the problem of typology. I must get into that problem, here, in time—for I intend just such an attempt, a decoding of the rebus, an explication of the book's poetics. If the novel were more ordinary, my subject would be termed narrative strategies, but if discussion of *Rings* were limited to the usual principles of narrative, the text would seem so impersonal, dreary, and tautological that its reading could never provide the satisfying, indeed compelling, experience it does.

Resolving that paradox, making sense of that impact, stands as the next project before Sebald readers. While it's going on five years since the man's untimely roadside death, the majority of critics and reviewers, including such esteemed figures as Ozick, have so far avoided the question of *how*, instead reiterating a ravished but unilluminating *wow*. Among the shorter assessments made during the author's lifetime, the most valuable was Susan Sontag's review of *Vertigo* (the German edition appeared in 1990, but in America and England the book was Sebald's third to be published, in 2000). Writing in the *Times Literary Supplement*, Sontag offered fine insights regarding Sebald's overlapping roles as narrator, protagonist, and author. But the reviewer's role also forced Sontag back onto frustrating vagaries of praise, like "extraordinary...unclassifiable... bewitching," reiterating the sort of puff we'd already seen a number of times, for instance from Roberta Silman of the *New York Times Book Review*, who claimed that *Rings of Saturn* was "like a dream you want to last forever."

Indeed yes. But even dreams can be analyzed—and then too, a useful interpretation need not be windy and abstruse. I mean that academic studies of Sebald are now starting to proliferate, and these have tended, predictably, to be clotted with theoretical backing and filling. Mark McCulloh titled his 2003 book *Understanding W.G. Sebald* (on Univeristy of South Carolina Press), but his exegesis, once you get past such bewildering coinages as "literary monism," offers little more than an introduction and a summary. Those who love Sebald's work need now to move toward true understanding, and not by means of a finicky demonstration of how sometimes the novels fit one critical theory and sometimes another. A more accessible elucidation is called for.

Not that *Rings of Saturn* doesn't make a point of defying analysis, in keeping with a thoroughly postmodern aesthetic. The jargon of theoreticians indeed applies, as the text breaks down anything approaching a "metanarrative" and allows plenty of echo-space for "heteroglossia." Rather than a unifying story of some personal-plus-social transformation (the metanarrative of a conventional novel), *Rings* presents what seems a meandering pastiche of literary and historical materials, repeatedly abandoning personal detail for appropriated passages from older texts as well as for fragments from the correspondence and biographies of those who wrote them (a heteroglossia, that is, of multiple voices and effects). No worthwhile explanation of this author's magic can ignore how he chose to work at the developing fringes of his art form. Elements of my own interpretation are drawn not from Aristotle, but from whomever it was who thought up recycling.

Yet I must also note, as a last defining point before getting down to cases, that in *Rings* this surrogate narrative, up-to-the-minute as its art may seem, has nonetheless a classic aspect. For throughout, Sebald relies on what used to be called "masterpieces of Western art," the likes of *Lear* and Flaubert. The most recent such case appears to be the Borges story "Tlön, Uqbar, Orbis Tertius," written in the 1930s and generally acknowledged as a benchmark of the past century's literary development. Thus I'll conclude my explication by identifying one of the book's subtler allusions, to a very cornerstone of the European canon—namely, an unstated yet fundamental allegiance with Dante's *Divine Comedy*.

Now, ordinarily, an author draws a correlation with the likes of the Florentine for thematic ballast, ideological muscle. Let me exemplify by means of another novel often termed "plotless," like Sebald's, yet profoundly different: In *The Catcher in The Rye*, J.D. Salinger invests adolescent pathology with *gravitas* by having his protagonist speak of *Hamlet*. But the strolls around mid-Manhattan that occupy most of Holden Cauldfield's Christmas holiday have a purpose poles apart from those of the narrator in *Rings of Saturn*, who claims he's assembling the "notes" he took after he "set off to walk the county of Suffolk" one August during the last decade of the twentieth century.

To begin with, the latter perambulatory novel largely eschews its form's common function, in the famous phrase adapted from James's prefaces, as the record of sensibility. Rejecting the comforts of the conventional long story, *Rings* never evokes an imaginary coming-of-age or other private transition intended to illuminate larger forces at work; from the first, rather, Sebald suggests that his own project comes too late for such cathartic hijinks. His opening recalls a pair of university colleagues who died more or less mysteriously (the first of many strange passings, in *Rings*) before completing their fanatical studies (the first of many obsessive cases). One of the deceased was at work on Flaubert, and yet the author of *Madame Bovary* prompts thoughts not of marriage, nor even *le mot juste*, but rather of inevitable destruction. Apropos of Flaubert's time in Egypt, the narrator takes a brief turn as Cassandra: "Sand conquered all."

Or rather, that *may* be the narrator speaking, extrapolating from the work of his departed colleague. We can't tell if, instead, the nominal storyteller is quoting the dead scholar directly. This lack of clarity about provenance sets yet another transgressive pattern, another skewing of novelistic norms, in which without distinctions of punctuation or format the primary narrating consciousness adopts the voice and vision of some subject. Our pilgrim lets others do the talking, often. This rhetorical instability underscores the vertiginous quality of what passes for story, a story which itself combines the scholars' feverish dedication—they surrender their own lives to that of their subjects—with the abrupt ironies of their actual twinned deaths. Given this pervading uncertainty, enhanced by a reader's first experience of Sebald's destabilizing effects, it's entirely appropriate that, when *Rings* then detours into a summary of Thomas Browne's gloomy *Urn Burial*, a paraphrase comes close to dismissing the more common order of novel:

...the history of every individual, of every social order...does
not describe an ever-widening, more and more wonderful arc,
but rather follows a course which...leads without fail down
into the dark.

"Destruction" is this author's "great theme," Sontag declared, in
her *TLS* review. Moreover, just as *Rings of Saturn* includes the Hamburger family tragedy, all of Sebald's books in one way or another address the Holocaust, that defining destructive episode of the century
just past. *The Emigrants* (German edition 1993, English 1996) is his
most direct address of that grim subject, and his reputation rests on
that book as much as on *Rings*. I should add, then, that the narrative
and rhetorical devices I identify in this essay certainly apply to the
earlier novel. As for *Vertigo*, it uses the same strategy but takes on a
less affecting subject matter; the later *Austerlitz* (2001) comes the
closest to straightforward cathartic narrative that this author managed, though it by no means abandons the poetics that are my concern. And both this author's best-known novels, at first encounter,
hardly seem to be about recycling or renewal. Instead, first *Emigrants*
and then *Rings* appear to address the polar opposite—namely, that
unavoidable drop "down into the dark."

The latter novel consists of one spectacular episode of efflores-
cence and decay after another. No sooner does our narrator define his
walkabout on the opening page than he adds that all over southwestern England he found himself "confronted with traces of destruction." Examples from the second and third chapters, wildly diverse
though suggested by places physically close together, would be the
near-extinction of the Atlantic herring and the collapse of the once-
fabulous, now-forgotten resort of Somerleyton. Here, as throughout,
the emphasis remains on the rot. Sebald's very name appears only in
archaic spellings.

So unrelenting a catalogue of woe, to be sure, would never be
rendered "bewitching" simply by means of the destabilizing devices

I pointed out earlier. A mysterious demise, whether of a colleague or a resort, is only so interesting, the less so when combined with many others, and the same admonition can be made regarding Sebald's fondness for maniacal singlemindedness, alternately laughable and horrifying, as well as for his borrowed voicings. Thus my explications must turn to style, perhaps the crucial resource for this medium. Consider, for instance, a sobering meditation about halfway through the novel. The passage may call to mind recycling specifically, though again by means of its seeming contrary, the devastation of forests:

> Our spread over the earth was fueled by reducing the higher species of vegetation to charcoal, by incessantly burning whatever would burn.... Combustion is the hidden principle behind every artefact we create. The making of a fish-hook, manufacture of a china cup, or production of a television programme, all depend on the same process of combustion. Like our bodies and like our desires, the machines we have devised are possessed of a heart which is slowly reduced to embers.

If what we read amounts to a wailing and a gnashing of teeth, what a celebration is its language! To put the point another way, if an author indulges in prophecies of doom, then he might as well take on the bearing of Scripture. Thus abstractions such as "the higher species of vegetation," more or less scientific vocabulary, fold with surgical exactness into the humane yet hard-headed business of "burning whatever we could burn." And if we're reading Scripture, an idiom of that solemnity and scope, it's Scripture carved into the sarcophagus of history. Note, in the passage above, the march of civilization, a brisk synopsis but by no means unfelt: from fish-hooks to porcelain to television.

This ambiguous text may seem at first a "novel" only for lack of a better word, since we have little here except rubble—the actual material of the seventh planet's rings, according to the epigraph. Nonetheless, at this level of rhetoric *Rings* can't help but recall Flaubert's messianic yearning for "a book about nothing," one "held together by the strength of its style" (from a January 1852 letter to Louise Colet). The 1998 book seems hardly to be about nothing, with its many imperial delusions and extraordinary individuals, and yet on closer scrutiny, these subjects fall apart like pointillist sketches. The strength of Sebald's style is an undertow, forever tugging us toward the spectral, the vanishing, thus undeniably subversive or "centrifugal," to use the metaphor of Mikhail Bakhtin; yet his sentences also prove redoubtable, python-like in the sinuosity of their grip around science, history, and "a heart…reduced to embers."

Just as the syntactical felicity throughout this text works against naysaying plain and simple, *Rings* also has little use for literary allusion as it functions in a run-of-the-mill novel—that is, as thematic support. Given the utter transparency of Sebald's moral, where would he begin? With Ecclesiastes: *all is vanity?* Yet it's hard to think of another work so rich in reference. The opening pages touch not only on Flaubert and Browne, but also on Kafka's "Metamorphosis," the Franco-Swiss poet and novelist Charles Ramuz (whose best-known title seems pertinent: *Presence du Mort*), the 1911 edition of the *Brittanica* (a note that itself recalls the rabid encyclopedia fan Borges), and Albrecht Durer's etching, *Melancholia*. As you see, the allusions are primarily, but by no means solely, to literature. And all the above-listed precede the text's first extended interrogation of a cultural "artefact"—a masterpiece of Western etcetera—namely, its meditation on Rembrandt's *Anatomy Lesson*. This miniature MLA paper begins by imagining the young medical student Thomas Browne in attendance at the public dissection of "a petty thief…hanged for his misdemeanors an hour or so earlier," and concludes by determining a subversive motive in the great Dutch painter's depiction of that gruesome spectacle. Rembrandt "alone" (Sebald repeats the word for classic affect, like a tolling bell) identifies with the young man put to death for such minor infractions; "he alone sees that greenish annihilated body."

A number of later passages in *Rings of Saturn* come round again (so to speak) to this painting, sometimes explicitly and other times by implication. Thus once the visual artwork stands revealed as both clinical and compassionate, it becomes definitive for the text in which that insight was achieved. What book but this would estimate the number of herring pulled from the North Sea in a single late eighteenth-century year (sixty billion), and then a few lines later startle us with cross-species sympathy: "The truth is that we do not know what the herring feels?" Indeed, the celebration of this lowly fellow-creature goes further: "Held against the light, the rearward parts of the fish appear a dark green of a beauty one sees nowhere else." Elsewhere, the mere sight of a water-strider crossing the surface tension of a well evokes "a shudder that went to the roots of my hair."

The moment may be taken as emblematic of the reading experience with this novel: one goes on tiptoe across precarious sustaining tensions, across disturbing-but-fascinating sketches of madness and denial on both the individual scale and the societal, staggered from time to time by disruptive gambits of style and voice, and also brought up short by unlikely sympathies and unexpected *memento mori*. In this way Sebald generates an engagement and even suspense that belies the ostensible narrative of ambling over trash.

His use of pictures, and of the occasional page from an older text (in alternative fonts, and in one case in manuscript), reinforce the affect. The anachronistic black-and-whites of *Rings* suffer a deliberate haziness; they are obvious reproductions, even the two-page spread of *The Anatomy Lesson*. As such they call attention to the tenuous nature of these "notes," a job of cut-and-paste. The illustrations wobble back and forth between clarifying details of the passage in which they appear and shifting those details, as the rhetoric does, once more toward shadow-bordered fragility.

Besides all that, these novelizing means are enhanced throughout by a skillful balance of polarities. An essential tactic for *Rings*, whether one considers it story-making or story-faking, this device is most clearly expressed midway through the journey, when the traveler visits what's left of the medieval port of Dunwich. Once a bustling seaside community, Dunwich has been largely lost to North Sea erosion, and the beachside remains of a monastery, at the current eastern border of town, trigger the perception that cities tend to "move west... and along that axis affluence and squalor are unfailingly polarized." So the book in hand adds to its sense of discovery, even while coming to foregone conclusions, by regular juxtaposition of opposites.

Another signal case comes when the author ponders his patron saint. The name appears as "Sebolt" and the holy man's story is coupled in the very next paragraph to the figure of a lone duck illuminated momentarily by lightning—another animal riding the storm, to be sure, and more than that a situation about as far from a conventional hagiography as can be imagined. Before that, too, Sebolt's miracle of lighting a fire with icicles digresses into an inversion of the earlier thoughts about burning down the world's forests:

> I wonder now whether inner coldness and desolation may not be the pre-condition for making the world believe, by a kind of fraudulent showmanship, that one's own wretched heart is still aglow.

It is by such paired oppositions, fire and ice, combustion and blooming, that Sebald maintains his own showmanship, keeping his book's sympathetic moments aglow despite the pervading gloom.

A disruptive polarization also rules some of the larger narrative choices in *Rings*. One striking sequence sets together two deeply divergent aspects of Chinese life in the 1870s: the agitation of the pampered Empress Tz'u-hsi, dithering around her palace in fear of usurpation, and the near-motionlessness, specifically noted as such, of the millions dying of famine in the countryside. Likewise that chapter ends with several pages on the bookish and reclusive Algernon Swinburne, a neurasthenic hypochondriac enthralled by sickness and decay, while the previous chapter spends considerable time with a figure at the opposite end of the writers' spectrum, the robust and prolific sensualist and world traveler Joseph Conrad.

Details of Conrad's life work especially well within the novel's dialectic between antipathies. Now he's at home and affluent, now he's at sea and penniless, and in this way his biography destabilizes, in keeping with the book's other aesthetic devices, sentimental responses to the primary material of the chapter—namely, the appalling story of Roger Casement. Casement is the man who, twenty years before his execution as an Irish spy, called attention to the central African exploitation fictionalized in *Heart of Darkness*. In relating the man's biography, Sebald presents his most breathtaking surrogate narrative. While never losing sight of the story's core tragedy, really many tragedies in one, the narrator achieves almost the playful quality of an exotic international thriller as he makes free with all his tools of appropriation and digression, borrowing from Conrad's fiction and memoirs both, leaping from then-mapless jungles of the Congo to "endless snow-covered fields" of the Ukraine. Isaac Newton declared famously that he stood on the shoulders of giants, and in this chapter of *Rings* Sebald may be said to go further; he leaps from one giant to its eternal enemy and then either back to the first or on to a third, a monster at odds with both the others.

This literary-historical hopscotch, I should reiterate, defines the postmodern. The game persistently deconstructs anything like authority, while at the same time constructing a new beauty out of recycled pieces of the scattered and broken statuary. A less obvious postmod-

ern benchmark, having to do with subject rather than form, may
be Sebald's pervading compassion for animals. Such compassion recalls a number of major accomplishments of the past few decades,
books by everyone from John Barth (*LETTERS*) to J.M. Coetzee
(*Disgrace*), but most notably Milan Kundera's *Unbearable Lightness of
Being*, in which the protagonist of the concluding chapter is the dog
Karenin, an embodiment of the unconventional love that has sprung
up between Tomas and Teresa. *Rings*, like *Unbearable Lightness*, can
be said to make a disquieting refutation of Genesis regarding man's
dominion over the animals.

Then again, when properly understood, Sebald's novelizing means
can be seen to possess a timeless aspect. After all, since *Oedipus Rex*
great drama has depended on creating improbable fellow-feeling. Aristotle would recognize much of the poetics at work in *Rings*: the
pity or terror achieved by means of a feint or two in quite another
direction, the mutually intensifying interplay of disorientation and
recognition. So too one declares the text a "novel" in part because
of certain elements that have defined the form since its emergence.
A work of prose nearly three hundred pages long, *Rings* nonetheless
proceeds mostly via lyric association, not by philosophy's logic or
history's chronology. This wanderer speaks of Roman roads but not
the Roman occupation, and though he makes mention of the larger
conflicts that had an impact on southwestern England, these come
up within a personal framework and are often embodied by often
minor details.

For instance, the air war against Nazi Germany happened to be
an obsession for Sebald the man; it was the subject of his last finished
book, the collection of essays *On the Natural History of Destruction*
(2002). In *Rings*, however, though Suffolk served as a primary staging area for the bombing runs, nearly all the narrator has to say on
the subject concerns two American Thunderbolts that crashed into
a local pond, as reported to him long afterwards by a friend. And in
a touch that would be typical either of postmodern destabilization

or of timeless storytelling pathos, this doubly fatal accident follows a staged dogfight, a playful moment "of sheer high spirits." If the aesthetic instruments at work in Sebald's best books take us toward notions of transcendent narrative art, it's because the novel's goal must be seen as that likewise enduring thing, aesthetic bliss.

The book offers any number of examples to explore, most telling perhaps the climatic visit with Thomas Abrams, building a miniature version of the Temple of Jerusalem as it was in Christ's time. This project offers the fullest reflection of the novel's own: at once small-scale and vast, existing outside time and pitiably ephemeral, forever under reconstruction and long since over and done with. But rather than reiterate more of the same paradoxes I'd like to point out a particularly subtle use to which Sebald puts his tactics.

From the circles in its title on through a number of likewise suggestive choices in perception and vocabulary, this novel makes recurrent references to another great story with a protagonist narrator who was both a historical figure and a pilgrim Everyman. This earlier traveler's tale also trips back and forth between the best and the worst of humanity and relies throughout on heroic or terrifying prodigies from the past. Dante's *Divine Comedy* seems to me a central reference here, an epic that looms behind the lyric *Rings of Saturn* like a planetary center of gravity behind its parti-colored satellites. The Medieval Italian poem is never mentioned directly, and in this may stand as a unique case for the contemporary German-born Englishman, otherwise so willing to reveal his devices, as postmodern etiquette requires. For a while Sebald toys similarly with *King Lear*, but eventually he names Shakespeare's tragedy outright, something he never does for the *Commedia*.

Naturally, a book so rich as this has other veiled allusions—for instance to Plato's cave—yet none are comparably ubiquitous. Sebald-the-Pilgrim is forever finding himself lost in some dark wood, and forever emerging to look up at the stars; I will cite just two of the most striking instances. Early on, a glimpse of lovers on a beach, at the foot of a cliff, has the narrator picturing a "many-limbed, two-headed monster" at "the bottom of the pit," an "image...which lasted an eternity." Contrarily, much later, a remembered limousine ride through the Middleton woods—the limousine was rented, and the forests have since been decimated—seems to take place in a "luxuri-ant...realm" of "clouds," and "above these, at a height the eye could hardly attain," there "hover" "delicate, feathery" flora suggestive of a Caravaggio angel.

To be sure, the more recent wanderer takes poetic liberties with his predecessor. Lucifer in the Ninth Circle has three heads, not two; but then two are more appropriate for an imagination so sensitive to polarities. Likewise the bléssed forest in the *Comedy* (as opposed of course to the dark wood), is the Earthly Paradise at the top of Purga-tory rather than the Celestial Rose of heaven's Empyrean; but then the summit of the purgatorial mountain is also a realm of angels, without sin, entered only after renewing one's soul in the River Le-the. In short, even when Sebald manipulates his referent (slightly) he remains on task, and thus respectful.

In fact, our turn-of-the-millennium masterwork has few words that recur so often as two terms which took on special resonance at the end of the Middle Ages, two concepts in polar opposition—"inferno" and "paradise," I mean. One wonders, on revisiting the novel, at the absence of the middle region. The word "purgatory" is nowhere to be found, in a text otherwise so plenti-ful with antique vocabulary. In that absence we can see how Se-bald continues to work his poetics of opposition, keeping things high-minded yet off balance, even when his language partakes of a resource he never reveals. Any direct connection between heaven and hell would interfere with his subversions, creating unity in a universe this author appears to have accepted, with an animal fatalism, as otherwise; his God's realm may be once in a while made gorgeous and supernatural by a lone lightning bolt, but it seems ultimately without direction, justice, or hope. Or, then again, perhaps *The Rings of Saturn* itself is this author's Purgatory, recycling all the rubble of worlds both imaginative and real into a mountain by which we might come closer not to Chaos, but rather to the Unknowable.

—*Southwest Review*, 2005

BREAKFAST EGG, SLICE OF DREAM: PAUL ABLEMAN & I HEAR VOICES

Paul Ableman, an esteemed British playwright and critic, originally published this travesty thirty years ago. His first novel (Ableman has published four more since[1]), *I Hear Voices,* originally appeared on the list of the Olympia Press, the Paris house that first brought out *Lolita* and *Naked Lunch.* American publication, late but welcome, is thanks to McPherson & Co., another small house of gumption and discernment.

Brief as it is, the novel's one long wake-up call—the protagonist never entirely makes it out of bed. The delivery of his breakfast egg, a recurrent set piece, would be a symbol in a less explosive exercise. But Mr. Ableman must constantly break his eggs, fragment his abbreviated roundabout world. His unnamed narrator (some variety of schizophrenic, perhaps?) may never get out from under his bed-tray, but the cryptic types who drop by to talk (nobody's idea of "characters," certainly) carry him further than many of us go in a lifetime.

Arthur, who seems to be the protagonist's brother, takes him into the world of affairs. Our eggman-narrator tumbles through elliptical factory visits and business meetings that turn into streamlined psychotherapy. "When the doctors arrive," Arthur advises him at one point,

---

1. True in 1990 and at Ableman's death in 2006. He remains unclassifiable: now working in avant-garde fiction, now in journalism, now in TV and radio.

"I wouldn't be quite so—so articulate. One doesn't say everything one perceives." As for Maria, sometimes a nurse and sometimes a maid, she offers affairs of another kind. She and Egg, now smitten with each other and now dying of embarrassment over some ludicrous faux pas, stumble through shopping trips that brim with erotic possibility. The brother and the lover by no means exhaust Ableman's catalogues of witty facsimiles. Whoever's along for company, the narrator's shifts from breakfast to weirdness and back provide the same effect as chapter breaks, and offer breathers in the onrushing slice of dream.

Anonymous commuter encounters will flare with offhand intensity. Party scenes prove sharply knowing about social give and take, even as they introduce such impossible figures as Cortex the Statue. The parties best embody the text's essential dialectic: breathtaking precision about states of mind played off against a hilarious vagueness about physical reality. Along the way, poetic tangents fly off in every direction: "There were far reports and others that leapt from brain to brain so that the sunset was pricked with doubt and signaled a spectrum of confused acknowledgement."

Is this in fact the mind of a madman? Is Arthur a doctor, a brother, or a business partner at wit's end and trying to close a deal? Wrong questions. *I Hear Voices* trembles at times on the verge of familiarity, in exchanges that suggest counseling or confession, but whatever grasp on the world they might offer is laughingly undone by the narrator's phantoms and leitmotifs. Ableman prefers the unexplained, the visionary; a number of passages recall Donald Barthelme in how they resist ossification into one thing or another. His novel stands as another example of the wild freedoms embraced by European fiction since 1945, freedoms still only fitfully understood on this side of the Atlantic.

—*New York Times Book Review*, 1990
—*Willamette Week*, 1990

A TORTUROUS HISTORY, A SUPPLE MEDIUM: ELIAS KHOURY & GATE OF THE SUN

It's a rare book that can embody a torturous history we all recognize yet at the same time come up repeatedly with on-the-button analogies for the medium of representation, the story of the history. *Gate of the Sun* has an epic subject, thoroughly painful. It relates the blasted lives of the peasants who composed the first wave of the Palestinian diaspora—the Fedayeen, just coming to adulthood in 1948, when they were driven from their orchard towns and fishing villages. Elias Khoury's handling of their sorrow may be meaty with incident, but it often seems less like a novel of recent history than like a rabble of images coming together to drive history to a fresh end; again and again, it insists on the direction and significance that narrative can give materials of utter devastation. A quarter of the way in, we read:

How am I to bear the death…and my fear, if not through telling stories?

And not much further:

Prison is a storytelling school: Here we can go wherever we want, twist our memory however we please.

And not much after that:

I discovered how it was possible to open the book of history,
enter it, and be the reader and the read at the same time.

Toward the end of his saga Khoury may even intrude authorially.
The final episodes make recurrent use of his own first name, the Arab
translation of the Old Testament "prophet of fire"—and of wheels
within wheels.

Certainly *Gate of the Sun* is a book of fire, crackling with gunplay and howls, throwing off intense heat. In particular it traces the
violent odyssey of two Palestinian guerillas. The warrior hero would
be Yunes, the Arab "Jonah," a bush fighter of legendary resourceful-
ness who also goes by Abu Salem and other names. The present action, however, finds Yunes stuck in a Leviathan from which he won't
emerge; he lies comatose in the threadbare hospital of the Shatila
camp outside Beirut in the late 1980s. And the narrator of *Gate*,
whose constant reflections on what he's up to goes along with a certain bumbling quality, is Dr. Khalil, a less venturesome comrade in
arms and a doctor without a degree. Sitting by the unconscious guerilla's cot in a makeshift private room—"a relative paradise in a relative hospital in a relative camp in a relative city"—Khalil tells Yunes
the stories of both their wandering lives,

The relative doctor hopes that the human contact will revive his
friend. More than that, Khalil seeks to make sense of the experience
they share with the rest of the uprooted Arabs of "Galilee." As the
narrator asks, in perhaps the most resonant of his many single-line
paragraphs: "How did we get here?" So the novel's accomplishment
can never be appreciated by the standards of straightforward war story, revenge tragedy, or refugee survival drama. It claims all these elements, a story of fire, but its magisterial impact depends equally on
its *lack* of closure and certainty, on recursive meditation and quixotic
probing into things unknowable. The novel questions not only the
route taken by its protagonists, but also its own reliability as a map.
Tales of lost homes and loved ones themselves lose direction; even

as *Gate* works toward repatriation-by-story, its style keeps leaping to aphorism ("the question of land sales in Palestine has 'no end and no beginning,' as they say") or to far-reaching speculations ("the only solution to love is murder"), both devices that have little respect for borders. Strands of narration twist till cause and effect yield wheels within wheels.

Not that Elias Khoury, himself a Lebanese Muslim born in '48, distrusts cause and effect. A professor at NYU and an editor for Beirut's daily paper, he has four volumes of cultural criticism and has often reported on human-rights issues in camps like Shatila. In the novel, his shaggy-dog narrator pokes his snout now into an assessment of Dostoevsky, now into the nuts and bolts—the scraps and rags—with which such a camp hospital is maintained. Yet Khalil's creator has also found time for ten previous novels and four plays. The Arabic *Gate of the Sun* (the title *Bab al-Shams* translates directly) appeared in 1998 and won ringing endorsements from the likes of Edward Said, as well as a number of international prizes, including Book of the Year from *Le Monde Diplomatique*. The near-decade it has taken to produce an American edition seems like another black eye for our publishing industry, the worse because no mainstream press would take on the task. There's better news, at least, in what Archipelago Books has done with the book, bringing out a scrupulously checked and crafted hardcover, in handsome desert orange, as part of their Rainmaker Translation series.

Perhaps the problem for commercial publishers was that Khoury's achievement depends not on simple reportage but on something less quantifiable, namely, sensibility—an imagination open to the power of both the ambiguous and the concrete. For this author must be counted a sensualist, composing a "Sort of Song" not unlike the one celebrated by Williams: no ideas but in things. Khalil's tangled yarns may take shape as scenes half-hidden in smoke, beneath which honor and shame can never be sorted out, yet the doctor always fixes quite specifically the humble rewards of its battlegrounds. The novel's first image for recovery is the branch of a fruit tree, brought to the displaced narrator from another destroyed hamlet. Elsewhere, bittersweet reductions of the vanished homeland are distilled from fish soup, from pillows stuffed with flower petals, from the odor of ground pork and onions simmering in olive oil. Details such as these, rendered with just a smattering of Arabic, bear out the quality of the translation by Humphrey Davies. Even the sex scenes, always difficult material, convey Khoury's distinctive blend of murk and nugget—of, for instance, a woman who "must be past sixty" yet whose "body became full, with…a complexion the shade of white wheat," who "started to shimmer and change" in lovemaking.

For love, in both its small gestures and large, plays so great a role in *Gate* as to suggest an earlier story sequence of what used to be called "Oriental complexity," namely, *The Thousand Nights and a Night*. Yunes, as befits his energy and charisma, has plenty of female attention right up through the evening of his stroke. The relationship that matters most—itself an epic of tenacity told in anecdotes, none of them quite complete—was with his late wife Nabilah, the mother of his ten children. Nabilah's and her husband's trysting place gives us the title: they meet in a cave they called Bab al-Shams, an underground that wound up taking them, like Dante's, to the sun. And romance may scar the storytelling doctor more deeply, even, than his so-called patient. Over time, we come to understand that Khalil's endless hours in this largely unknown private room have a less-than-altruistic second purpose. The doctor fears reprisal for his part in a saga of betrayal, as intricate as all the others here, involving his unfaithful lover, Shams. Not long ago, the woman was gunned down by the family of one of the other men in her life.

Yet Khalil's love for Shams comes across as genuine. Her name too partakes of the intimate sweetness in the title, as well as being the word for the sun that defines this hardscrabble land. Then, too, the doctor's not nearly so worldly as his manifold wanderings and wallopings might suggest. Khoury generates a terrific jolt, and underscores the toll taken by a life in exile, when it turns out that his narrator's not yet forty.

Given such subject matter, it's not surprising that another of this novel's fixing particularities, along with foods and fruits, are tears. A widowed mother declares early on that "tears are our remedy," and more than once Yunes—so philosophical a guerilla he recalls Jay Cantor's Che Guevara—remarks on how the Palestinian after-dinner liqueur goes by the same word as "tear," *arak*. Khalil, for his part, meditates on the artificial tears with which he doses his unresponsive friend, and so arrives, as always with the natural rhythm of talking to oneself, at perhaps the loveliest of his self-reflections: "All the stories of the exodus have collected now in your eyes—shut over the tear-drops I put in them."

The crux of the novel's success is how it rises to the challenge in the first half of that statement, how it chronicles nearly half a century in the wilderness without stinting on the joy and lamentation implicit in the second half. Emotional richness, after all, goes hand in hand with narrative complication, and the novel's fugal construction draws out a number of provocative shadings, many of them surprises. Khalil, all hemming and hawing aside, proves a cold-eyed recording angel when it comes to the repeated failures of other Arab nations to back up the Palestinian cause. And Yunes opposes the famed Black September kidnapping in Munich, and he can't abide "the hijacking of airplanes…and the killing of civilians." Even after joining Fatah, late in his career, he remains a soldier rather than a terrorist. "If you don't respect the lives of others," Yunes declares, "you don't have the right to defend your own."

And respect, for this fallen warrior and his doctor, extends as well to the women of their culture. If we consider this novel a tragic pica-resque—a paradox, to be sure, but then a masterpiece usually pres-ents a paradox—the figures that deepen it from adventure to tragedy turn out to be, by and large, the wives and mothers and girlfriends.

Nothing Yunes or Khalil suffers haunt them so stubbornly as when they cross paths with another abused or rootless woman.

After all, their brother Fedayeen help to map the route of their *hejira*. Indeed, their travels include more than a few returns to former villages. Such visits must be surreptitious, but again and again guerillas go on foot through old stomping grounds: a vivid demonstration of just how small a region has given rise to so much wailing and gnashing of teeth. The opening maps establish that "Galilee" occupies a rectangle about fifty miles by thirty. What's more, in spite of how the displaced peasants mourn the loss of their olive groves, much of the land remains barely arable. In such close, sparse quarters, the chronic mistreatment of those supposedly nearest and dearest to the fighting men can't remain hidden. Battered women turn up at every winding of these spiral stories, here "the Madwoman of al-Kabri" and there Kahlil's own beloved Shams, suffering "humiliation and…beatings" at the hands of the man she was forced to marry as a teenager. The most decent among the male characters can't ignore the moral vacuity of their position, and early on Yunes admits that "degradation of our women was the root of our failures, our paralysis, our defeats." At the end, if Khalil is restored to something like faith, to believing he can climb "ropes of rain…and walk" back to wholeness and home—walk on water, yes—he's been brought to this miracle by two women, the first an actual hospital colleague and the second a dream visitor to his kitchen and bed. Elias Khoury must know that, according to tradition, angels have no gender. But he knows better, too, and his *Gate of the Sun* illuminates a womanly host.

—*Michigan Quarterly Review*, 2007

CHESSBOARD & CORNUCOPIA:
40 YEARS OF INVISIBLE CITIES

As you head south and east, with your back to the sea, the city of Alvito draws you uphill along ever-smaller roads, tightening spirals and switchbacks that soon have you confused over what's the approach and what the close-clustered town itself. Around just which curb-hugging rise and turn did you finally arrive? Nothing so defines this metropolis as its precipitousness…

The above concerns an actual place about an hour outside of Rome, a "city" insofar as that's defined by culture and close living quarters. The *style* of my description, however, the parody I'm attempting—respectfully—that's what Americans will recognize before they think of any Italian reality. It's the style of *Invisible Cities*, of the cities within *Cities*.

Fifty-five thumbnails, the longest a few pages, the shortest half a page, take up most of Italo Calvino's slim text and supply its defining innovation. Indeed, their bulk proves *part* of the innovation. Plenty of writers have set fictions in fantasy downtowns, but none have dreamed up so many at once. One metropolis in the 1974 novel comes alive as a memory of young love; another presents faces of the unhappy dead. One hangs in hammocks, another stands on stalks, another contains a museum of its own ideal forms, forever perfect, and another remains eternally unfinished, nothing but abandoned plumbing. Each miniature is rendered with improbable specificity, in bits and pieces now exotic, now mundane. Each brings off a small tale of discovery, a bracing single shot of narrative.

Sets of ten cities open and close the book, and these bracket seven sets of five, but enclosing the whole there's another sort of bracket. There's a sketch of a story connecting the city sketches. Marco Polo, footloose merchant, shares his travels with the stay-at-home emperor Kublai Khan. This frame device turns out to be itself about framing, since the Khan seeks a better sense of his domains "to discern," as the novel's opening has it, "through the walls and towers destined to crumble, the tracery of a pattern so subtle it could escape the termites' gnawing." This premise alone sets *Invisible Cities* far beyond ordinary storytelling. Still, nothing's so striking as the cities themselves, a Baedeker unparalleled in its variety, forever playing peekaboo with pattern—now you see one, now you don't.

And this game has continued for forty years. First publication came at the end of 1972, and hardly eighteen months later arrived the English translation, the pinnacle of William Weaver's career, scrupulous yet songlike. By the end of the first print run, American novelists as far apart as John Barth and Gore Vidal were hailing Calvino an international grandmaster, beside the likes of Grass, Naipaul, or Garcia Marquez.

Those reputations, however, are based in the tradition of the social novel. *A House for Mr. Biswas*, for instance, generates story out of well-known tensions. It's about race, colonialism, and money-grubbing, and while the narrative includes a touch of formal experiment, its primary task remains to embody a place and a people. *Cities*, on the other hand, tends to *dis*embody. Merchant and emperor do without psychological backing and filling, and their dialogue makes no pretense to the ring of the street. The two men scuffle, toward the end, but their pushing and shoving may take place only in dream, and after that the frame tale itself is rendered irrelevant. It turns out that the Emperor has an atlas. Throughout, too, in place of rising action, Calvino has rising numbers. His cities are presented according to the Fibonacci series, a mathematical pattern rich in suggestion—though one that remains largely undiscussed by fans and celebrants.

Granted, the meditations on cities eventually develop a resonance within the world we know. The final ten towns include Procopia, where a population explosion crowds the view with "an expanse of faces" (an image that also suggests the proliferation of media), and Penthelisia, which has no center, only endless sprawl, "one limbo [after] another." Many critics have noted these nightmares of collapse and the way they build to Polo's closing: a plea for the liveable city. We must "give... space," the traveler warns, to "what is not inferno." Yet as Calvino's twentieth century recedes, his foremost accomplishment hardly looms as a contribution to urban studies. Rather, *Cities* has become a benchmark for narrative.

William Gass, in an encomium that rolls on like a caravan, struggles to place the book in some alternative genre. He settles for "one of the purer works of the imagination," and indeed, placed alongside *Invisible Cities*, other recent achievements in the long story can look adulterated. Even *Infinite Jest* or *The Elementary Particles* at once reveal their debt to classics of the form. Not surprisingly, then, the last four decades have seen more and more authors trying to steer by this willowy new landmark. More and more book-length fiction has taken the form of variations on a theme, in which the consistency of a motif matters more than the depth of a character. The model proved especially congenial for Gilbert Sorrentino in his last novels, but a better-known case would be Zachary Mason's *The Lost Books of the Odyssey*. Mason's debt to *Cities* was especially clear in the original, on Starcherone Press, which included a frame tale excised for big-house publication. Indeed, cuttings off Calvino's rootstock flourish on the smaller indies; an exemplary case would be Matt Bell's *Cataclysm Baby*, but the approach doesn't exclude bestsellers either. Alan Lightman's *Einstein's Dreams* and David Eagleman's *Sum* are pop confections whipped up *Cities*-style, substituting comfy metaphysics for urban rough edges.

Other authors have left their stamp on the art form, to be sure. Garcia Marquez introduced a contagious strain of magic, and no doubt we'll soon see knockoffs of Thomas Bernhard's hundred-page paragraphs, all bile and erudition. Still, the nearest analogue I can see to what Calvino did for the novel is what Beckett did for theater, in the decades after he stripped it down to rags.

Nothing so defines this metropolis as its precipitousness. Throughout Alvito, homes hundreds of years old stagger upslope and down, each striving to boost itself above or between the others, and yet the stone-bound claustrophobia of these palazzi and the winding stairs at their feet will open up, with a step onto a balcony, at a turn in the stair, to airy vistas of the farm plains—green, black, dappled, dun—far below. At a glance the gritty and fecund stacks of basaltic rock fall away, and you could be a hawk, idling spreadwinged and scouring the fields for prey...

Another measure of the novel's impact is how often it brought the author to the United States. Back in 1960 Calvino had swung through the country on a Ford Foundation grant, but this was for his work as an editor. He'd championed exchanges across the Iron Curtain and overseen major translations (among Americans, Bernard Malamud). His creative output kept pace, though, starting with *The Path to the Nest of Spiders* in '47. This debut verges on the surreal and has traces of fable, yet it's a war novel; it draws on Calvino's time with the guerillas of northern Italy, combat that left him, he later claimed, with "an unparalleled sense of the human." Still, it took *Invisible Cities*, Calvino's tenth or eleventh work of fiction (depending...), to make him a Distinguished Visiting Writer. Barth, at Johns Hopkins, arranged the first visit early in '76. After that, for the nine years left to

him, Calvino came over often. The project on his desk at his death—
not yet sixty-two, multitasking as ever, and smoking, smoking—was
a series of lectures to be delivered at Harvard.

These were *Six Memos for the New Millennium*, something of an
aesthetic manifesto, but concerning *Invisible Cities* the author's nearest thing to full disclosure came in the spring of '83, at Columbia.
The talk is difficult to find in English, but it's transcribed in the Italian critical edition of *Cities*. The sentences, despite their everyday vocabulary, coil something like those in the novel. Calvino begins with
his habit of keeping file folders of occasional reflections: "A folder
for objects, a folder for animals…one for historical figures, one for
heroes of myth…" Whenever a folder grew full, his job became "to
think of the book [he] could pull out of it," and as the 1960s ended,
his fattest folders had to do with cities.

The decade had begun with the American visit, and in a letter
home he claimed he wanted his tombstone to read "newyorkese." In
Italy he bounced from Turin to Rome to smaller centers like Alvito,
trips abroad included Tripoli and Havana, and in '67 he settled in
Paris. On an earlier visit he'd met the woman who would become his
wife, the woman he called Chichita, a multilingual Argentine Jew
whose actual name was Esther, and the year following the relocation,
as a wave of youth revolt shook cities everywhere, the worst upheav-
als came in his new home. Rioters pried the stones from the streets
and chanted *La vie est ailleurs*, "Life is elsewhere."

Amid this turmoil, Calvino's folders began to reflect both the actual and the elsewhere. One collected places he'd known, "life-pas-
sages for me," while another held cities of the imagination. Together
these "became a diary that traced [his] moods," now a metropolis
like "a sky full of stars" and now nothing but "garbage." Everything
in his experience ended up in "images of cities," and "carried along
behind," he sought to discern the tracery of a pattern.

A creative spirit so restless as Calvino's could never settle for
memoir. Rather, he began to sort his notes in groupings that,

nearly half a century later, remain familiar: *Cities & Memory,
Cities & Desire...*

These first two he knew to be "fundamental," but another of
his initial attempts at categorization, *Cities & the Form*, he rejected
as "generic." He preferred the concrete, such as *Cities & Eyes*, and
he didn't want the text's *percorso*, its way home, "completely dis-
connected" from his original, more personal order. By the time he
developed his *Hidden* and *Continuing* sets, the author was working
"*apposta*," deliberately building on the form he'd glimpsed first in
the juxtaposition of memory and desire. Polo and Khan emerged as
a natural complement, another set of contraries, in an initial lump
of "material" that Calvino then dispersed among the rest, "each to
its own part." Polo's thirteenth-century *Travels*, after all, is known
in Italian as *Il Milione*, "the million," for the number of lies it's supposed to contain. For a certain sort of novelist this very quality made
the text accommodating: "an imaginary continent in which other
literary works find space."

Finding space, in the '83 talk at Columbia, also comes to mean
finding a direction. The *percorso* proved central to the creative act:

> A book...is a space in which a reader can enter, turn about,
> perhaps lose himself, but at a certain point find an exit....
> Some of you may tell me that this definition better suits a
> novel of plot, and not a book like this....All right, but I would
> claim that also a work like this, in order to be a book, must
> have a certain construction, in which it's possible to discover a
> plot, an itinerary, a resolution.

As for that word "plot," remarkable under the circumstances, the
Italian is "*intreccio*," which also translates as "weave" and "nest." Out
of gleanings from what he'd known, what he still wished for, and
what he saw under threat around him, the peripatetic magpie Calvino wove a new home for his imagination.

At a glance the gritty and fecund stacks of basaltic rock fall away, and you could be a hawk, idling spreadwinged and scouring the fields for prey. No scrambling small rodent below, however, is quite so helpless as the farmer. His parcels of orchard and vineyard and eggplant, which once rolled on for miles beneath the city, keep collapsing together into consolidated holdings. Agribusiness in its far-off capitals, casting its web of finance models, demands ever-more systematized growing cycles, more single-crop dependency. And with each fresh demand, another family farmer abandons what was once the far-flung ducal territory of Alvito, and with those farmers there disappear folks from the city, their own livings dependent, one way or the other, on the valley's former diverse haul, here olives, there truffles, there pig. The locals can no longer cling to the mountainside; the gravity proves too much.

What then is this "itinerary"? The author was uncomfortable with the way critics reduced the text to Polo's final admonition. To protect what's "not inferno," to Save the City—even William Gass treats this as the book's ruling purpose. Yet for an argument like that, wouldn't we do better to read Jane Jacobs? *The Death and Life of Great American Cities*? Worries about our disappearing downtowns, our degraded quality of life, go back considerably further than the Paris riots, and Calvino himself, during his Columbia talk, argues that his work is something else, "polyhedral." He claims that "all its folds" offer potential concluding insights, "no less epigrammatic." He wraps up his remarks by pointing to chapter five, "the heart of the book," where he locates "a theme of lightness, strange in its association with the theme of cities."

Lightness is a cardinal virtue for this author, one of those upheld in *Six Memos*, and in *Cities*, it's a sylphlike set of five he singles out. The chapter includes Octavia, dangling on webs above an abyss, and Baucis, standing on "long flamingo legs." One city, Leandra, comes close to holding a mirror to nature, its political squabbles sound familiar, but they're the nattering of fairyfolk. Chapter five is introduced, moreover, by Kublai's dreams of "cities light as kites...cities like leaves' veins." When he wakes, he hears of a town with "slender pinnacles, made in such a way that the moon in her journey can rest now on one, now on another."

A lovely fancy—but one Calvino had imagined before. Over the decade preceding *Cities* he produced a number of titles, but most collected odds and ends; in '68 he not only refused an award for one, *T-Zero*, but also asked that his name be withdrawn from all other award considerations. The only recent work that mattered to him seemed to be the '65 story sequence *Cosmicomics*. In that book, "The Distance of the Moon" brings off a similar bi-play between planet and satellite. At one point the moon sways atop a pole, and the touch is made poignant, part of a bravura narrative of adultery, night-sea voyages, and gathering the lunar cheese.

Narrative rules in *Cosmicomics*: the fictions demonstrate expert command of situation, complication, and climax, all the more impressive given their material. '*Comics* has even less recognizable reality to work with than *Cities*. Stories consider the beginning of the universe, the formation of the galaxies and the Big Bang itself. The narrator in every case is some particle of Essence that's been around eternally. Yet his tales render Freytag's Triangle with such dash that two appeared in *Playboy* (pieces devoid of sex, I should add) and the first US edition, in '68, was labeled "Science Fiction." Now, still, some Calvino readers prefer *Cosmicomics* to *Cities*. Others point back to another triumph of story over situation, namely, *The Baron in the Trees*, from 1957. *Baron* concerns an eighteenth-century aristocrat who moves out of the manor and up into the trees. His arboreal travels at times anticipate Polo's, and weave an *intreccio* in which the Enlightenment arrives at the point of a bayonet and a love affair tumbles with the beauty of a November leaf.

In all the work back to *Nest of Spiders*, Calvino's allegiance was to *both* wild ingenuity and story satisfaction. In the process he could raise philosophical issues, in particular issues of the good society (in *Baron* especially), but these worked through conflict to a dramatic resolution. This author had earned the authority to claim that a book should have "an itinerary, a plot." Still, by his early forties, the later 1960s, his sensibility had grown restive.

He married and left Italy, but as he reveals in the rueful "Hermit in Paris," the move never generated that "inner landscape for the imagination to…turn into its theater." His introduction to the City of Light had been the cracking yarns of the Musketeers, but to live there reduced the place to "a series of practical problems." So too in *Cities*, again about midway along, the glory of Phyllis dwindles to "a door here, a stairway there, a bench where you can put down your basket." The author needed more, new material for the interior theater, and as he and his wife worked on a translation of Raymond Queneau, Calvino entered the French author's salon—his "workshop for potential literature," Oulipo.

The relationship with Oulipo can be seen as symbiotic: the group enabled Calvino's break from story, and he brought them greater stature. *Invisible Cities* was his first wholly new work out of the affiliation, and no other title linked with the salon (such as Georges Perec's *A Void*) enjoys anywhere near its esteem and influence. *The Oulipo Compendium*, put together by Harry Mathews, certainly includes numbers-based exercises, suggesting what Calvino does with the Fibonacci series. Certainly, by the mid-'70s the author was into a fresh series of texts, all original and coherent, and all radical breaks from narrative. The best known, *If on a Winter's Night's a Traveler* (English, 1981), proceeds by first setting up intrigues not unlike those that sustain the earlier works—steep, strange challenges—and then cutting them off.

Still, the shift in aesthetic had to do with a lot besides Oulipo. The Italian, the hermit in Paris, wasn't an active participant. He'd begun exploring writers like Queneau long before, and during this same period his reading often took him in the opposite direction, to the ancient forms of fable and fairytale. Starting in 1970, he edited collections of the Brothers Grimm and others, writing several prefaces. The best-known is his *Italian Folktales* (English, 1990), praised by the arch-conservative John Gardner. The power of *Cities*, in other words, was forged in a tension between old pleasures of the text and a recognition that those pleasures no longer suited his energies. The *percorso* he'd always followed had reached a dead end.

> Locals in Alvito can no longer cling to the mountainside; the gravity proves too powerful. Along the city's byways, there tends not to echo a clippity-clop but a schlip-sch-sschlip-schlip, as only the old shuffle by. More and more, a palazzo's double-doors, wide enough to welcome a carriage, thick enough to absorb a musket-ball, depend on a heavy padlock to hold them in place. Archways sprout weeds in the mornings, bats in the evening, and even the castle on the mountaintop doesn't so much crown the little metropolis as offer a way-station up the slope towards the ghost town: the gloom just overhead. Small wonder that lovers can't get enough of the place. Small wonder that no sooner does the light start to fail than the cars rise grumbling into the disused *centro*, with two to every car, and a fair number of the Fiats and Audis borrowed from a friend in order to escape detection.

The lightness of *Cities,* in short, must never be mistaken for fluff. Its cloud castles are streaked with storm; the plea to hold off the inferno should be taken also a stay against creative failure, and rickety, on stilts. This quality again recalls Beckett, his long shelf of last words, but Calvino has none of Beckett's austerity. Each cup of city arrives brimming, even the cemetery-town Agria. Most offer a taste of the fresh-made, a display of the Baroque, or—the most common refreshment—some inkling of a lover. Sensuality occurs in such variety, it can't help but suggest the author's homeland, and no doubt he suffered the absence at his desk in Paris. The book he pulled from his folders emphasized, above all, two aspects of *Italianità*.

The first is the Fibonacci series, where each term is the sum of the previous two in the series. The opening (0, 1, 0+1=1, 1+1=2, 1+2=3, 2+3=5...) provides the sequence for the sets of cities.

Their stagger-step up to five and down follows a pattern scientists know as the Golden Ratio, because it occurs in many natural forms, from the uncoiling of a snail shell to the clustering of sunflower seeds. Of course, to test the ratio required technology far beyond that of Fibonacci himself, a twelfth-century mathematician out of Pisa (a contemporary, that is, of Marco Polo's father). Still, his figures have proven correct, placing most flora and fauna on a grid—or a chessboard, to use a recurring image from *Cities*. The board of course belongs to the Khan, "a keen…player," who believes that winning at chess will allow him to "finally possess [his] empire." As the novel arrives at what would ordinarily serve as climax point (the eighth chapter of nine), Kublai orders Polo to stay at the palace and play. Farfetched travelogues will profit the Emperor less than mastering the game. But the hours over the board leave him in crisis, his values bankrupt:

> Each game ends in a gain or loss: but of what?...At checkmate, beneath the foot of the king, knocked aside by the winner's hand, nothingness remains: a black square, or a white one….[T]he empire's multiform treasures were only illusory envelopes.

Illusory forms, empty, as if the scent and hue of a flowerbed, its spices and thorns, were reduced to the numbers game of some old Italian. The bleak vision suggests as well an artist's despair, when inspiration goes lifeless, and consequently no moment in *Invisible Cities* feels so heartening as when Polo, in the closing frame of this same "climax" (the chapter's closing dialogue), begins to refill the envelopes. Where the Khan saw scorched earth, his guest envisions a garden. "Your chessboard, sire, is inlaid with two woods: ebony and maple." The Venetian reseeds the barren black and white; he imagines buds, larva, woodsmen, and the artisan at his lathe. In no time Kublai is left "overwhelmed," his senses reawakened by "rafts laden with logs...women at the windows..."

In this exchange resides the essential dialectic of the text, between Form and Content. The Emperor sits alert to any sign of a controlling pattern, believing that "on the day when I have learned the rules, I shall finally possess my empire," and the merchant comes and goes, toting an ever-changing urban cornucopia. It's Polo who spies a woman in what was, a moment before, a rectangle in a blank wall. The Venetian plays the hero, you could say, since he gets the final, restorative word, both at the (surrogate) climax and the (sort of) conclusion; he provides a happy ending, you could say. Indeed, John Updike dubbed Calvino "the sunniest" of twentieth-century fabulists, in his review of *Cities*. Yet while the compliment's not out of line, it's over-simple. This novel can't be read like some episode of *Star Trek: TNG*, in which sloppy humanity defeats the regimented Borg.

Only an Emperor of Forms, after all, could supply the Fibonacci stutter-step, a ratio one also detects in chess combinations. The sequence propels our reading, a timekeeper, like the threes and nines in Dante's *Divine Comedy*. Besides that, at another fold in the book's middle, it's the Khan who intuits how Venice informs all of Polo's fabulations. The voyager's "first city" is "implicit" in them all, and the insight proves sharp enough to set the merchant doubting his goods: "perhaps, speaking of other cities, I have already lost [Venice], little by little." It's a moment when Content comes out the loser, in the biplay—and when Kublai stands in for a good reader, who senses Calvino's doubt and fears. Then there's the great irony of the Khan's atlas. This last surprise reveals actual cities ("Granada, the streaked pearl of the caliphs; Lübeck, the neat, boreal port") and creates further ambiguity. "Your atlas preserves the differences intact: that assortment of qualities which are like the letters in a name." To suggest paradise and inferno are merely tricks of the alphabet undercuts Polo's dominance of the closing; it maintains the essential tension.

Calvino's task entails a rigor far beyond that of any earlier book of lists. Old Possum's charming *Practical Cats*, Bierce's snarky *Devil's Dictionary*, have nothing like this text's accumulative power. Still, in the end, appreciation of *Cities* must return to the cities, their serendipity and brio. It's a city that best exemplifies the second element crucial to the book's continuing enchantment.

Pyrrha, #3 of the "Cities & Names," comes roughly at midpoint—that again. Polo admits that years went by before he visited, but over that time he'd "conjured" it "through its name." He'd done the same with others: "Euphrasia, Odile, Margara, Getullia." Thus the narrative of his visit explores how the actual place supplanted "everything [he] had imagined." It's all mills, Pyrrha, including windmills, and these recall another wayfarer who didn't know what he was looking at. Like Quixote, Polo still sees a chimera, the city of his imagination. That place has lost its name, but it haunts the same crannies of the mind, "a fragment or glimmer," and once more it calls up four odd names: "Euphrasia, Odile, Margara, Getullia."

The sojourn provides, first, yet another masterly miniature, evoking a subtlety of our inner life in a bit more than a page. What's more, that lingering glimmer of what we once believed illuminates, in this case, a dream lover. Odile would be the object of infatuation most English readers recognize, the trickster of *Swan Lake* (and by extension the prostitute Odette, from Proust, casting her spell over the well-born Swann). Also the names contain Shakespeare's Juliet, in Italian Giulietta; the girl was from Verona, after all. In that city, too, "Margara" echoes a common expression of regret, *magari*, "if only..." The word appears in a thousand love songs, and "Euphrasia" probably turns up in a couple as well, since in both Italian and English the term retains its Greek derivation, "an excess of happiness." More commonly, the word refers to an herb and its extract, eyebright. A few drops and you look like you've been crying for joy.

Life is elsewhere, cried the rioters of Paris '68, but "elsewhere" often takes the form of a shadow-love. To settle down is a Pyrrhic victory; you win comfort and lose the dream. If you're a married man, no pairing's so natural as cities and desire. In Pyrrha the Ghost Lover may be only a "glimmer," but its gestures indicate, once again, the author, whose fiction began to find its new form when he was both a new husband (as of '64) and father ('65). After that he appears never to have strayed, but as a younger man he'd been active, in the style of other European intellectuals. Affairs included a movie actress and, according to his letters, "a sweet and embarrassing bigamy" in his twenties. Later, though happy with Chichita and his daughter, Calvino's work often had him traveling alone, and each new city must've raised, faintly, a siren call. Each allowed him to experience the paradox embodied by Isidora, one of the first visits in his developing text: a place where "desires are already memories." Hence the project that resulted wove together all his wandering, going back to his days as a guerilla, in a vision of living arrangements constantly going to pieces, of "cities like leaves' veins." Our luck as readers depends on his exile: at every stop he sensed his discoveries were at terrible risk, and he sketched each with awe, with love.

No sooner does the light start to fail than vehicles rise into the disused central square, always two to a vehicle, and sometimes in Fiats and Audis borrowed from a friend, in order to escape detection. After that, on benches of crumbling stone, before the view from Alvito's first plateau, couples nuzzle and coo beneath gargoyles, or what used to be gargoyles, before their teeth wore off, or before the monsters' faces were obscured by the smoke of the lovers' cigarettes, often enhanced with a smatter of hashish. More serious encounters, meanwhile, take place up along the spiral networks of alley and stair. There's always a door that's come off its hinges, and once inside, what do you need besides a blanket, a candle, a half-bottle of booze or a smatter of hashish—what more, so long as love keeps you nubile and willing? The sighs and giggles, the chink of a belt-buckle hitting the tile and murmurs of no, and no, and yes-s-s, these fill the shelves of the abandoned libraries, they echo like prayers through the deconsecrated chapels, imbuing all the moldering leftovers with such excitement as to seem the guiding purpose, the ultimate resolution, of the centuries upon centuries previous, with all their struggle and decay.

—*Ploughshares*, 2014

FRESH TIDE

CHE SARÁ SARÁ:
JAY CANTOR & THE DEATH OF CHE GUEVARA

According to Marx, history and the individual grapple perpetually. The individual strives to make history even as history guides his hand. The ideal revolutionary, then, must try to cleanse himself of the past. He may even go so far as to drop his given name, the way Ernesto Guevara did when he became a guerrilla, identifying himself instead by a mere blurt, *Che,* "an empty sound that might mean anything, that anyone might fill in as he wishes." That's how Jay Cantor describes it toward the beginning of his magnificent first novel, *The Death of Che Guevara.* But Che pursued a quest that seems, to choose an analogy the book itself invites, as doomed as Ahab's. Consider the history.

Che Guevara was killed—executed without trial, on the command of a field officer—on October 9, 1967. Two companies of the Bolivian Army, so reliant on US support that they even wore our Rangers' Vietnam-issue boots, caught up with Che's decimated band of twenty or so near the mountain village of Higueras. For most of the previous year the doctor-turned-guerrilla, Fidel Castro's indispensable second during the Cuban Revolution of '58–'59, had been trying to establish the first of what he termed "many Vietnams." Starting in Latin America, he'd been trying to demonstrate why the struggle against imperialism had to be global. But until his death, Che's presence in Bolivia had been at most a rumor; he'd become, to borrow a pertinent metaphor, the specter haunting *la causa*. At the time of his murder he posed no obvious threat, hobbled by a thigh wound and struggling with asthma. Yet the death required confirmation via a notorious photo, with an officer pointing at the fatal wound. After that Guevara's hands were cut off and put in a jar, so that his fingerprints might be taken, and after *that* his corpse was burned. John Berger, in an essay inspired by the photograph, pointed out that the Bolivian establishment's fearful behavior accomplished just the opposite of what was intended. Thanks to these barbaric funeral rites, Guevara's legend grew: he became something of a Christ, and something of an artwork. The image of his murder challenged the viewer in much the way a great painting does. "In the face of this photograph," Berger argued, "we must either dismiss it or complete its meaning for ourselves."

Jay Cantor's book turns all these concerns—the making of revolution and revolutionaries, of new Christs and novel challenges—to account. A number of fiction writers have treated Fidel, for instance Jon Krich in 1982,[1] but Cantor gets greater mileage from the man beside the dictator, in a tome at once omnivorous, rigorous, and explosively dramatic. *Death of Che* needs every homely metaphor, every sonorous repetition, every subtle probing of guerrilla motives. It seeks nothing less than to make sense of history.

Cantor opens, closes, and separates the two books of his novel with brief passages entitled "Dates." The three inserts suggest, year by year, possible directions taken by events: "1952…In Bolivia a force made up of Indians, peasants, and cadre of the Movement for a National Revolution smash the regular army and bring Paz Estenssoro to power (Pieces of a new interpretation: …In Latin America the peasant will be the base of the Revolution)." But the bulk of the novel concerns the pieces of one man's interpretations. In the first half, the present action is set in 1965, on an island off Cuba.

---

1. The list went on after 1983 as well, at least through Norbeto Fuentes in 2009.

There, on hiatus from his deepening squabbles with Fidel, Che composes what might be called a fictional autobiography; he reshapes the ways in which the years through the start of the Cuban Revolution shaped him. At the same time, we're allowed an occasional peek into his journal—though over time it becomes clear that Che's entries have been edited by a fellow guerrilla, rather a disciple. A black Cuban who took the name Ponco, this sidekick has even written a few pieces of his leader's history for him. Journals also provide the material of the novel's second book. Here the subject's the fatal Bolivian expedition of '66–'67, seen now in reflection and now in the heat of the action. The daily entries are mostly those kept by the soldiers of Che's meager "army"—though again the acolyte Ponco looks over everyone's shoulder, editing, selecting. Ponco was one of those who escaped the last stand in Higueras (improbably, though in keeping with the facts of that day), and he's working over these "piles of paper" back on Cuba in summer '68. He has excerpts from Che's speeches, each appended with Ponco's ideas for edits and improvements. Also there are the poems and songs the Bolivian cadre composed to distract themselves from their hardships. There are two absurdist plays, Ponco's own work, but our reading of these is interrupted so that the playwright can make changes. The novel itself ends, before the final "Dates" passage, with ten additional "Notes for Revision." Thus this attempt to understand history is at the same time an attempt to understand itself. It's unfinished, decadent, ambiguous: precisely the sort of art that a Marxist ought to avoid.

Cantor, in short, is smart enough to open with a man in crisis and then to sustain the difficulty. In Book I, '65, the rift with Fidel has left Che rethinking his commitment. As he drafts his autobiographical sketches, he worries over what's "best" and what's "true" as much as Ponco. At this point Guevara's a fairly standard protagonist in convalescence. He has little taste for food, his asthma interferes with sleep, and he doesn't want to think about the work gangs here on the Isle of Pines. Enemies of the State, or inmates of an insane asylum? Che wonders which category he belongs to, and expressing his doubts with a characteristic grim flourish:

> For a bad moment...I thought of the factories—my ministry's responsibility—many of them idle or half used, hobbled for lack of raw materials or trained workers, or spare parts. The Revolution was an old engraving I saw once, as a child: a pensive bearded man, a broken god, with a ruined city in the background, a collection of useless instruments around him, a magic square whose impotent charm means nothing beyond itself...

Cantor has so thoroughly assimilated the Latin American ambiance that he's taken on its music: hyperbolic and exclamatory, free with metaphor and repetition, always ready to snap off an epigram ("Everything," Che admits early on, "goes into my sausage machine for epigrams"). When these qualities combine, as during the "bad moment" above, they can raise an experience or a character to cosmic proportions. And this mythmaking inclination is in time reinforced by the insistent artificiality of the novel's documents. Guevara reshapes his past to suit his present quandary; Ponco has to ask why the reminiscences make no mention of Che's brothers and sisters, and why Che's father has been killed off when in fact the old man is still ministering to the sick down in Argentina. Che himself is striving to fill his "empty sound" with significance, even as he doubts the effort. A note in his first journal excerpt: "Endless redefinition instead of the activity itself."

Yet something more than endless redefinition, more too than style with all the stops out, propels us through this palimpsest of memoir and myth-making. Ponco's interrogations establish what's true as well as what's false. A key discovery for the first book, for example, comes when Che rejects his earlier Gandhian pacifism and kills his first man during the US-backed invasion of Guatemala in 1954. When the guerrilla reaches that point, it doesn't matter that the journal packs impossibly long paragraphs of suspenseful meditations around the act, a bit of gunplay that must've transpired in seconds. The moment is Che's point of no return; he's entitled to dwell on it as long as he likes.

Another way in which these reminiscences remain true even after they're proven to be lies is their insight into the contradictions of personality. One character is described as "an atonal concerto of conflicting voices," and the same might be said of anyone to whom this novel gives space to breathe. Ponco was born a loquacious liar (a natural at fiction, one might say), but a war wound has made it painful for him to talk. Che's mother suffers the most extraordinary contradictions, and yet she's the first figure here to rise to allegorical stature. In a hilarious imitation of Eva Peron, during young Ernesto's last dinner at home, she renders herself both queen and clown, both a steel-trap rationalist and a stiletto-wielding master of domestic revenge. This sort of emotional clout never lets up. Five hundred pages in, after executions and suicides and murders enough for an entire hot and bloody continent, the death of a single member of Che's Bolivian cadre stings as if he'd been the first to go down, thanks to the striking variances, the alternating silence and repetition, of the journal excerpts.

Also, the author has his details down cold. Cantor knows what newspapers were available in La Paz in 1952—their names, their politics, and how each was printed. He knows how Cuba's Rural Guard would set up a barracks guard post in 1957; he knows what was wrong with those Vietnam-issue jungle boots; he knows the taste of monkey meat. During the first half of *Che* the emphasis is so much on interiors, on criticism of self and other, that one doesn't notice the density of detail. It's a Proustian effect, really, and Cantor may drop a sly reference or two to the French Modernist. But unlike Proust's narrator, Che eventually emerges from his convalescence. "The words, the deeds, the people live in separate houses," he concludes. "Where is the man whose actions could call them together?" The novel's first half reconstructs Che, at last, as that man.

The second book is the more active, the more sensual, and by far the more bizarre. While one could almost use these diaries and other scraps to construct a how-to on guerrilla warfare, Che's Bolivian campaign nonetheless comes across as a tragicomedy of errors, its strategy dubious to begin with and doomed thereafter by tactics one might charitably call harebrained. Che is arrogant: he alienates the intellectual communists in the cities, people whose help he must have. He's careless: one of his own cadre betrays him (a twist Cantor handles with admirable indirection). Worst of all, he's unable to adapt. In one strange encounter after another, rendered in a style both gothic and cartoonish, Che proves a failure at enlisting recruits from among the upcountry Bolivian Incas. His zeal to haul these subsistence farmers into the twentieth century either scares them off or induces them, in the novel's richest irony, to construct a myth of their own out of the wheezing and tattered guerrilla. For them, Che becomes something both Incan and Christian, another heroic human sacrifice. And yet, and yet…Che's troops emerge from the jungle highlands to win their share of engagements. They draw U.S. advisers to Bolivia, with their boots and their helicopters. For a few astounding months they carry on a "second Vietnam."

It's only natural, then, that this miraculous tale has four gospels. Book II of *Che*, that is, has four principal sources: Guevara's journal, the journals of two Bolivian recruits, and a variety of writings by the loyal Ponco. Now (a word the novel suggests belongs in quotes: "now…") it's the summer following Che's murder, and it falls to the black-skinned former servant to make sense of history. Yet no matter what Ponco does with his ragtag bundle of documents, no matter how he selects and orchestrates, interrupts and explains, still the War of Liberation remains aborted, and the hero's life and death remain ambiguous.

"This isn't a story where things simply are as they were," Ponco complains. No, Che agrees, or his ghost does: this is art. Elsewhere, his mother claims in a letter: "I have always thought you had more of a taste for literature than actually politics? But woe woe woe when the realms are confused!" Or perhaps this letter is only another of Che's fabrications, another self-important lie to convince himself that his life hasn't been a self-important fabrication. "In... silence," he writes, "my worlds my words unraveled back past the present to nothing."

Endless redefinitions. The *implied* center of all these documents and details, the implied moral and message of history, has been Guevara's spiritual and political growth, and it's hard to imagine a novel that demonstrates more effectively, or sympathetically, the way a Gandhi might mature into a guerrilla. Yet every doubtful entry in Che's journal, every sunless day in the Bolivian jungle, threatens to undermine that development. In claiming he can change history, is Che so different from the rabbit-eyed Incas who call him Christ? So the *actual* center of Cantor's *Che* is that doubtful silence. All the redefinitions may be no more than aesthetic choices, absurd attempts to fill in an essential emptiness. Cantor's refusal to ignore that possibility places his novel among the most maddening but deeply rewarding works of our time.

John Barth would term those redefinitions, because they are an explicit and dramatically functional part of the text, "self-reflexive." Indeed, one of the few recent North American novels that can match *Che* for historical sweep and Protean shape shifting is Barth's *LETTERS* (1979); others that comes to mind are Thomas Pynchon's *Gravity's Rainbow* ('73) and William Gaddis' *JR* ('75).[2] Cantor, despite the richness of his rhetoric, recalls most the down-home garrulity of Gaddis. The self-reflection is an intrinsic part of the Che & Ponco Show; the author never intrudes with a flourish, as do Barth and Pynchon. Overall, though, *Che* belongs with such books, match-

---

2. Twenty-five years following *Death of Che*, this short list wouldn't be much longer. Recent candidates would be Wallace's *Infinite Jest* ('96) and DeLillo's *Underworld* ('97).

ing a vast scope to an iconoclastic form. In this, it also leans on an earlier American masterwork, nothing if not excessive and myth-minded, namely, *Moby-Dick*.

Barth, in *LETTERS*, relied on a Melville connection to underscore the central allegory of man vs. nature. Cantor, on the other hand, is working with the motif of a doomed quest, both heroic and comic in its obsessive self-sacrifice. Some of the allusions are explicit: Ponco reads *Moby-Dick* throughout *Che*'s first half, and both he and Che draw the parallel between guerrilla leadership and Ahab's captaincy. But one subtle reference is even more revealing. During one of Che's most bizarre and pathetic appeals to the Incas, a mad boy in the crowd exclaims that "he was a bloody man, he had a bloody hand, and he would have revenge." Thereafter the line becomes a gruesome rosary for Ponco and the other guerrillas, and one of Cantor's most disturbing repetitions, as the men wonder whether they've been reduced to mere supporting actors in Che's drama of self-destruction. It's a chorus of doom, really—and it's lifted directly from Charles Olson's 1947 study of Melville, *Call Me Ishmael*. This seminal and poetic work of criticism insisted, in almost every sentence, on turning literature to myth. Olson's thesis: "History was ritual and repetition when Melville's imagination was at its own proper beat." Even the subtlest reference, the most esoteric aside, helps deepen Cantor's vision.

Neither are Cantor's novelistic forebears solely North American. *Che* is also a response to *El Boom*, the literary renaissance from south of our borders. His cha-cha chronology and exhortatory prose recall, in particular, *The Death of Artemio Cruz* (1962), in which Carlos Fuentes managed to weave all Mexican history into the tale of a cutthroat's change from revolutionary to oppressor. Che never becomes an oppressor in the usual sense, but throughout the novel's latter half, one wonders at how he pushes around the men under him. The readers knows Che must die, and so the suspense lies elsewhere, in seeing how he kept Ponco and others true to a quest that every day appeared more quixotic (Che even names his horse Rosinante, and when throat-sore Ponco struggles to say something, it's hard not to hear Sancho Panza). And there's Baudelaire and Neruda, in each case poems about escape to a better life. Cantor refuses to let any giant from the past intimidate him.

Yet he won't drop an allusion simply for its own sake. The novel's few weak spots have to do with shortchanging personality rather than overloading the literary baggage. Every once in a while the other guerrillas' journals sound too much like their leader's, and the betrayal of the cadre may be handled too brusquely. The reference to Hollywood, at that point, seems too quick and sneering. But then who should Ponco and the others sound like, if not their maddening and charismatic leader? And doesn't Hollywood provide a perfect image for the revolutionary vision turned hollow? Certainly Omar Sharif's star turn as the guerilla, in *Che!* (1969) comes nowhere near the man's paradox and tragedy.[3] In short, this text is one of the rare ones that contains all its own alternatives, that exposes both its immoral promptings and its moral justifications— a book with a whale's breadth and strength. *The Death of Che Guevara* stands as heartening evidence that there exists a generation of younger writers in this country that can rise to the highest challenges of the novelist's art.

—Boston Phoenix, 1983

---

3. Benicio del Toro, in *Che* (2008), does better, as does Gael García Bernal in *The Motorcycle Diaries* ('04), but another of the lasting pleasures of Cantor's text is how it demonstrates the depth, the interiority, only a novel can achieve.

SAILOR & SON: BARTH & THE LAST VOYAGE OF SOMEBODY THE SAILOR, *CANTOR* & ON GIVING BIRTH TO ONE'S OWN MOTHER

Should a good device reveal its own devising? Should I say, before attempting to point out the often-mystical gyrations of John Barth's new novel, that I've twice taken classes with him? Yes: a semester apiece in Boston and in Baltimore. At the time the author's latest was *Chimera*, winner of the '73 National Book Award, and the most useful comparison with his new one, *The Last Voyage of Somebody the Sailor*. Working with Barth triggered a private metamorphosis. Before those seminars I was your typical Big Man of Letters on Campus: Beat-besotted, Dylan-dreamy, Kafka-cantankerous, Melville-megalomaniacal. After, I'd become smaller and yet tougher. Aside from timeless lessons (humility, study, perseverance), I'd learned what was then a new coinage, the term *Postmodern*. Postmodern work, I'd learned, does this and that—and reveals its own devising.

In this, postmodernism challenged the aesthetics of the previous era. A time that might be bracketed between the poems of Baudelaire and the movies of John Huston took it as art's ruling purpose to create a detached perfection, a Chinese box which only another expert could unlock. By contrast, the postmodern offers show and tell, collage, the exposed simplicity of an Erector set. Consider, for instance, the stage show of most rap groups. And while this impulse to demystify is neither entirely new (*Don Quixote* did it), nor important to everyone (Paul McCartney couldn't care less), it's certainly an honest reaction to recent history.

No matter how an informed artist constructs this century, his or her own work in it must seem suspect. Marx derides most art as a toy of the privileged. Freud warns that it may be no more than a spectacle, before which personality turns passive. In Jay Cantor's new collection of essays, *On Giving Birth to One's Own Mother*, the author considers film in relation to the Holocaust. "Art must be," Cantor argues, "from now on, poised on a knife's edge, aware of its own blandishments, its dangerous penchant for deception, its implication in catastrophe."

And yet, perversely, Cantor goes on making artful things. *Giving Birth* offers belle-lettres at the level of William Gass or Susan Sontag—or, for that matter, of John Barth's twin essays, "The Literature of Exhaustion" (1967) and "The Literature of Replenishment" (1979). But Cantor is significantly younger than those bellwethers. His essays include insights about Dylan and Vietnam and Allan Bloom. He's young enough to have been in Barth's seminar himself, and these two books offer an opportunity to understand how the Postmodern torch has passed.

Critics have been kind to *The Last Voyage of Somebody the Sailor*, in general recalling the excitement Barth generated with his *The Sot-Weed Factor* ('60). This success must be, in large part, a response to the new book's emotionality. *Somebody* presents a spooky Moebius strip of realism and fantasy, fascinating as a good sailor's knot, but it's drenched with passion. There are bittersweet tradeoffs between growth and loss, genial insights concerning changes and challenges, and above all fevered sexual couplings, sweet or unwilling, approved or taboo (incest is a recurring motif). The plot turns on a raucous storytelling contest, mortally threatening and surrounded by deceit.

"Somebody" is Simon William Behler, a contemporary American who's somehow survived a near-drowning in the Indian Ocean to find himself—a fifty-year-old grandfather, a sober survivor of divorce, and a successful if uncertain journalist—in the world of the Arabian Nights. Behler's reminiscences offer Barth at the top of his form: brisk, clamorous, forceful, smart. Then there's the American's opponent in the storytelling contest, none other than Sindbad the Sailor, rich but weary after six terrible voyages. Sindbad retells Scheherazade (not badly, though at first his tales risk merely trotting through their assignment), and so eventually reveals his own devices. The sailor's narratives outline a moral dissolution; his rocs and snakes and cannibals turn out to be elaborate cover-ups for piracy and worse. Juicing things further are the stories of the man's concubine, Jayda, who knows all the secrets of her unsavory lord but remains committed to him. Then there's the story hidden from both those two, the secret love that's bloomed between Sindbad's daughter, Yasmin, and this man out of time, Behler. An ingenious formal experiment, *Somebody* nonetheless throbs with blood and dark laughter.

Emotion, its absence, has been a problem for Barth's work. That's the perception of many recent critics, at least, all of whom make the same complaint about postmodern fiction generally. Revealing the device severs cathartic connections, goes the argument; the Erector set lacks attachments to the heart. Barth, as one of the Americans who more or less created the new aesthetic, has been saddled with the responsibility for that breakdown. In *Somebody* he's particularly caring about those bonds, about caring itself, and most reviewers at least have given him credit. In fact, however, this author has been finding new ways to work more emotion into his fiction for years now. Texts like *Chimera* and its predecessor, the story collection *Lost in the Funhouse* ('68), are among the most technically experimental in our literature. Their substance, paradoxically, is often drawn from classic material like Greek myths and the *The Thousand Nights and One Night*, and indeed if there's such a thing as a "postmodern classic," it's the title piece of *Funhouse*. But the Barth of this era can also read like Euclidean proofs of theoretical notions, peculiarly late '60s in its freaky excess. To some extent, then, a critical backlash was inevitable. *Chimera* provides an extraordinary scenic route, but also a dead end—as does, for instance, Frank Zappa's '69 opus, *Uncle Meat*.

But the backlash ignores how this author has made his experiments more humane. He followed *Chimera* with books rooted in the tragedies of our times, in particular *LETTERS* ('79). That novel and *Sabbatical* ('82) are in many respects "social novels;" they might fairly be shelved with, for instance, the Dos Passos *USA Trilogy* (1930–36). Their stories work terrorist drama into very real Chesapeake Bay settings, along with charged family sagas. *LETTERS* in fact may be the man's greatest accomplishment, Melvillean in its vision and complication, despite relatively bad press.

Somebody is a more modest book, accessible and kind. It's Barth's most direct assertion of the feminist argument implicit in his fiction since *The End of the Road* (1958), and it's lovely stuff, really—a late-career peak, with fugue-like spirals of physical death and spiritual cleansing. But I for one miss the stick and grit of lived history that distinguished one or two of his other novels.

For stick and grit, see Jay Cantor. History haunts the eight long essays collected in *On Giving Birth to One's Own Mother*. Meditations on the contemporary impact of Marx, Nietzsche, and Freud open the book (Cantor calls them "patriarchs of the tribes of the modern"), and the author closes with the wish that he could say Kaddish for the dead of the Holocaust. There is one humorous piece here, a deliciously nasty birthday greeting to Mickey Mouse from Ignatz Mouse, the brick-throwing wise guy of the old comic strip *Krazy Kat*—also the eponymous protagonist of Cantor's second novel. But this touch of comedy serves as the exception which proves the rule, and it concludes with Ignatz driving nails into his palms in order to avoid falling under the smarmy spell of Mickey's cartoons. Ha, ha.

In fact *Giving Birth* is modeled on the polished high seriousness of the patriarchs, more than on the naked scaffolding of the postmoderns. This is by no means a handful of occasional pieces (as was Barth's '86 collection, *The Friday Book*), but a coherent attempt at durable and work-shaping insight. While not above a smart aleck aside or a sudden tart touch of contemporeana, Cantor's tone remains by and large noble and deliberate, unapologetically eyes on the prize: "I reread my past by the light of the patriarchs' ideas, and allow my past and its bewilderments to interrogate their works, so that, after the long sleep of the past decade [roughly, '75–'85], I can reknit my involvement with these texts and look for what they might still ask our present."

This rereading recalls that of Cantor's superb and challenging first novel, 1983's *The Death of Che Guevara*, which "reread" a century of armed Marxist struggle, recasting its famed protagonist as Ahab and Quixote and Christ. *Krazy Kat*, in '87, had a zanier, more abbreviated take on the civilization. *Kat*'s metaphors came from pop culture, starting with that same Sunday-comics love story and spiraling out into Hollywood, black music, and a lot else. Ignatz and Krazy even enjoyed a few bouts of S&M: kisses and bricks. The novels share a central obsession—each depends on what might be called the Sick Patriarch. Offissa Pup wastes away in *Kat* (and with him the childish hope for eternal comic simplicity), and throughout *Che*, the Revolution seems to be on its last legs (as does Che himself). Thus the present essays arise out of the writer's most persistent concerns, his deepest fears over what's wrong.

Not that Cantor sees nothing to like in the Now. He takes pains to understand his comic strips, his Aretha Franklin, his protests against Vietnam, and to distance himself from conservative broadsides like *The Closing of the American Mind*. He understands that an inspired pop artifact is a self-sustaining, time-arresting "gadget"—as capable of meaning, in its way, as *Thus Spake Zarathustra* is in its. Comparisons like that illuminate, especially, the essay "Looking High and Low," which ought to be required reading for anyone trying to wring insights from so-called "low culture."

Yet during "the long sleep of the last decade," Cantor has suffered a nightmare. He's seen the highest ideals of aesthetics, and the most profound things said by the patriarchs, turned into a mere "pattern-book," a source for "quotation"—a way of proving an artist's hip without ever confronting whether he or she is wise. Yes, Marxism resulted in the Gulag, but does that mean our reflections on it now it should be nothing more than shrugs and quips? Yes, Nietzschean search for ecstasy and the Superman took us to Treblinka and Auschwitz, but does that mean our seeking now should go no further than the local heavy metal show? Cantor's particularly disturbed by the notion that ours has become a "society of spectacle" (the phrase is from Guy Debord), our sensibilities MTV-empty, rejecting any real transformative confrontation with our core paradoxes in favor of passive attendance. Finally, *Giving Birth* is an outcry on behalf of renewed transformation, renewed belief in the possibility of transformation, all the braver because it's raised despite full knowledge of past failures.

This inability to shake off what has gone before seems, for better or worse, a defining characteristic of the younger postmodernist. Compared to Cantor, Barth seems happily unencumbered, outside history: his man is an island. But Cantor is young enough to have witnessed the intensifying critique of postmodernism—*Giving Birth* twice mentions Barth, in lists of "the best contemporary work"—and smart enough to understand the lack of human connection which caused that critique. Thus younger writers of equal ambition (and there are others, among them Carole Maso) feature history as part of their wit and designs. To reveal the device, these days, means first to reveal how human hardship has forced it into being.

—L.A. Weekly, 1991

JAIMY GORDON:
TAKING FEMINISM TO "FANTASTICOES"

If literature were politics, Jaimy Gordon would be the victim of a cabal. When she took home the 2010 National Book Award for her racetrack novel *Lord of Misrule*, the larger literary forums blinked at the news, astounded. At the *New York Times*—the daily, not the Sunday *Book Review*—Janet Maslin didn't resist the cliché "bolt from the blue." Maslin did go on to praise *Misrule*, calling it "assured, exotic," and "an incontrovertible winner," but her review also threw in a sneering parenthesis about the shoestring publishing house, McPherson & Co. Overall, the effect was rather a backhanded compliment. The novel came off like a hothouse flower, lovely but out of the way, for special tastes only. Indeed, Gordon's books have yet to draw notice in the *Sunday Book Review* or *The New York Review of Books*, among many other places, and if literature were politics, there could be no denying how this woman's been shunned. Her name has never been linked to that of some Manhattan angel. For decades she's taught in the hinterlands of Kalamazoo, and she's published little journalism or criticism, those bite-sized pieces of sensibility that can cause readers to hunt for more.

Indeed, this author has been slow to produce anything. *Misrule* is only her fourth novel since 1974. A couple of experimental dramatic pieces can be tracked down, as well as a few poems and shorter fictions. The most notable works are a pair of historical narratives, one a farce about Civil War Reconstruction, *Circumspections from an Equestrian Statue* (1979), and the other, free verse, a fantasia about Prohibition-era gangsters, *The Bend, the Lip, the Kid* (1978). Both run no longer than the average chapter of a best-seller.

Yet it does this writer a disservice to measure her accomplishment the way Andy Warhol would, ignoring the substance and measuring the inches. Neglect is endemic among serious authors, and Gordon's done better than some. She's enjoyed attention in magazines like *Gargoyle* and *Context*, and she's raked in a starry array of blurbs, from writers as diverse as Gilbert Sorrentino and Jayne Anne Phillips. She's won grants, awards, and an inclusion in *Best American Short Stories* (with a piece that became part of *Misrule*). The 1990 novel *She Drove Without Stopping* (Algonquin) was named a Notable Book by the American Library Association, and in 2000, *Bogeywoman* (Sun & Moon) made a similar short list at the *Los Angeles Times*. These two will get a close look here, along with the title that's made the woman famous, or sort of famous—and the point is, fame and its vagaries can't be the primary criterion in assessing what she's accomplished.

Without Stopping, *Bogeywoman*, and *Misrule* have more durable qualities. Their style alone achieves rare enchantment and risk, even in an incidental description like "cowbells bouncing down a glass staircase, that was her laughter" (an aside in *Bogeywoman*). Brief passages cast such a spell that they can cloud the seriousness of the larger project, a coming-of-age without end.

The young women at the center of Gordon's full-length narratives struggle within the rubbery confines of the white American middle class. All three have Jewish roots, and this has a bit to do with their inability to accept, to settle. Their more profound unease, however, stems from their bourgeois conditioning, not to say cushioning. Each starts out a well-off, well-educated Baltimore girl—the protagonists of *Bogeywoman* and *Misrule* are sisters—and they're more than smart enough to see they have advantages denied many others. They never fail to notice, in their roughly Southern environs, the more limited resources of the nearby African Americans, leading a dray or pushing a broom. Yet the girls end up betrayed by their intelligence and privilege. When they forage beyond its limits, in the hallowed pursuit of happiness, they blunder into the School of Hard Knocks. Though each girl makes it into her twenties, she's lucky to get that far. While the novels must be considered comedies, that's the only word for them, each turns a Suburban Suzy to a creature of myth. She faces down monsters but achieves nothing you'd mistake for the American dream.

Gordon hit this stride in 1990, with *She Drove Without Stopping*. Her lone previous novel is something else again, a man's initiation, in an alternative universe. The eponymous fledgling in *Shamp of the City-Solo* (1974, reissued on McPherson in '93) shrugs off his stultifying hometown of "Bulimy" (ring a bell?) and takes on a more challenging dystopia, "City-Solo," the "Big Yolk." There, following as best he can the lessons of masters like the "Topical Tropist" Sergei Shipoff, young Shamp finds his calling as a kind of performance poet. Shipoff ships Shamp off (to employ a fitting tongue-twister) as a "novice lector." The apprentice scuttles down Caligari byways, sits through nuthouse oratory, and finally takes the podium, speechifying with his life on the line at the "Arslevering Ox Roast." In this citywide competition, literally do-or-die, Shamp emerges victorious.

His reward reveals something about the game afoot, in that it recalls that other surrogate cityscape, Monopoly. The winning "soloist" at the Roast is given a great hotel in a posh district. Boardwalk or Park Place, one wonders? Anyway, Shamp rejects his trophy. He prefers an abandoned subway station, and this closing dissonance may be the most illuminating aspect of *City-Solo*, so far as this author's later work is concerned. Later, her initiates earn their scars, but they too wind up ambivalent. No one simply cashes in and folds away the board.

To put it another way, the clown act of Gordon's debut arrives finally at serious feeling. What critical attention it's gotten has dwelt more on the off-kilter setting and fine-tooled language. Keith Waldrop, in a 2001 essay for *Context*, noted the many allusions, "classical, biblical, historical," and made comparison to earlier high-style exercises like "[Thomas] Urquhart's Rabelais and [Richard] Burton's *Thousand and One Nights*." Gordon herself mentioned such "forebears" in a 1983 interview with *Gargoyle*. Our present perspective, however, reveals a more recent model for *City-Solo*, another shaggy-dog story from an author with a Baltimore base. That would be John Barth, close friend of John Hawkes, Gordon's mentor at Brown University. Her *City-Solo* owes an obvious debt to Barth's 1960 novel *The Sot-Weed Factor*, a book that likewise foregrounds a baroque language. It makes mention of both Rabelais and Scheherazade; it puts a holy fool through madcap ups and downs. Yet Barth delivers his poet picaro to a decidedly ambiguous "success," and *Sot-Weed* ends up a love story, a work of serious feeling. Naturally, Gordon and Barth have many differences, but in order to understand what the younger author has gone on to do, it helps to see her first book's connection to another radical experiment that, on one filigreed sleeve, wears a bleeding heart.

She Drove Without Stopping too is a picaresque. What's more, its protagonist Jane Turner delivers a ringing peroration. About two-thirds of the way along, Jane reiterates the title clause several times as she bolts from Baltimore to L.A., struggling to break out of the rubbery comforts to which she was born:

> She drove without stopping for twenty-four hours, midnight to midnight, except for a hypochondriacal consultation at a rundown one-pump station...[and afterwards] she drove off warily, trying to overtake her happiness now by sheer perseverance instead of velocity....

Jane, or more precisely Janet, middle name Kaplan, Jewish on her mother's side—Jane will never overtake that happiness. The way she's been raised has set an impossible, indeed orgasmic standard. Hardly have we met the girl when she reveals: "I masturbated every night from age beyond memory." At that point, the opening of the second chapter, the pleasure remains innocent, freed from "any sense that I was...pantomiming a conjunction of far more complex terms." It's Eden, where a girl goes naked unashamed and uses the personal pronoun.

But *Without Stopping* gets going even while Jane's too young to drive. Her Paradise is swiftly lost, the first time her father refuses to kiss her on the mouth. He's "not a criminal," Philip Turner, "not even a bad sort." Jane never suffers abuse, but rather unrequited love. The first time Dad shoves her off, and "I was suddenly six feet away, blinking up at him, holding scraped elbows," is the last time she uses first person, for more than three hundred pages. The innocent becomes "the adventuress," in search of an alternative paradise.

Importantly, these adventures lack for anything surreal, outside of Jane's overheated mind. Even the brief passages above demonstrate how Gordon's second novel constitutes a departure *into the ordinary*, with one-pump stations and scraped elbows. Once Daddy and Mom divorce, once his rejected baby hits her teens, she acts out just as you might expect, "trying hard to be a bad girl." Not that her boyfriends aren't interesting, sharp-witted misfits beneath Jane's status. Not that her vicissitudes don't take an odd slant. I've never encountered so comic a rape as in *Without Stopping*, and the startled laughter kept coming throughout the Mutt and Jeff response of the police. Still, the system fails the girl in ways all too typical, and soon it feels like a "whole megillah." The rape's the turning point, actually. Wary of its "black cloud," Jane climbs into a rattletrap and drives without stopping. Only out by the Pacific, slinging booze in a dive bar and risking commitment to the faun-like Jimmy, artist and mystic and beach bum, can she have "her true adventure." Only there can she shake the false promise of her upbringing and come to terms with how "even an adventuress cannot choose her father, her first lover, the one least liable to be forgot."

The point is, Gordon's 1990 opus may be a grab bag, in which one page offers Jacob wrestling with the angel (Jane takes Hebrew lessons) and the next Brown vs. the Board of Education (she shares a homeroom with some of the first "colored" to attend her school), but, taken together, it reveals the outline of what once might've been acclaimed a parable of Women's Liberation. Jane travels amid '60s paraphernalia, there's even sort of a commune, but the majority of such details connect to the Civil Rights movement. The novel's first lines mention Martin Luther King, raising the idea of liberation, and providing specific historical context for this rematch of Yahweh and Lilith. In the climactic explosions, out in L.A., the most volatile elements are an African American and a Native American.

Yet the narrative never starts to feel like a political cartoon. Gordon's bravura style allows for no such broad strokes, and when this Eve makes her peace with the serpent, it's personal. For the final talk with Dad, the final break, she's once more using the pronoun "I." Still, Jane comes out of that conversation into a glaring reassertion of social and economic status, during a court hearing. The black whores around her all receive a thirty-day sentence, but Jane's public-drunkenness charge is quickly dismissed. The judge needs only one look at her "white skin, glasses, curly hair" to recognize her as "a child of the upper middle class. His class."

Indeed, isn't the protagonist's cross-country ride a "moneygreen Buick"? Doesn't she need the occasional check from Dad? Even out west, she can't get free of "reproaches from the unimprisoned creature she might have been." She does publish her first poems, in a smudged and wacky venue, yet even this emblem of self-actualization takes her to economics. Her L.A. boyfriend may be a romantic hero, a starving artist—but after Jane sees print, she admonishes him: "I only started to be a poet so I wouldn't think it was my duty to pay your rent." A

wonderful quip, one of many that raise the novel above simple dia-
tribe. Feminism emerges, rather, like a monster from the id:

> She could see what was coming. This would sweep her off
> to the world, which was suddenly altogether compelling and
> necessary, loaded as it was with human males. She would be-
> come a prowler... a centripetal force, with gravity in all her
> excentric orbs....From now on she would put herself into the
> hands of men without fear of disappearing, for she was the
> cunt from outer space.

She Drove Without Stopping can feel like the "women's classic" that
more famous cases hoped to be. Its heroine comes unshackled only
to confront a fresh set of irons, heavier still, and so takes risks beyond
those in, for instance, Erica Jong's *Fear of Flying* (1973). Too bad, then,
that the book's *what* lacks the intelligence of its *how*. Its first third never
quite transcends that predictable bad-girl pattern, the collapsing domestic circle and the child crazy to break out. Once Jane breaks out,
too, some elements do seem drawn from a counter-culture scrapbook,
such as her California boy. Nevertheless, in her first full-length fiction,
Jaimy Gordon laid claim to the visionary knocking about, Bible-in-
flected, that American male writers have always taken as their entitle-
ment. When the story fails to satisfy, it has to do more with limitations
of the road novel than with those of the author.

Bogeywoman took ten years to appear after *Without Stopping*, and
this wasn't entirely due to creative struggles. Also Sun & Moon Press,
though a distinguished imprint, lacked the resources to produce more
than a few titles a year. Such delays are common in small-press publishing but deserve to be noted in a case like this, because the novel is so
well made. Here Gordon solves the structural problem implicit in the
previous book's title. Free of Kerouackian meandering, *Bogeywoman*

confines its drama to three not-unfamiliar Northeast settings: a girl's forest camp in Maine, a psychiatric hospital outside Baltimore, and the Great Dismal Swamp along Chesapeake Bay. It occupies a few eventful months of self-discovery for the sixteen-year-old Ursie Koderer. Ursie, Ursula, narrates a coming of age by way of coming out. Her first attempt at taking a woman lover leads her to disaster, but her second, while bumptious and terrifying, delivers her to (relative) safety. Indeed, the neatness of the drama proves surprising. A reader needs to step back to see how plausibly reaction suits action, in just a few key scenes, because the experience on the page seems all "humid longing," feverish in its mood swings: "All at once my heart opened up like a peacock's fan, I knew all the colors of love."

Now, that sentence pulls off quite a performance, with its active metaphor and surf-like *all-all-l-l*. Yet the tone's serious, and while this seriousness suits the moment—Ursie's first meaningful encounter with Dr. Zuk, the woman who will save her—by far the majority of the well-turned phrases in *Bogeywoman* traffic in laughter and surprise. The laughter may sag with pain, the surprise may pack a threat, but isn't such paradox natural to the best comedy? The novel brings off an open-throated new demotic, omnivorous in its attention to detail, especially sonic detail, and this constant celebration feels comic.

Consider the few lines leading up to the peacock moment. In these lines, the "you" is sister Margaret (the central figure in *Lord of Misrule*), on a visit to the psychiatric facility, Rohring Rohring. Maggie has come to convince the younger Koderer to check out ("I know you're not buggy, Ursula"). To that end, she's giving her disheveled sib a haircut. But Big Sister knows at once what's up when she sees Ursie share a loaded look with Dr. Zuk.

Trouble dented your forehead. Your idled scissors snipped air, tinka tinka tink. Dr. Zuk, having blessed me with that look, was already squinching out the door in her silver sandals. I watched, the familiar systole diastole of her muscular but-

tocks, the flickering curves of her soccer player's calves. All at
once my heart opened...

Rich as this stuff is, here wiseacre description and there spellbound
epiphany, it does without some of Gordon's most enchanting coinages.
In particular, it does without "dreambox mechanic," *Bogeywoman*'s
term for a psychiatrist. The expression occurs first in the opening lines,
and it was mentioned in all the novel's few write-ups, though these
tended to be brief (in *Publishers Weekly*, for instance). One can't help
but wonder how many reviewers simply lacked the patience required
for such neologisms to come clear. Gilbert Sorrentino blurbed the
work as "radiant with energy...a radicalization of language," but it's just
such language that tends to scare off a larger audience.

A shame, because *Bogeywoman* also deserves the encomiums
that have to do with emotion, such as (in Sorrentino's case) "funny"
and "bittersweet." Gordon's phrasing may suggest a Rube Goldberg
contraption, but it's always in service to her character. Her opening
evocation of "Camp Chunkagunk, *Tough Paradise for Girls*" feels
moist, redolent, altogether woodsy, yet isn't such lush business appropriate to a sixteen-year-old who suddenly finds herself abrim
with illicit desire? "From that moment," she declares on the second
page, "I saw everything in a different light, murky, as through a
dark lake. From then on I was a * Unbeknownst To Everybody,
and that was the meaning of Bogeywoman." The oversized asterisk
looks queer, and the prose includes one or two other typographi-
cal oddities, tricks one might consider signs of postmodern experiment, the brand of fiction that's supposed to keep us from caring
about characters. But then, the girl who dreamed up these off-the-
wall constructions *is* queer. Ursie's far from the only gay teen to
prefer living "unbeknownst." She's far from the only one to make a
mantra of keeping mum: "Lemme die first."

To put it another way, Gordon has not lost touch with the ordinary. Ursie may speak in tongues, but we recognize the tomboy

type, a "Wood Wiz" who loves "what a feast run amok the whole earth was." We understand when her first kiss and cuddle with another camper causes the "girlgoyle" to act out like the Kaplan Turner kid. She raises a great hue and cry over a tryst (hetero) between two of the staff, and they in turn discover what she has up her sleeves. The Bogeywoman has taken to self-mutilation. Such behavior lands her in the "bughouse," but it never gets in the way of sympathy.

Is it Ursie's fault, after all, that she's surrounded by such names, at once goofy and significant? Isn't she herself the bear in the woods, delighting in camp tales of "giant Gooskuk?" Then once the girl's goose is cooked, she's sent to a facility to assuage the Rohring Rohring in her head. This verbal gamesmanship (admirable in itself) is set off, always, by tragedy. Ursie can't be sent home from Chunkagunk, for instance, because her mother's dead and her father's on tour with his experimental troupe, Merlin's Puppets. And who's kept dancing at the end of the magician's strings if not his daughters? Ursie and Maggie don't hate their performer dad, but, "for Godzilla's sake," he can be distant.

Small wonder his younger daughter has been left hungry for "the feast of the world." Small wonder that, in the hospital, Ursie and others form a band, banging on homemade instruments and sending up cries for help. These are the Bug Motels, and their Kafkaesque torments also get a compassionate, though hilarious, fleshing out. Their songwriter is the Bogeywoman, and her greatest hit may be her piece for the anorexic heartbreaker Emily Nix Peabody, "refusal was her middle name."

Because I could not stop for lunch,
It kindly stopped for me.
The van read PIZZAS BY HASSAN
FAST FREE DELIVERY...

It's two years later now and I'm
Still tryna put away
That eighteen-inch cold pizza
Known as immortality.

Again, the tomfoolery cuts unexpectedly deep, in its concern with outcasts. In the starveling Emily and in Emily Dickinson, in immigrant food and its on-the-fly counterfeit by other immigrants, the song dwells on the American fringe. Another in the Motels' repertoire tosses in, wouldn't you know it, a bit of Hebrew: "*Ma nishtanah* hullo whozat?" Also Ursie must negotiate favors with Reginald, "the Regicide," a very cool cat of an African American attendant. He enables her eventual escape with the help of two "Ayrabbers," the black ragmen who park their wagons across the street. By then, as Reginald puts it, the girl herself is "persona niggerata" around the facility. She may have killed one doctor and she's the underage lover of another. Dr. Zuk in fact has ducked into the wagon beside the girl, putting at risk (to say the least) her research fellowship from "Caramel-Creamistan."

The climax in *Bogeywoman* includes, to be sure, sexual climax. For the lovemaking the rhetoric rises but never loses its oddball integrity, such as the recurring reflection that Zuk's body is "like Central Asia." And by the time the runaways make it to the doctor's family lodge in the Great Dismal Swamp, where Zuk must sit down with her diplomat cousin and face the consequences of her infatuation—consequences that include Ursie's fortified sense of self—by that time, every incident is poised between comic and serious. The dialogue between Zuk and her cousin sounds as if it were lifted from *Duck Soup*, Gordon creates yet another demotic, but in their country homosexuality carries a death penalty. The swamp may recall good old Camp Chunkagunk, but here the Woods Wiz must pick her way between burning peatholes that could swallow her whole.

Has the girl come full circle? She's come out, among family and friends; she's no longer "Unbeknownst." Yet in acknowledging that hunger, has she brought on a new "hunger for difference"—meaning someone besides her Svengali? Ambivalence like that pervades the ending of *Bogeyman*. After the girl returns to Baltimore, she learns of the twins born to Reginald and one of his charges, the nymphomaniac of the Motels, and those twins embody duality: "boygirl, blackwhite, buggysane." As for their blackwhite, buggysane mother and father, they marry; their story has a happy ending. But what of the larger story? Was Zuk the crazy one, falling for love's fairytale? Once the doctor sees the error of her ways, she abandons the girl in the Great Dismal, where snakes crawl in the shadows and flames burst from the ground. It's an inferno, and the Bogeywoman's journey proves the reverse of Dante's. Starting out in a child's paradise, she moves on to a purgatory of souls in arrested development, and at last she achieves the hell of adult desire, gnashing its teeth while bound, inescapably, by rules and obligations.

Jaimy Gordon dares stand *The Divine Comedy* on its head and yet delivers a potent philosophical comedy all her own. The Bogeywoman may reconnect with family, she may make herself a place among the sane and straight, but she takes pride in the fading scars of her self-mutilation.

> I think of my arms as my monster ticket...in case the whole world goes the monster way and monstrosity comes into its own. I'll be there. I'll be ready.

She remains a warrior, even lying dormant. The novel closes *diminuendo*, as the grown girl coolly demystifies what she had with Zuk, and yet at the same time she affirms her belief that, as her renegade lover put it, "*the heart is khan.*" So too, Ursie allows her older sister the final pungent summary of this magnificent novel's core value, in an adage appropriately Janus-faced: "An ounce of positive desire is worth a pound of negative regulation."

In *Lord of Misrule*, Gordon still flourishes postmodern colors. She does without quotation marks, and the sex, while hetero, is all eyebrow-raising B&D. There's challenging vocabulary like "xanthous" and "hierodule." Early on appears what seems a neologism, "goofer," and many pages go by before a clarification emerges. The word turns out to mean an herbal potion to hex a horserace, a traditional magic among black trainers of the old South. The goofer's effect, however, is always unpredictable, and so too, remarkably, this novel casts an old-fashioned spell. Despite occasional devices that foreground experiment, *Misrule* impresses most in its command of story structure.

No longer does our author rely on a hand-me-down drama. Even *Bogeywoman*, as if to compensate for its brilliant *bizarrerie*, steers by the landmarks of initiation. A growth experience does figure prominently in *Misrule*, after Ursie's sister Maggie, "around 25 years old," arrives at Indian Mound Downs, a no-account track and stable in West Virginia. She learns the race game and gains the strength to break free of the rakish gambler Tommy Hansel. But then Hansel's in thrall himself, "challenged" by his girlfriend's "monkey-green eyes." The two young people, "bound in slavery of the man-woman kind," have fallen into sadomasochism, in scenes that match the trysts of *Bogeywoman* for their commingling of flesh and mind:

> ...had he read her mind? Maybe because he had that empty space where her own drawers and pigeonholes were stuffed with words, he often, spookily, out of a silence, echoed back to her her most treacherous thought....In an almost soothing gesture [he]...brought that hand down behind her, and suddenly he was binding both her hands together with the leather shank, then the chain.

Also Maggie very nearly joins Jane Turner as a rape victim. The novel's "monster," the hoodlum Joe Dale Biggs, slips her a horse tranquilizer. The young woman does get free, first from Biggs and later from Hansel, but she'd never have managed either without the intervention of an old family friend known as Two-Tie. The nickname, naturally, suggests an angel's wings.

Two-Tie's actual name is Jewish, we learn via clever indirection, and his connection to the Koderers is another of Gordon's brushes with that ethnic identity. Yet Two-Tie reflects mostly his own Jewishness, not his friends', and he never mentions the younger sister by name. In this novel Maggie may carry the author's banner of Women's Liberation, but unlike Jane and Ursie, she's not the whole parade. She's not our sole vehicle of consciousness. *Misrule* also enters the personalities of Hansel, Two-Tie, and others, in roving third person. A few brief passages even seem to sample the wicked thoughts of Joe Dale Biggs—but those are actually another case of mind reading, courtesy of the novel's true protagonist, the weary racetrack veteran Medicine Ed.

One of the "old-timey negroes from down...in the hunt country," Ed offers sharp insights into everyone. Yet at seventy-two he finds himself closest to "Mr. Boll Weevil...*He's looking for a home. He's looking for a ho-me.*" The folk-song refrain not only provides pithy expression for the old man's tragic yearning, but also places him at the head of Gordon's African American chorus. He's more fully realized than *Bogeywoman*'s "Regicide," or its "Ayrabbers," or any of the dark-skinned strays in *Without Stopping*. It's Ed who comprehends the "slavery" that binds "the frizzly hair girl" and "the young fool" with the "crazy look." It's Ed who provides essential background in the sport, the economics that underlie the drama. He knows about "goofers," too, from bitter experience; he's seen how fickle their magic can be. We share his regrets and refusals—he's sworn off magic, and booze along with it. We share what passes for his home, a half-crushed Winnebago decaying at the edge of Indian Mound. In

Medicine Ed, *Misrule* brings off an act of imaginative sympathy that's nothing short of sensational.

The characters who make things happen, to be sure, tend to be younger. Just as old Ed suspects, Hansel's a hustler, with his own failing stable in another state. He's come to West Virginia to cash in on a few of his horses; as unknowns, they'll run at long odds. As the scheme strays into complications, Gordon handles things with the skill of some racetrack-*noir* professional, another Dick Francis, scattering clues like a trail through the woods. But speaking of babes in the woods, doesn't this Hansel have a Gretel? Doesn't he think of Maggie (Margaret, Gretel) as a "long-lost twin," and doesn't the heroine wear her hair in braids? She likes to use the oven, too, though she's "not the homey kind," rather "the restless, unsatisfied, insomniac kind." She's got a lot in common with Jane and Ursie, that is, as well as with the lost girl who kicked the cannibal witch into her own oven. So one night as a pot of beans bubbles beside her, Maggie thinks how beans "were lots in the lottery for Lord of Misrule and his Lady, king and queen of Saturnalia, when the order of the world turned upside-down." With that, she turns rightside-up. No longer the child victim, she's "free to fly about the snowy skies on her broomstick."

Gordon may have become a pro at plotting, but her artistry remains complex. The touch of allegory, something else *Misrule* shares with its two predecessors, again gets treated with playful high-handedness. Maggie may escape destruction and come into power, but the journey proves bumpy indeed. After Biggs slips her a Mickey, as she fumbles for a way out, once again the author fetches laughs where you'd least expect: "She had to try, of course. Nowadays you couldn't just let some Black Bart tie you to the railroad tracks and walk away." So too, Lord of Misrule turns out to have a life outside the "drawers and pigeonholes" in Maggie's head, a rambunctious life, as a racehorse with a reputation for winning. Once the black nag arrives on the scene, Medicine Ed declares him "the devil." Who trucked Misrule in from Nebraska, after all, if not Joe Dale Biggs, that "monster in a labyrinth?" For the climactic race, monster and devil are in cahoots, Biggs intends to win, and he strongarms the old trainer into breaking his vow and mixing up one more goofer. "I don't want no uncontrollable factors," the gangster snarls, and in that line this complex multi-voiced narrative reveals a simple central irony. What could be more uncontrollable than magic?

The uproar at novel's close proves apt, well-nigh supernatural, and it comes with a threat. This time it might be murder into the bargain, for Maggie. The final confrontation does resolve itself as comedy, again, and again distinctly Gordonian. Its blessings are mixed, and besides, the conclusion leaves us up in the air about the fairytale's ruling spirit, Medicine Ed. Has Ed found a home? The last pages are his, as were the first, but both show him working at the Downs and sleeping in the crippled Winnebago. Perhaps "home" requires a new definition, a metamorphosis, something like the way the natives reshaped the earth, building mounds to house the spirits. Or like the vision Maggie had, whenever she groomed her horse.

> She knew…this one thing: She could find her way to the boundary where she ended and some other strain of living creature began. On the last little spit of being human, staring through rags of fog into the not human, where you weren't supposed to be able to see let alone cross, she could make out a kind of home.

Love would be another term for it, this belonging beyond "the last spit." But *love* would be the more common term, hence pitted with cliché, and Gordon's careful with it in all three of her mature comedies. The happy ending never leads to the altar; not even Ursie gets her "girlgoyle." Rather, once this author outgrew her explorations in other genres (among which I'd include *Shamp*), she began delivering her women to mystery. They change, passing through those "rags of fog" we call myth and fable, the smoke that trails from all classic literature, but the ultimate shape of their metamorphosis remains "Unbeknownst." In this, Gordon's texts make a much-needed contribution to the American novel of a woman's self-actualization.

From the doomy brooding of Kate Chopin's *Awakening* (1899) through the sexed-up capering of Erica Jong, and from there on to the vengeful ferocity of Marge Piercy and the more complex cross-cultural materials of Louise Erdrich and others, fiction about a woman's place in the world has tended to omit the spiritual, the Unknowable. Instead such narratives emphasize social issues: political, economic, or otherwise. Erdrich's work provides the closest thing to an exception, and the best correlative for Gordon's. Granted, a novel as violent and admonitory as *Love Medicine* (1984) could never be called a comedy. Still, in that book and others, while Erdrich never ignores class or money or *Realpolitik*, no more than Gordon does, nonetheless she leavens their oppressiveness with magic and miracle, sometimes Christian, more often Lakota. In the process, she also risks formal experiments, at the level of both sentence and structure. She too had early exposure to John Barth, as a graduate of his program at Johns Hopkins, and her fiction demonstrates what he argued for in his "Exhaustion" and "Replenishment" essays: a postmodernism that can "have it both ways." The work, that is, both calls attention to the dream-making artifact in our hands and sweeps us up in a dream.

Still, Jaimy Gordon presents the more freewheeling case. Literature as potent as hers will outlast any cabal. Every story sustains a strong feminist element, and yet none collapse into lecture. The author can roar like the literary equivalent of a punk-rock Riot Grrrl, still she remains open to the least tenderness. And that tenderness may be a simple gesture of sisterly caring, ordinary as Baltimore, yet any gesture can set us wondering, with the Bogeywoman, "how many fantasticoes dare we hope…from any one family?"

—Ploughshares, 2012

SOUL IN THE SF MACHINE: RICHARD POWERS & GALATEA 2.2

Ursula LeGuin, possibly our country's greatest gift to science fiction, rejects the label. In a 1977 essay for *Antaeus*, LeGuin argued that a better category for novels and stories like hers would be "speculative fiction," and she pointed out that in Europe the masters of such fiction, like Orwell and Huxley, are seen as masters in the larger sense. In America, meanwhile, "sf" still tends to be considered commercial fluff. LeGuin went on to grumble that, more's the pity, American practitioners and fans both seemed to prefer their sci-fi fluffy and pop. Stateside, whether sitting before the keyboard or browsing the bookstore shelves, we'll take Captain Kirk over Big Brother.

With LeGuin's complaints in mind, *Galatea 2.2* by Richard Powers might once have been called a breakthrough for American science fiction. Its plot depends on technological development still beyond us—last I checked.[1] But the many games of *Galatea* are expertly and evocatively played, suffused with feeling and resonant with culture; the book scales some of the steepest challenges of storytelling while keeping anyone along for the climb on a good, tight leash.

To be sure, the same might be claimed for Powers' third novel, *The Gold Bug Variations*, from 1991. The story combined computer science, genetic coding, and high orchestral art—is that title book

---

1. True at the time of this review, and still true fifteen years farther on.

or Bach? His first, *Three Farmers on Their Way to a Dance*, and his fourth, *Operation Wandering Soul* (like *Gold Bug*, a prize finalist), were likewise shaped in part by far-reaching extrapolations. Since the beginning of his career, well before he won the MacArthur "genius" grant in 1989, Powers has been making those extrapolations. The wilder the possibility, the more the suspense; his imagination tends to expose the scary fragility of the here and now. In this, Powers isn't alone, either. A number of Americans of his generation make drama out of what could go wrong with our comfortable place in the world. Those dramas might be worlds apart, otherwise, ranging from the *noir* of Jonathan Lethem to the kink of Katherine Dunn. But it's better to take *Galatea 2.2* not as something wholly new but as another contribution to this movement, reclaiming pop materials for serious purposes: a younger generation's therapy for the schizophrenic culture LeGuin complained about.

What's most remarkable about *Galatea*'s contribution may be that business of keeping readers on the leash. The story materials seem, in outline, to frustrate emotional engagement. A critically esteemed but non-commercial novelist, recipient of a lucrative fellowship, returns to the Midwestern university of his youth. He haunts "the Center for the Study of Advanced Sciences," one of those vast hives of research sharing a state-of-the-art computer mainframe. Here, as "the token humanist," the novelist finds it easy to muffle his mid-life crisis: having lost his love, he's hit writer's block.

A novel about a blocked novelist, in an academic setting—that's two strikes right there. And the narrator Powers chooses is named Powers, Richard Powers, and to make sense of his current crisis he must explicate, one by one, his four previous books. The first was inspired by the famous August Sander photograph from 1913 or '14, "Three Farmers on Their Way to a Dance"…Strike three? Astonishingly, no: *Galatea* proves as entertaining and full of heart as a two-out rally.

Part of the reason is plain mastery of the craft. Powers demonstrates a terrific supple swiftness, his tale unfolding without chapters, in snippets rarely longer than a few pages. Yet along the way he seems to uncover every aching similarity between past and present a heart-sore loner can think of. Whenever fictional "Richard" veers close to sentimentality over his lost love, some irony of his success spices the moment. The sorrow he feels over a former professor and surrogate father, now dead, is undercut by bitter ambivalence over his alcoholic actual father, also gone.

The more unusual player in the book's success is the science fiction element. Early on Powers embroils "Powers" in a bizarre computer-training contest at the Center. As he emerges from his own cocoon, the narrator warms up to another Center inhabitant little more socialized than he. This is an old hand at thinking machines, name of Philip Lentz; in time, perhaps, this prof can fill up the lenses of the hollowed-out novelist. Soon enough Lentz and Powers accept a bet to teach a computer to make sense of literature. In less than a year, their machine will have to write an essay for the school's Masters Comprehensives as good as any human's.

The computer scientist is great fun, his reading and smarts more than a match for our token humanist. Even when it comes to worldly experience, Lentz easily outpoints the hothouse-flower colleague he scornfully calls "Marcel." This master of artificial brains has a wife with a brain permanently broken, and a grown daughter who blames him for it. Thus training the story's sequence of "Imps" (implementations, see, to the basic mainframe) soon becomes therapy: the two damaged men minister to each other. As Powers comes out of himself, out of paralysis, his first baby steps result in a classic tumble. He develops an infatuation with an English grad student half his age, never mind that he's smart enough to see where that leaves him: "A Humbert Humbert. One of those old fools in Chaucer, Shakespeare....I meant to make an idiot of myself." And when Imp H, a.k.a. "Helen," starts to understand the poetry that Powers reads to her, in particular this quiddity called love, things really get interesting. Indeed, the talking machine emerges as a fascinating minor character—plus a better helpmeet for this recluse-in-recovery than that pretty face over in the English Department.

It's at sentence level, of course, where all this must percolate into life. Or no, "percolates" refers to the wrong technology. *Galatea* prefers computer jargon: at sentence level the novel's input layer must connect via hidden neural networks to create a full-blown cognitive economy. Got that? In fact, after ten or twelve lively pages here, a reader does get it. That's the craft again, as Powers fuses nerdy data and narrative drive considerably beyond what he managed in the DNA-saturated pages of *Gold Bug Variations*. In the same way, the novel's summaries of its four predecessors are kept pertinent to the breakages and mendings at hand. The phrasing, while never dense, relies on Anglo-Saxon abruptness and when focused on character can take off in flights at once abstract and perfect:

> I told her in one clean rush, as only a twenty-one-year-old still can. Of my father's slow-burn suicide, stretched out over fifteen years. The man's long, accreting addiction that made every day a sine wave of new hope crushed. How hope, beaten to a stump, never died. How it always dragged back, like an amputated pet, its hindquarters rigged up in a makeshift wagon.

Powerful stuff, even with the scientist's touches like "accreting" and "sine wave." At such moments, equal parts brainy and hurtful, Richard Powers isn't simply delivering a better brand of science fiction. Rather he's pointing up timeless perplexities, in particular the difference between simulation and the real, with new means and new panache. He's proving again that the best artists remake their chosen form and genre rather than shrinking to fit convention. If Ursula LeGuin reads this novel, I'll bet she smiles.

—Portland Oregonian, 1995

SOARS, BOGGLES, DANCES: POWERS & GENEROSITY: AN ENHANCEMENT

An international student is pleased that her professor doesn't consider himself religious. "Good," the young woman responds. "I'm nothing either. I'm a Maghreb Algerian Kabyle Catholic Atheist French Canadian on a student visa."

Richard Powers always has a lot going on, but he's never attempted a vehicle so jerry-rigged as *Generosity: An Enhancement*. This student's rapid-fire border-hopping suits his latest, his tenth novel and closest brush with comedy. Not that either the girl or her novel lack for tragedy. Thassadit Amzwar, twenty-three years old, has lost both parents. She herself barely survived the post-colonial "Time of Horrors" in Algiers. Yet even that grim story eventually undergoes an "enhancement," a reconfiguring. Every element of this narrative experiences some modification as Amzwar connects with four other major characters, each from a very different place. And everyone's tailed by a ubiquitous Author. This figure's intrusions include quick cuts to imaginary textbooks, websites—and the future. Powers even subverts his own project, his readers' expectations, when a TV personality here describes her cable program as "*Scientific American* meets *Gotterdammerung*." Encounters like that have defined this author's work from the first. His 1985 debut, *Three Farmers on Their Way to a Dance*, considered the dangers of accelerating technology, and his National Book Award winner from 2006, *The Echo Maker*, considered how little we know about the brain. Powers has always warned of coming twilight, and this time he raises an unnerving possibility of gene science.

The story postulates a "happiness gene" that would enhance the whole species. Thassa Amzwar, improbably happy despite her suffering, might be the gene donor who will usher in "the coming age of molecular control." Yet the novel's affect, first to last, isn't admonition so much as amazement, that word buried in the girl's name. *Generosity* may be jerry-rigged, but it's genius: it soars, it boggles.

Powers breaks us in gently. Our introduction to the imperturbable Maghreb, etc., comes before she generates any hullabaloo, via the subdued Russell Stone, her Chicago professor. Thassa studies film, but she's enrolled in Stone's seminar in Creative Non-Fiction (a form whose ambiguities prompt stinging Authorial asides). It's the teacher who first marvels at the girl's "eerie contentment," her "promiscuous warmth." Not that Thassa's actually promiscuous, or on drugs, or blessed with great looks. Still, "her glee is a dance," and the writing assignment in which she details the Time of Horrors ends in a lighthearted remembrance of Algiers, "So crazy with life." Her classmates designate Thassa "Bliss Chick" and "Miss Generosity."

The title character demonstrates how this novel represents a departure. Karin Schlutter and Gerald Weber, central figures of *The Echo Maker*, were all inner torment. And Russell Stone is something new for Powers as well, a literary artist, though lapsed. The writers in previous novels were, like Weber, researchers who published. This time the actual author must shuttle between another who's a conventional flawed character and yet a third, that prankster Author who isn't Powers but nonetheless knows a good deal beyond Stone's ken. Such a metafictional game was anticipated in *Galatea 2.2* (1995), which had a protagonist named Richard Powers, but here the play gets so complex—the Author, for instance, follows the future storyline to the edge of the Sahara—that it requires a simple narrative frame. So the professor asks himself, the first night of class (in these pages, the point of view is with him), "What in the name of second chances was he thinking?" Much of what follows, and by no means just for Stone, boils down to an answer. Renewal for the prof comes in the form of Candace Weld, a college counselor. Weld too gets knocked sideways by Thassa, her "peak experience...*all the time*," and, as a single mom peeking out from under her bandages, she draws toward Stone. The couple come together with the exquisite slowness implied in the image for their first kiss: "Lowering a bucket to a well." Thassa has played Cupid, in short, and seems set up for her own second chance; she's looking to work in film. But so close a student-teacher-counselor friendship makes the college nervous. Other students put up internet posts concerning the Bliss Chick, bringing her ever more into the public eye, and before long administrators sever her from Stone and Weld. Orphan, immigrant, trauma victim—though upbeat as ever—Thassa is left vulnerable to someone else who found her online, namely, the genome researcher Thomas Kurton.

Kurton and his work have been a part of *Generosity* from the beginning. It's he who argues for gene implantation. These fringy speculations are presented, fittingly, via the fanciful visuals of a TV program about him, a descriptive method that also distances this Science Guy from the gloomier variety found in earlier Powers novels. Kurton enjoys his celebrity, and in any case the fabricated drama around him ends up delivering the McCoy. He and his science-gal interviewer, Tonia Schiff, confront second chances of their own, each having to do with Thassa. Schiff in particular emerges as a superb oxymoron, a figure of depth who works in two dimensions. She cuts back on recreational sex and starts to worry about the unsophisticated foreign girl; Thassa's happiness starts to seems fragile, something that would wither in the media glare.

Tonia's change of heart suggests a classic movement toward catharsis, and the same structure might be sketched for Kurton, Stone, or Weld. But *Generosity*'s first climax offers nothing so simple, a daredevil reimagining of the Oprah show, a funhouse mirror.

Between laughter and drama, *Generosity* takes us to the conundrum of representation vs. reality. Can a narrative both sweep us up in imagined lives and acknowledge their artificiality? Powers answers, here, with a laughing affirmative. His Chicago resounds with hard knocks, so vibrant as to recall *Augie March*, yet his Author admits: "This place is some other Second City…Chicago's in-vitro daughter, genetically modified…" (indeed, the primary literary allusion is to an Algerian city-book, Camus' *The Plague*). Likewise many of the personal touches enchant, such as everything about Weld's son—yet the boy's Wii game turns metafictional. Thassa points out that its virtual landscape is the one she grew up with, the semi-arid lands around Kabyle. Is this magic realism? It's a striking experiment, at the least: a narrative instability that Powers might once have found too distracting, back when he always had an eye out for *Gotterdammerung*. But this time Jeremiah dances a genie's double-helix.

—*Bookforum*, 2009

ASSERTING THE FABULOUS: DON DeLILLO & FALLING MAN

In *Falling Man* we have the fourteenth novel by Don DeLillo, and more pertinently his third shorter fiction since *Underworld*. That 1997 masterwork capped a fifteen-year run that began with *The Names* and has few if any peers for sustained literary accomplishment, and the opening chapter alone, a brilliant ballgame setpiece, would've taken up two-thirds of the current book. In the '80s and '90s DeLillo poured even his shortest shot, *Mao II*, a couple of fingers deeper than *Falling Man*. Now, in light of the even briefer twosome that preceded this one, *The Body Artist* ('01) and *Cosmopolis* ('03), it's clear we need to start expecting something different.

Falling Man is a 9/11 novel, beginning and ending on that awful morning in lower Manhattan. It opens with a bravura flourish typical of this artist:

> It was not a street anymore but a world, a time and space of falling ash and near night. He was walking north through rubble and mud and there were people running past holding towels to their faces or jackets over their heads. They had handkerchiefs pressed to their mouths. They had shoes in their hands, a woman with a shoe in each hand…

The juddering poetry we've savored before: rich in consonants, stumbling over near-repetitions, emphasizing both motion and monosyllable. Likewise familiar is how DeLillo sweeps us at once into an utterly American *medias res*, like the Moonie wedding at the start of *Mao II*.

As the first sentence indicates, the attack ushers survivors into another world. The theme goes through many iterations—by the standards of an ordinary novel, in fact, the concept is more fleshed out than the characters. According to the estranged husband Keith, the man walking uptown at the outset: "These are the days after. Everything now is measured by after." The wife Lianne, who was seeing to their child Justin when the planes hit, couches the idea in more intimate terms: "It was…the only interval she'd known in these days and nights that was not forced or distorted, hemmed in by the press of events." Thus the project of *Falling Man*: to delineate the forms created by so titanic a "press."

Among them, none engages sympathy like Lianne. Her we experience as a full personality, now bristling with panic, now venturesome with love, defining a recognizable space between a caring father who took his own life and a mother too much of a Brainiac. Lianne searches out informed discussion of the 9/11 attacks, and her quest, along with her writing workshop for Alzheimer's patients, affirms language and story as a means to wholeness: "This mind and soul, hers and everyone's, keep dreaming toward something unreachable." Lianne's "days after" dramatize the need for the unreachable, the Unknowable, more vividly than anything DeLillo has tried before. Only *The Names*, with its series of ritual murders, rivals the new novel for its concern with God.

In the husband Keith, however, *Falling Man* embodies the opposite: renunciation and the aleatory. The novel opens and closes around this disagreeable axis. In contrast to our time with Keith, the visits with Muhammad Attah's cell—a terrifying skeleton extrapolated from very few bones—come across as suffused with spirit, for all their perversity. But Keith proves a husband and father in name only, his deepest emotions reserved for another survivor, a "light-skinned black woman" whose briefcase he wound up carrying. The case's return leads to…well, you wouldn't call it *healing*: inconclusive talk, inconsequential sex, and fisticuffs with a stranger who may have made a racist remark. Keith soon finishes with New York altogether. He comes to prefer Vegas and professional poker. In these episodes the recurring phrase is "A fresh deck rose to the tabletop;" his new Towers are built of cards, not God.

In *Mao II* DeLillo came up with the provocative notion that the role of the novelist had been taken over by terrorists. In *Falling Man*, when Attah's crew gets incinerated and Keith Neudecker rises to the tabletop, the point isn't that terrorists have now been supplanted by card sharks, but rather that the rejection of human value which defines the jihadist's sacrifice keeps finding fresh embodiment. On 9/11, convinced that Western life had no meaning, the hijackers flew down the Hudson Corridor "carrying their souls in their hands"— like cards. A few years later, Keith's poker buddy describes a game as "like a forbidden religion springing up again."

So the new book takes on the austere outlines of a parable. On one side is a "religion" that reduces the soul to a card or a box-cutter, and "then there's the other thing," as Lianne puts it, "and that's the family." Deliberately, DeLillo keeps his elements basic, setting this life versus a life beyond.

Such simplicity, I would argue, informs all the rough-cut work since *Underworld*. The aesthetic is no longer that of the novel, exactly, though its author is one of the practitioners who stretched core novelistic elements like social and psychological insight to a new postmodern jaggedness. This text however reaches for another affect, that of the fable—or of the Falling Man, a performance artist of the "days after." The artist (an invention of DeLillo's, to be sure) drops in harness, then replicates the famed Richard Drew photo of a man falling alongside the Towers. The performances aren't about anything so novelistic as nuanced emotion.

Thus I can see why critics like Maureen Corrigan and Michiko Kakutani have dismissed *Falling Man* as "spindly" and "shellshock alone," since it frustrates the desire for psychological development. Yet I prefer to consider the work a starkly drawn reminder that its author has always been less of-the-moment than critics have claimed. Yes, *Mao*'s Yankee Stadium opening concludes with the ominous slogan "the future belongs to crowds;" but then *Underworld* begins in an even more crowded ballpark, and the year is 1951. For all DeLillo's analytic sharpness, his reportorial precision, he's fundamentally an artist of the imagination and lately he's asserted its primacy. That sketchy figure in the air above the ashes—could it be flying? Something fabulous?

—*Rain Taxi*, 2007

SAVAGERY AESTHETIC & PUBLIC: LANCE OLSEN & HEAD IN FLAMES

How weary, stale, flat, and unprofitable seem the uses of Western Civ! Surely the husks of Renaissance and Enlightenment need "slashes of verve;" they need "aesthetic savageries," in the raucous and polyglot twenty-first century. And savagery would seem, at first glance, the aesthetic at work in Lance Olsen's exciting new novel, *Head in Flames*. A chapterless—not to say relentless—narrative, *Head* unfolds in three alternating typefaces that actually look like slashes, no entry longer than a few lines and many a single barbed scratch. Each typeface streams a different consciousness: that of two men intent on spilling blood and another trundling oblivious into his murder. Such a text offers next to nothing by way of scene setting, and while there's character development, it can be tricky, hidden behind the narrators' posturing.

Besides, these are characters reined in by the facts. The business about slash and savagery comes from the most famous of the three interior monologists, Vincent Van Gogh. The great Impressionist has a turbulent turn of mind on the day we visit it: that July day in 1890 when he shot himself in a cornfield, then staggered to his boarding house to die. Yet the other two on are on track for worse. One is Van Gogh's filmmaker descendent, Theo, riding his bike through Amsterdam on the November morning in 2004 when the third narrator, Mohammed Bouyeri, waits outside the Dutchman's studio, in one pocket a 9mm Glock and in the other a serrated blade.

The murder and beheading at the end of Theo's commute, combined with Vincent's eventual passing, deliver a tripartite climax with prickly satisfaction to rival that of any conventional novel. Olsen's entire rare construct delivers, its imagination exploding through its constraints. I've rarely experienced so deep a chill in reading that sets such a formal challenge.

Olsen has worked within similar constraints before, especially in *Nietzsche's Kisses* from '06, a backward journey through the philosopher's experience. His *Anxious Pleasures*, from '07, provided group therapy for the family of Gregor Samsa after their breadwinner turned into a bug. Before then, Olsen tended to American subjects, toying for instance with cyberpunk, but his brisk European sojourns have opened his sensibility to new power—he's never done anything so hard-hitting as *Head in Flames*.

The worst blows, to be sure, are those of Mohammed Bouyeri. From the first he's in a place where "words don't count," where all that matters is "the weight inside your fist inside your pocket." Bouyeri's transformation into holy warrior holds no great surprises, but Olsen leaves glimmering details in his narrative claw marks. We learn the ethnic slur preferred by the Dutch, a monkey's name, "*Makak*;" we witness a new version of that lose-lose conflict, a strapped immigrant father versus a son born to the promise of a new land. Yet while Bouyeri's reflections generate sympathy, they don't soft-pedal his viciousness—in particular, his faith-based misogyny.

What prompts the murder is one film in particular, an outcry against the brutalization of Muslim women. For this the twenty-first-century Van Gogh worked with a Somali-born woman who's served in the Dutch parliament, Ayaan Hirsi Ali. Ali remains one of Europe's foremost spokespeople against Wahhabi Islam, but here the potential heroine is encountered only at a remove, via Theo's memories.

The filmmaker's hardly a saint; he wrecked his marriage with philandering and currently has no intimate life outside of Amsterdam's red-light district. Theo knows himself, however—"I'm the village idiot"—and with his acerbic wit and his affection toward his son, he'd be the central consciousness of an ordinary novel. Olsen's sentences often feature marvelous verbs, and the best occur in Theo's passages, such as the man's "belly wubbling in glee" under a whore's ministrations. Then too, Theo provides the most horrifying stuff in the text—and I don't mean his murder. Worse is his recollection of Ayaan's recollection of how she was "made pure" as a six-year-old: tied down by fundamentalist aunts and worked over by a butcher's scissors.

Given such material, and the persistent reminders that European tolerance may have invited in a "Trojan Horse" of "De-Enlightenment," when "by 2015," more than fifty percent of the continent's population will be Muslim—given his insistence on the culture clash that most defines the present—what's crazy old Vincent doing in there? What's 1890 got to do with it? Yet the painter gives us the book's title, a device he rigged up for night-work, a candelabra worn as a hat. Then too, when it came to women Vincent had terrible problems, rooted in his religious training. The most notorious case got bloody.

Olsen isn't about savagery after all. Rather, for all his ambition, he's subtle; he teases out the link between the tortured artist, driven to self-slaughter by an "experiment in writing our own lives," outside God's will, and the deluded murderer, who acts in hopes that God will revisit his own degraded "soul…in its ragged sheet of skin." No small accomplishment, and I daresay *Head in Flames* has set a new standard for the social consciousness of postmodern narratives.[1]

—Rain Taxi, 2010

---

1. Olsen expanded the postmodern social consciousness further with *Calendar of Regrets*, another exceptional piece of work, the following year.

OTHER GRAVITIES

'TOONS TAKE ITALY & THE WORLD:
DYLAN DOG

Fellini lore includes a wonderful bit from a 1960s interview. Asked about the influence of James Joyce, the filmmaker declares he's never read Joyce. *Davvero, mai*—truly, never—though one should never admit such things, continues the *Maestro*, since it presents a bad example for the young. Next, however, Fellini points out that of course he knows about Joyce anyway. Joyce is everywhere now, he claims; you even see him in advertising.

Or in the comics. Thirty years on, the Italian talent for shock and image appears to have found a new field for the synthesis of high art and low: not the big silky screen, but the small paper panel. Up and down the boot, everyone's snatching up a comic book called *Dylan Dog*.

Or "comic book" is the closest American equivalent. The Italian *fumetto* signifies a softbound serial picture book of about hundred pages, and it's rarely some simple Superman or -woman. *Dylan Dog* sells horror, essentially, with such standard fare as zombies hungry for living flesh and sicko scientists with power over weaker minds. It sells humor: the dark sarcasm of its handsome ghost-hunter hero (no dog), and the loonier cracks of his sidekick, a Groucho Marx lookalike named Groucho Marx. It sells sex: no episode is without its starlet, playing a monster or monster prey, and Dylan beds his share. But the series accomplishes these unremarkable goals with remarkable style, a masterful *noir* complexity peppered by sophisticated elements at once media-wise and unabashedly postmodern. Joyce—and Kulchur generally—is everywhere.

A rough stateside correlative might be *The Simpsons*, as a country-wide comics phenomenon, but *Dylan Dog* succeeds in cheap black and white, without the benefit of TV. There are T-shirts and conventions. Spring '94 saw the release of a movie, *Dellamorte Dellamore* ("Of the death of love," later released in English as *Cemetery Man*), in which Dog was played by the actor on whom he was modeled, British heartthrob Rupert Everett. Devotees buy as many as four publications a month: the ongoing new series, reissued numbers from the past, expanded special editions, and "little sister" extras. Kiosks from Palermo to Venice stock a backlist. With a monthly print run near three-quarters of a million, in a country whose total adolescent population runs ten million, this constrained but skillful creepshow has achieved a dream market penetration. *DD*'s selling in London too, and in Paris. New York outlets like Forbidden Planet are looking for an American distributor. [1]

Prime mover for this extraordinary success is Tiziano Sclavi. Back in 1986, Sclavi was the thirty-something author of undistinguished thrillers—novels, in print—when he hit on *Dylan Dog*. He does the storyboards. An illustrator named Angelo Stano was instrumental in establishing the look, but there's no significant falloff in those issues for which others do the drawing. Primary credit must go to Sclavi.

As it happens, the man's a recluse. His only word on *Dylan Dog* has been an unlikely magazine quote: "I am neither Dylan nor Groucho. I am the monsters." No doubt his publishers, Sergio Bonelli of Milan, sympathize all the way to the bank. More tellingly, Sclavi's reticence recalls that of Bob Dylan, the figure most people think of when

---

1. Since the mid-'90s the rise of computer media has eroded the popularity of *Dylan Dog* a bit. But the series flourishes still, with other artists succeeding Sclavi and an American translation on Dark Horse Comics, as well as another movie: *Dead of Night* (2010), starring Brandon Routh.

they come across these books. Then again, the series title may owe more to Dylan Thomas, whose work includes the scabrous *Portrait of the Artist as a Young Dog*.

Whatever; this Dylan's his own man. Based in London, he works as an "Investigator of Nightmares." His ghastly nemeses and the havoc they wreak of course get the benefit of a Hitchcock-eyed presentation. Groucho too cuts quite a figure (always in the jodphurs he favored in *Animal Crackers*) as do Dylan's lady friends. But it's the chiseled young *indagatore* who dominates the page. Lank and easy in jeans and open-necked shirt, in limp sport coat and undone hair, he's part Sam Spade, part slacker smartmouth. He's a pop star.

The nature of his presentation seems at first nothing special. It's black and white commercial design, the shadings atmospheric but never obscure. This workmanlike clarity, however, proves crucial. Plots whirl along head over heels, decaying corpses and naked breasts pop out unexpectedly—yet there's always something rather dry and precise about this twilight zone. *Dylan Dog* doesn't have much truck with the explosive graphics of American comics and their movie adaptation. Scalvi's people take their cue, rather, from Industrial Light & Magic. They run a clean operation, parceling most of the action into well-composed pages of five or six panels, and they're demons on the accessories. See, for instance, the unfinished model of a Spanish galleon that sits on Dylan's desk.

Now, that galleon is a hand-me-down from Dylan's father, and the dual-generational guilt trip—the ship's never finished, remember—is typical. If this special investigator has become an icon, it's largely because he holds his own while careening up and down dizzying layers of life, death, and who knows how many stages in between. Every new issue comprises a single story, ninety-plus pages without advertising inserts or other distractions. First impressions can call to mind an archeological dig in some busy Italian acreage. In one corner we unearth a frieze of zombies, in another a totem of a sicko scientist, and over here a painted potshard on which—*per carita!*—a woman's face putrefies and falls away.

The gore's a factor, certainly: *DD* sells horror. Among the least sophisticated fans, a good scare is good enough. But the *fumetto* reaches deep into every market there is between the ages of thirteen and twenty-five. For this audience, *Gruppo* MTV, a winning pop enterprise needs to see the gore and raise it. It needs to take its play into the more entertaining realms of media and mind.

Post-*8 1/2*, Sclavi gives us a perpetual *8 1/2*: Dylan plays the gifted but blocked Guido (Fellini's surrogate, portrayed by Marcello Mastroanni), trying to follow his muse in a din of resonances at once personal and cultural. One episode may resuscitate Edgar Allen Poe, and the next go to the *traum* root of Freudian analysis. New storylines give way to old, living lovers to dead enemies, or to dead Dad. The compatibility with film *noir*, in which "nothing is as it seems," only adds one more layer to the mounting strata Dylan must make sense of before it smothers him. And—speaking of personal—many an issue wrestles with the ambiguous position of comic books and their makers. Dylan's gun may melt in his hand, even as the ghouls close in, because, as Groucho explains: "It's our new model, the Soft, designed to cut down on the violence in comics."

Selling humor, yes, that too. The wit reveals a tough-minded comprehension behind the surface bewilderment. Groucho gets most of the best lines, though the sidekick spends a lot time offstage. Dylan himself, typical gumshoe, prefers stiletto asides that deflate the grand sepulchral ambitions of his enemies. But a lot of the humor doesn't belong to one of the characters, but rather erupts from the madcap juxtapositions and turns of events. Such gags are in keeping with the anarchy of adolescent humor; they upend the status quo. On another level, the wit operates like the cleanliness of the design. It's another drying agent, toughening the blood and guts into something else, a net in which Sclavi can catch more interesting stuff.

As for *Dylan Dog*'s sexual content, the contrast with American comics again proves illuminating. The girls of *Tales from the Crypt* bulge in their halter tops, and those of *X-Men* in their superheroine spandex—but none of them let us past the tease. Worse, American comics offer unreal tease, muscled-up, D-cup tease. Dylan on the other hand sees his honeys naked. Not that *DD* is pornographic; *fumetti* that show sex in detail in Italy are no different from those in America. But this hero beds his heroines every second or third episode. And the girls, compared to Catwoman or Lana Lang, seem only a trifle better than average. Like Dylan they wear long-sleeved shirts and sensible shoes.

These affairs, in this medium, come across as down to earth. They're *realistic*, strange as that sounds. So too, for all its supernatural grotesquerie, *DD* enjoys a general absence of gunfights or fistfights (even in episodes without the new Soft-model pistol). Violence runs far below the level found in American comics.

Thus the last significant element in *Dylan Dog*'s appeal, affiliated with its humor and its Speilbergian clarity, is a pervading low-key quality. Homely faces never look out of place, among these skulls and hooded cowls. Dylan must shift from passion to problem-solving the same as the rest of us. Though first impressions are of sheer outlandish splatter on a flat Postmodern plate, of "multiple subjectivities" multiplying out of control, Sclavi takes us back in the end to the dreary reassurances of making do. Most stories end with a final vision of the episode's now-familiar brokedown world—and with Dylan no longer in the picture. The artist or his surrogate is more likely to have the last word; as for the hero, his job is done. Having guided us through inferno, he leaves us at purgatory gate.

It's all very Italian. Adult fans of the series, according to both Italian news sources and the *New York Times*, include the Bologna-based polymath Umberto Eco. Not only does Eco's favorite comic fit classic models like Dante and the *Decameron* (the background for which is a city racked by plague), along with more recent ones like those of Fellini, but also it provides a balloon-dream representation of an ongoing national crisis. During the late '80s and early '90s, when *Dylan Dog* took off, Italy saw the worst excesses of the vast bribery scandal known now as *Tangentopolis*, "Bribe City," described in the *New Yorker* as "tantamount to a coup d'etat." *Tangentopolis* brought down the coalition of parties that had ruled since the end of World War II. Nonetheless, the very worst that the scandal revealed—the way respected politicians had "kissed the hands" of Mafia kingpins— seems by no means a thing of the past.[2] The "leadership" of Silvio Berlusconi appears more buffoonish which each passing year. Small wonder disenfranchised youth turn to an Investigator of Nightmares. Generations X and Y, throughout the West, suffer diminished expectations and lack of faith, and in Italy they confront a ruling order of sicko scientists, in a land well-nigh overrun by zombies. We should only be glad they're going to the *Dog*.

—*millennium pop*, 1994

---

2. More contemporary corruption is grimly detailed in the '06 book (and '08 movie) *Gomorrah*.

TROUBLE & BEDAZZLEMENT: "THE ITALIAN METAMORPHOSIS" AT THE GUGGENHEIM

I work on a darling little computer. The color is industrial gray, the casing construction-site rough, and yet the trackball[1] and keyboard invite the touch, smooth and gleaming. The impression is of a subdued, shadowy elegance that contains both the far edges of science and my own *lumpen* makeup in a single handsome, handy packet. And while the name of this machine is Anglo, ending in the hard *k* that doesn't exist in Latin countries, I know its forebears were Italian.

To see where the laptop came from, look to Rome. The design models for the computer age remain the materials of a Fellini set circa *8 1/2*—that is, 1963. Consider for instance the Vespa scooter, bug-like yet sleek, still the model for any city-wise runabout though it was designed by Corradino D'Ascanio in 1946. In the '50s came Marcello Nizzoli's trim Olivetti typewriters, in the '60s snug portable televisions designed by Marco Zanuso, and all have since proved the shape of things to come. Certainly the Japanese knew a good thing when they saw one. Honda and Sony owe an obvious debt to Fiat and Vespa, and to the appliance designs of Zanuso or the Castiglioni brothers. Anyone who needed proof had only to visit New York while the Guggenheim Museum was showing "The Italian Metamorphosis: 1943–1968," an exhibit that included over a thousand objects in just about every medium.

---

1. Why not stick with the terms of mid-'90s technology?

Too much, too quick, and yet full of light and laughter, the event showcased a culture swept up in a transformation as radical as any this century. More than that, it demonstrated that the ways in which Italy handled its "Metamorphosis"—in artists' lofts or on draftsmen's tables—left a notably workable blueprint for how to live at this crowded and changeable turn of the millennium.

But if the world has come to fit Italy's boot, that same culture proved a tight squeeze for the Guggenheim. An art museum after all, the Gugg set aside its Rotunda space (its signature mushroom spiral) for the art *per se*, the sculpture, wallpieces, installations. Climbing the central ramp, one passed two or three isolated pieces every sixty degrees or so, a thinking-friendly pace. But something like the Design section, where the Fiat and Vespa were on display, was shunted whole into one of the side galleries. Indeed, half a gallery: Design shared its space with Photography. The crowding left cinema coverage, in particular, shortchanged. The Film section offered nothing more than screenings of a few classics, wonderful yet shopworn, plus a couple sets of self-congratulatory clips from *CinéCitta* and a winding corridor of poster-plastered walls. Yet that splashy narrow corridor was, as well, a clever touch. It was an imitation Roman or Florentine alleyway of the period, a bit of Italian street life brought in-house.

Certainly you could carp at the show's limitations. Where was the historical grounding, the samples of '20s Futurism and monument-happy Fascism? Where was the better work by '60s iconoclast Jannis Kounnellis? But such carping would ignore the unique challenges posed by the "Metamorphosis." Curator Germano Celant had to make like Fellini, whirling a whole fractious world into a single prolonged dance. Simply to have pulled off something coherent would have deserved praise. But Celant did more: He got the alleyway into the house. His cramming left room for wit.

———

Wit was about all Italy had left after 1943. The urge to create is always in part contrary, a renunciation of whatever's too true, and art-infected Italians at the end of the Fascist misadventure found themselves with more than most to react against. The country was bankrupt, its finest minds in exile or dead. The claim that Mussolini made the trains run on time proves, alas, elitist folklore; he poured money into the luxuries enjoyed by his generals, like first-class trains, but left the rank and file to sink into a cultural backwardness unmatched in Western Europe. After that, during the Allied drive up the peninsula, more than one eyewitness reported that the triumph of democracy often reduced local life to near barbarism.

Small wonder that most of those in the first wave of talent to have an impact following the War had played some part in the leftist resistance. They reacted not only against the hollow exaggerations of the "blackshirts," however, but also against the mannered swoops and coils of Bruncusi and the Futurists, which seemed hopelessly out of touch. Instead they embraced a harsher credo: *Get real.*

The Neo-realist movement, best known in this country via movies like Rossellini's *Open City* (1945) and De Sica's *The Bicycle Thief* ('48), seems at first glance far removed from the suave tech of something like my laptop. The Guggenheim's photography section, for instance, began with the grim urban scenes of Alberto Lattuada; these suggest, to a present-day visitor, the footage out of devastated Mogadishu. Over in the high arts, meanwhile, the back-to-basics impulse led to the *composizioni* of Alberto Burri—some of the most arresting pieces around the Guggenheim Rotunda—cobbled together out of materials like burlap and charred wood. Even the '46 Vespa is nothing if not down to earth: the name means "wasp" and repair requires no more than a jackknife. Then how does one get from such naked postwar homeliness to the fine Italian hand of, say, mid-'60s Ferragamo shoes? The sequence makes sense only to those who can open themselves anew to the dizzying power of its initial step.

The exhibit's film clips, even edited so as to send everyone home happy, couldn't entirely neuter the movement's power. The agitated faces and bodies onscreen shook off even the smarm caked over them by a thousand imitations. What most sets these originals apart from their followers, one saw again, is the women. Even a great disciple like Martin Scorsese must rest his reputation on men's roles, and lesser American attempts at capturing the Italian feminine mystique prove blandly Hefneresque.[2] But when Ingrid Bergman abandoned Hollywood for Rossellini, in 1950, it wasn't because of any nonsense about Latin lovers. It was because of what he'd done for Anna Magnani and the young Loren. The women of this movement were true screen sirens: encouraged to a raw emotionality actresses had rarely if ever been allowed. Dramas were pursued down to the root: money, shame, family.

At the Guggenheim show the sheer muscle of Neo-realism had its brute way once more, not just in the Film section but also in Design and Photography and elsewhere. It's no small measure of the exhibition's success that, by unearthing this old touchstone, it achieved a startling cross-cultural insight. It demonstrated that postwar Italian realism uncorked the same genie as early rock 'n' roll—the magic of the organic and libidinous.

With that in mind, the later modulations of this Metamorphosis seem natural. On the one hand, by insisting on the streetwise and bottomline, engaged imaginations moved toward practicality and flexibility. Thus Ferragamo, unencumbered by the limitations of his materials in 1944, combines scraps of suede and chunks of cork to make a patchwork high-heeled slip-on that remains a staple of boho fashion to this day. On the other hand, by putting a premium on impulse and the back of the brain, makers and doers were carried away from the constraints of logic and unity. Thus about 1960 the

---

2. At this point I cited the John Mellencamp video for "Dancing Naked;" a more up-to-date example would be the movie *Nine*.

artist Mimmo Rotella develops his "Décollage" style, in which layers of wall posters are peeled away in pieces in order to reveal startling colors and perceptions.

By the early '60s Italy had entered a heyday of money and sensibility known as *Il Boom*, surfing these twinned waves of adaptability in the marketplace and fidelity to human dimensions. The high arts, too, broke away from realism, and from any leftist dogma that might demand it. At the Guggenheim, the manifestos of that break and its reactions (and counter-reactions), made up much of the exhibit on "The Literature of Art." Including everything from novels to graffiti-style notices, in one sense these literature collections amounted to little more than a flag display, under glass. But then again, they constituted the flags of a new universe, parti-color testimony to the country's leap from Third World to First.

Even the most extravagant excesses of this moment, the most cutting-edge assemblages, imply an awareness of donkey carts, a feudal Mafia, and public health disasters that most of Europe hadn't encountered in a century or more. Thus Missoni's rainbow tunic-dresses, though made of rayon and associated with the '60s jet set, nonetheless derive unmistakeably from Sicilian and Saharan peasant gear. Having begun in naked human outcry, the Metamorphosis kept finding ways to keep hands and bodies part of the changing formula. Industrial design had a trademark asymmetry, jamming the rounded against the flat, the fleshy against the mechanical, and it moved always toward basics, so that a TV would appear nothing but screen. Yet its other defining element remained something then called "aerodynamic," now known as "biomorphic," but in any case natural, down-home, *simpatico*.

In high arts, as more and more unusual materials found a way into assemblages, they did so with humor. The Guggenheim Rotunda featured a delightful Piero Manzoni confabulation of fake fur and charcoal bricks. At times, too, the work achieved mythic Mediterranean resonance. The very title of the New York show pointed toward legendary benchmarks of the civilized animal: Kafka's twentieth-century bug and Ovid's first-century transformations.

The exhibition's choice of closure was in some ways arbitrary. In Italy the dislocations of the sudden postwar jump into the future continue to this day—as do their creative responses. Yet 1968 was indeed a watershed year, as Rome and Milan, like Paris and Mexico City, saw strikes and protests. Cantankerous freethinkers, at that point, began to react against the very boom they had helped create. To put it another way, the Guggenheim show provided a fresh example of a familiar cultural pattern: following do-it-yourselfers who seize the foreground through the golden triumphs of their initiative to the moment of their inevitable disillusionment and return to origins. That return was *Arte Povera*, "poor art," with installations made of things like treetrunks and sandbags; it was as usual echoed in other media, for example in Joe Columbo's gleaming plastic stacking chairs, in-your-face childish and disposable. Those chairs suggest what's notable about the Italian version of retrenchment, namely its lightheartedness. Although the same era produced the deadly serious Red Brigades, in the arts and the media reaching out to the disenfranchised remained a game rather than a duty.

That last juxtaposition, the terrorist cell and the happy craftsman, may provide the most revealing and sobering image out of the entire event. An energetic expansion of the museum mission—and as such a great success—the exhibit also couldn't help pointing up the ongoing crisis in its source country. During the show yet another Italian government collapsed, one that had been elected on the promise of ending the previous half-century of corrupt and inefficient administration.[3] As breathtaking and influential as the country's creative

---

3. This was the first administration of Silvio Berlusconi, 1994–95. Twenty years later, many Italians still consider him a force for honest and responsible government.

minds continue to be, they seem to make their way as much in spite of their homeland as because of it. At the Guggenheim, the least interesting room covered architecture; even the wall-text there, while noting figures like Mario Rodolfi and Carlo Mollino, spoke of a "general sense of failure." And it's a telling failure. Architecture more than any other medium depends on civic cohesion, on a community commitment that exists in some better form than extremist cabals. From Turin to Naples, however, the postwar artist seems to thrive on such cabals. Or he works entirely solo, fiddling on ancient instruments or new while his city burns. One hopes that this won't prove another of the international models to emerge from the protean bedazzlements of the Italian Metamorphosis.

—*millennium pop*, 1995

DINOSAUR IN THE TRAIN STATION: FOUR YEARS INTO THE SOPRANOS PHENOMENON

As the fourth season of *The Sopranos* unfolded,[1] a deflating question loomed for anyone who loved the show and felt moved to respond. A question that cut a critic down to size as swiftly as a baleful glare from the Jersey mob boss himself.

What's left to say?

What, really? By now a bookstore browser can find easily a dozen titles having to do with the HBO series. Psychologists (*On the Couch with Tony Soprano*), theologians (*The Gospel According to Tony Soprano*), and academics of every ism (*This Thing of Ours*, on Columbia University Press) have all by now taken their cracks at this "Mafia show," the brainchild of a tele-savvy writer-director named David Chase. And does anyone still need to know that Chase's immigrant grandparents changed their name from DeCesare?

For an Italian American especially, the gladrags in which *The Sopranos* was once arrayed have faded. Even with the comparisons to Scorsese and Fassbinder, even with having won every Emmy in sight (except Best Show, an inexcusable slight), during the first hours of Four, Chase's television *noir* could feel as if it had lost its fine onyx glitter. The work started to seem familiar—as did the response.

---

1. The show continued for another season and a half, to be sure, but coming episodes didn't alter the qualities sketched here, or the social context. I've let the essay stand.

Onscreen, the season began with another sparring match across the breakfast counters and the sunken den, James Gandolfino as Tony vs. Edie Falco as Carmela; their marriage appeared, as ever, both a prickling of forked tongues and a commingling of wounded hearts. Yet even as this exquisite *pas de deux* unfolded, out in the larger world we witnessed another lumbering stomp of protest from some group connected with the Italian-American community. Their complaint remains the same: namely that the show perpetuates an ethnic stereotype, the gangster whose name ends in a vowel. The Italic Studies Institute has likened Tony Soprano to Stepin Fetchit. The chair of the National Italian American Foundation, Frank Guarini, has asserted that his "goal is to get *The Sopranos* off the air." And this fall, before the Columbus Day celebration in New York, the Coalition of Italo-American Associations (headed by the arch anti-Chase, William Fugazy) objected vociferously when Mayor Bloomberg invited two of the show's principals to join the parade.

By now, my Neapolitan relatives would treat such matters with a sigh: *Cos'è queste scenate?* What are these wild scenes? On the one hand *The Sopranos* makes critics dig for their rarest superlatives, while on the other a second gaggle of professionals—themselves well-meaning and educated—cry for the video equivalent of a book burning. We sigh; this radicalizing has become routine.

Early on in the current season, the controversy was recast as *opera buffa*, in an episode that relied less on the thrill of violence and more on the pleasure of laughter. Tony's henchmen, incensed by a Native American protest against their local Columbus Day march, mounted a blundering protest of their own. The episode's final scene was a riotous colloquy on the "whining and crying" among American minorities, including theirs, between the *capo* and his second-in-command, Silvio Dante. Silvio of course is played by the Bruce Springsteen guitarist Steve Van Zandt, something else nobody needs to know. But I must take a moment here for the diabolic beauty of Silvio's principal expression, a depressive glower. As Silvio starts to think his lower lip juts like the lead-weight embodiment of cogitation, pulling his eyes, his entire head, down and forward. This expression has deepened over the seasons, so that now the man seems congenitally incapable of an honest smile (an impression made more rich and strange still if we recall his ecstatic mugging in many a rock video)—and of course Van Zandt/Silvio fell back into this same meta-frowning at the end of this Columbus Day episode, while he and his current Boss tried to talk. Their give and take became itself a fascinating microcosm of the failure to accept one's own place and that of others in American society, a failure Tony was failing to communicate, even to his No. 2. God help the *capo* who must rely on such a *consigliere!* The scene cut to the closing credits at the moment of greatest possible zing, accompanied by a likewise perfect choice of soundtrack, Frankie Valli and the Four Seasons. Not only had Silvio and his boss just been speaking of Valli, not only had Valli begun to show up in the series as a rival mobster, but also the opening lyric of "Dawn (Go Away)" registered with greater significance than its Brill-Building composers had ever dreamed: *Girr-ll, we can't change the places where we-e-e were born…*

Funzione, is what I'm saying. It works, still, Chase's black-hearted, bright-minded creation. As this latest season developed I enjoyed renewed admiration for what his "crew" has brought off, the many arguments pursued—most disturbingly, the coziness between apparent pro-bono politics and the criminal world's unrelenting search for yet another way to score some easy money. And always, these arguments mounted to fine ironic shocks. First a murder-for-hire was called off even as the gunman and his victim met in a Miami elevator, and then a couple of episodes later the very man who'd dodged a bullet down south suffered an end more vicious and irrational up in Jersey.

Week after week, I experienced a nodding eagerness for Sunday evening. The show works, still, and even after the many critiques in various media there remains a word or two to say about why. I see three elements that need some thumping, some praise, and some explication, and in each case I'll try to express the point provocatively, boldly.

Get pretty and get whacked. With this line, I don't mean simply to applaud the show's frankness in its treatment of mob women—creatures of pure skin, most of them, no better than sex toys. That frankness deserves to be commended, surely; Chase even went so far, in a much-discussed episode from Season Three, as to screen the beating death of a young stripper with Silvio's Bada Bing Club. The girl's murderer got off with no more than a slapping around from the boss, and such brutal sexism should be understood as a ruling theme of Three, during which this lowborn Italian variety of *droit de seigneur* damaged even Tony's daughter, Meadow. In the season's closing moments, the last we see of this hyper-aware Columbia undergraduate, she's drinking way too much and staggering into traffic (while her Uncle Junior, in another stinging musical parallel, keens a Neapolitan ballad of love gone bad, "Ungrateful Heart").

Happily, during Season Four Meadow rebounded, and the thug who killed the Bada Bing girl learned, at Tony's hands, that what goes around comes around. My point however has nothing to do with just desserts. Rather I'm talking about just depiction: the show's frankness in all things, the sturdiness of its social realism. *The Sopranos* offers a dramatic mimesis as true to money-driven and family-saddened American dynamics as the Arthur Miller at his homeiest; an episode or two have even suggested a comic *View from a Bridge*. The show's accomplishment must be considered from within this tradition, that of the kitchen sink and the right-on colloquialism.

Of course, what sets the publishers pumping out cookbooks and anthologies is that Chase & Co. have carved their new benchmark in this old aesthetic via a pop medium. They've done it while reaching tens of millions of viewers. Indeed, the working method has been the classic one for American TV, namely, freewheeling collaboration. Scripts are hashed over in committee, scenes have been reshot at the last moment, and a single season may see as many as eleven different directors.

But Chase's expertise around the workshop (his c.v. includes a number of strong but network-neutered shows, among them *The Rockford Files*) shouldn't distract us from the essence of his gift. He's an empiricist, a Lasik surgeon helping us see more clearly. And the corollary holds true: whenever *The Sopranos* has tried something too cute, too pretty, it's caused a problem. The least satisfying sequence of episodes was the second, the season that climaxed with Tony's murder of Big Pussy, his old friend turned FBI informant. The relative weakness of Two had to do with its indulgence of narrative discontinuity and pop-referential trickery, stuff more characteristic of a pomo anti-story.

In the final episode of that season, the chief's recognition of Pussy's betrayal comes via a sequence of fever-dreams, laced with references to the *Godfather* movies; what's more, the dream-sickness was brought on by a lesser treachery, namely, the tainted mussels served him (without FBI collusion) by another old pal who runs a restaurant. The parallels are clever, but the whole effect's not nearly so pointed and right as the season's previous climax, when Tony's termagant sister Janice blows away her mobster fiancé. Janice's murderous impulse erupts mere minutes after she sat gushing happily over the coming marriage, and the feed lines to her sudden rage tap the core of her and Tony's family tragedy. Rubbing out Pussy, by contrast, felt imposed. The social realist's demand for reliable evidence was sacrificed to the circus-master's dream of a socko finish. [2]

This is what *This Thing of Ours*, the collection of academic essays on Columbia UP (to use proper MLA format), gets wrong: the

---

2. Complaints about the dream sequences were such a staple of *Sopranos* criticism that Chase appeared to take this as a challenge. The last season and a half featured several such sequences, one lasting most of the hour. These were great, actually—TV's richest dream material ever. But, as drama, they remained a problem.

key clan loyalty, among Chase and his crew, is to an old made man like Emile Zola. *Naturalisme* rules, not any more recent French craze involving intertextuality or Lacanian mirrors. I freely acknowledge that the compromises of this "waste management consultant" do indeed constitute a running commentary on late capitalism, and that our protagonist forever recomposes himself before the delusional language-based mirrors of "subjectivity." But by and large the contributors to *This Thing* overlook a core issue. Worthwhile contemporary realism like Chase's will inevitably embody the better insights of recent theorists—but such insights should never be understood as more than the tasty seeds sprinkled on the crust of substantial dramatic bread. To detail the show's implications for "female narrative authority," or for the "cultural geography" of North Jersey, reveals more about the viewer than about the show's intrinsic power. Should Chase himself ever put theory before catharsis, should he ever get too cute...whack!

Gary Cooper was gay? My second praise-point derives from the first, since the show's realism entails a free-range tunneling, like Marx's old mole, through a multiplicity of economic strata and cultural environments. The sweeping social canvas of *The Sopranos*, however, reveals a more scarifying panorama, in which one travels to the heart of darkness in a minivan, then houses it off the cul-de-sac—and keeps the dangerous organ alive via an abuse of the very thing intended to reduce its evildoing, namely, psychotherapy in all its forms.

In the recent Columbus Day episode, during the closing give and take between himself and Silvio, Tony tries to make a point by referring to Gary Cooper. As part of his Jeremiad against contemporary American sniveling, against so many constituencies crying victimhood, he asks what's happened to "the strong, silent type." If Gary Cooper were alive today, Tony says, "he'd be a member of some group, the...abused cowboys, the gays, whatever the fuck."

At which point the *capo* gets interrupted from the back of the car: "He was gay, Gary Cooper?"

It's a fine comic moment, all the nuttier because neither the hood's drunken question nor Tony's furious response alleviates Silvio's grave numbskull pouting. But it doesn't change what originally set the boss off, either. Tony's angry tonight because it's precisely this sort of thinking—the notion that his ethnic group never gets a fair shake—which has been manipulated against him. He's just found out that another shady wheeler-dealer has taken advantage of this vulnerability in the Soprano crew and used it to wangle a costly favor.

Every Sunday evening, some similar venal manipulation corrupts the very instruments that our comfortable countrymen use to develop better control over their personal demons, to become more fulfilled in spirit, and even to grow more just as a society. Therapy in all its forms, from the talking cure to the public demonstration (both, after all, means for seeking wholeness and redress), proves only another means of avoidance, denial—or worse. More often than not, the men and women of *The Sopranos* use the tools of therapy to better extort and exploit. Through most of Season Three, Tony grew in his skill as a mob leader thanks to his reading of Sun-Tzu's *Art of War*, a text recommended by his therapist, Jennifer Melfi (Lorraine Bracco, another of the show's standouts, all the more impressive for how the role requires she hold back). As the current season came to climax, Tony and his own *capo,* Carmine, almost found themselves maneuvered into a bloody showdown by a greedy second-tier hood, a man who tried to take advantage of both bosses' ill-developed impulse control, their anti-social personalities.

The show's cynicism about psychotherapy underscores its benchmark status, since in almost all so-called "psychological drama" before this, characters have achieved some breakthrough or other in fifty minutes tops. As Chase said in an interview for the *New York Times* as this season was starting, "my problem with a lot of what I see [is]...

people communicate perfectly...everyone is saying exactly what they feel." His series, to the contrary, constitutes a running challenge to the notion that people can ever send and receive unmixed messages, even after years of couch-work.

What's more, the attack on the promises of analysis darkens further the view of America. Despite the eager references to the *Godfather* movies among the denizens of Chase's underworld, their homeground bears little resemblance to the operatic realm of Francis Ford Coppola. The Soprano crew dwells rather in the *mondo cane* of Scorsese's *Goodfellas*, a drama all about the limits of mob lives, about a stunted social circle based on a threadbare outlaw code. Within the circle, anybody can "flip" and turn informant, even an old sweetheart known as Pussy. And for those outside the cabal, the Mafia remains a natural predator, a phenomenon of the disenfranchised working class, in which men with few options extort everything they can from those with still fewer.

Throughout Seasons Three and Four, Tony's fortunes have risen. He's bought a racehorse and put an assemblyman in his pocket, yet any number of scenes have emphasized that it's others in his life, including Meadow and A.J., who rub shoulders with the truly wealthy and powerful. Tony may object, with more than a hint of violence, to his daughter having a mixed-race lover—but this boy has the clout of a Hollywood lawyer father behind him. The "butterhead" gets the girl, and later drops her, without consequences. A young woman's assertion of her identity outside of family is only another aspect of psychology of which to take advantage.

In our country the Shrink now seems as fallen a figure as the Don, which may explain why *The Sopranos* first appeared at the same time as the Billy Crystal comedy *Analyze This*. On the small screen, Dr. Melfi at first seemed like an exemplar of success within the system, a foil to Tony's self-definition as an outcast. Yet over the course of the therapy we've seen several instances of integrity in her patient beyond anything in the therapist's own "ego structure." The principal storyline of Season One had to do with the failure of analysis when confronted by Tony's mother, Livia, an embittered first-generation immigrant who eventually provoked an assassination attempt on her son. The doctor's failure bore out the enduring pain of the uprooted life, and so in its own ghastly way invested Tony's cynicism with... well, the mob word "honor" seems appropriate.

Compounding this irony, the ex-husband of Tony's therapist is a spokesman against Italian-American defamation. During an episode of Season One, the former Mr. Melfi leads his broken family in a Thanksgiving toast "to the twenty million"—the vast majority of Italian immigrants who had nothing to do with the Mafia. It's a moving scene, and *The Sopranos* takes pains to show how the implications reach beyond this particular ethnicity. Tony must contend with a Rainbow Coalition of illegal activity. Hasidic Jews pose one kind of problem, Russians another, and then there's the African-American rap star who styles himself a "gangster." To Tony, hyphenated Americans are locked in perpetual unhappy striving, with no holds barred even in later generations, and no one ever rises above their worst weakness. Tony's police informant remains nothing but "a degenerate gambler;" his priest "'sgotta be a fruit." His own Thanksgiving must be for the natural-born wit and the store-bought firepower that allows him to turn other people's natures against them. His fellowship is cold-war style: a mutually assured destruction.

Insofar as *The Sopranos* works against psychology, the most pointed expression of its admonition comes via Tony's marriage. Carmela Soprano might be seen as the capper on that series of housebound but powerful TV women begun by Lucille Ball, but of course her permutation of the role offers a complexity like nothing before it. If Tony has ever for a moment freed himself from his gun-happy hall of mirrors, from his resident-alien unease, it's been via the long relationship with Carmela. But of course marriage American-style has its ambiguities too. The series has often presented the household as a mere accommodation for the sake of gain, especially this season, when Carmela mooned after Tony's Neapolitan henchman Furio and looted her husband's cash reserves.

Nonetheless, she and Tony lasted longer as a couple than his therapist and her ex—until the last episode of Season Four. This year *The Sopranos* once again proved its mettle by following through on the season's mounting marital discord with a hitherto-unthinkable breakup. In a drama predicated on lives outside convention, to uproot its one anchor in societal norms had a shattering affect (and its leads rose to the occasion, working up fresh embodiments of pain and anger from their established patterns for these roles). The scenes played like the ultimate assertion of a selfhood beyond the reach of head-doctors. When the heartbroken Meadow suggested "more counseling," also setting a suspense hook for next season, it sounded like a straw offered a drowning man.

Without the Mafia, there is no Italian-American story. No wonder the show makes people nervous. It presents its nightmare of anti-assimilation via full-access realism, turning its own doctor's assurances that "this is America" to empty palaver. And it delivers this message not in some hectoring documentary on a public-access channel, but rather with a humor and humanity that pull in more viewers each season. That said, as the son of an Italian—one of the 20 million who never had dealings with the mob—I want to return to the issue of my immigrant group. Not that it would ever occur to me to take Tony for a model of "my people;" I would argue that any viewer with half a brain understands that this crew chief is to most Americans of my descent as his mumbled Neapolitan obscenities are to the actual language of Dante and Leopardi. Yet insofar as *The Sopranos* can be called any one group's accomplishment, it's an Italian-American accomplishment (indeed, the tumultuous atmosphere in which Chase and company have worked recalls nothing so much as Rome's Cinecittà during the heyday of Fellini). And though Chase himself has spent his working life securely in the mainstream, nonetheless when he had the opportunity to do something on his own, he turned to the Mafia.

Hence my final point, which isn't so much about the show, its craft and vision, as about the artist. Again I put the point boldly: Without the Mafia, there is no Italian-American story.

Chase's essential dilemma is that, like Stephen Dedalus, like the best artists in any medium, he wishes to forge the conscience of his race. Thus he cannot avoid what it has always meant to create a moving and honest portrayal of a world; he cannot work without addressing the misfits and pariahs. Jennifer Melfi's story, though it has its triumphs and failures, would be that of any determined professional of any ethnicity. The same can be said for the membership of the National Italian American Foundation, surely. But an artist who looks beyond the individual to larger shaping forces must go where comfortable assumptions give way. To choose just one recent correlative case, consider the novels of Toni Morrison. In the best of this minority American's work, in *Sula* especially, communities of color set their own mainstream, oppressed by the larger society, against their own still-more-isolated pariahs.

In a nation composed of transplants, a place Ishmael Reed calls "MultiAmerica," it's the failed graftings that must be understood. Such failures have often been transformed into bad art, as in TV's *The Untouchables*, with its parade of cartoon Mafiosi. But a logical corollary to Chase's skepticism about therapy, its way of reducing all aberrant behavior to the same core issues, is that artistic vitality requires that page, canvas, or screen make space for what's worst about a culture. The refusal to recognize that vitality in *The Sopranos*, and its significance to any Multi-American, is the true disservice done by the complaints against the show. Conversely, it's the willingness to see a place in the arts for the hoodlum and monster—and thereby a place in our own self-definition—which distinguishes the only worthwhile book among the recent outpouring on the HBO series, Regina Bar-reca's anthology *A Sitdown with the Sopranos*.

Barecca, as her name might lead you to expect, has put together a collection of Italian-American responses to the show. The best-known of her contributors is Jay Parini, a man of letters who gives the lie to any thuggish stereotype, and yet he swiftly admits: "I marvel at the richness of the whole." Parini's "The Cultural Work of *The Sopranos*" is no mere *feuilleton*, it works toward unhappy conclusions about violence and American manhood, but it's suffused with admiration. Overall Barecca's anthology shares that feeling, as its writers never fail to acknowledge the characters' occasional incidence of honest warmth and supportiveness, and every contributor shares the rueful-yet-mature knowledge that Little Caesar and the Don are a now inescapable figures of the Italian-American cultural landscape. Everyone has reached, to use the therapist's word, acceptance. As Michael Flamini puts it in his essay, "Pa Cent'Anni, Dr. Melfi:"

> One cannot truly understand Italian American culture without understanding the Mafia. One need not embrace its legacy of crime and violence, but one must face it, understand it, and incorporate it into the view we hold of our community.

Si, fratello mio. Yes, my brother—though I can't help but note the irony in the stable and integrated personality implied by that passage, given the way this drama relentlessly dumps all its characters, if not our entire psychology-happy nation, off the couch. I believe the final point has more resonance if expressed as Chase would put it, in a story. For this I choose a very different sort of story, not at all realistic, a marvelous extended parable by the Italian genius Italo Calvino.

Calvino's 1965 book *Cosmicomics* presents a series of linked stories about the beginning of the world, and one considers the last surviving dinosaur. This former predator must now dissemble in order to keep from becoming prey himself. He must pretend to be one of the new ruling species, in the new world he's come to, and over time his deception succeeds. Meanwhile, though, the Dinosaur comes to realize that those around him remain terrified of the creature he once was, a corollary to his own terror of them, and so he sees the paradox of his adopted life: that in "the labyrinth of...thoughts," the monster still holds sway. His hoofs and horns have been internalized, as part of the natural order. At story's end, the Dinosaur arrives at a train station and is "lost in the crowd"—somewhere, no doubt, between Jennifer Melfi and Tony Soprano.

—*North American Review*, 2003

'HOOD MEETS WORLD:
W.S. DI PIERO & THE "SOUTH PHILLY" SEQUENCES

It's not as if, in his work before 2001, the sensual yet deeply meditative poet and essayist W.S. DiPiero had never written about South Philly. After all, by the turn of the current millennium this Stanford professor and contributing editor with *Threepenny Review* had six books of poetry and three collections of criticism and personal essays, in addition to award-winning translations from Italian and ancient Greek. Certainly the early poems of *The Only Dangerous Thing* (1984) addressed cultural transplantation, the immigrant agony of his parents' generation. More pertinently, in *Shooting the Works*, his 1996 collection of essays, reviews, and journal entries, there appear two *ars poetica* pieces, "Pocketbook and Sauerkraut" and "Gots Is What You Got," essays which locate determining factors for his art in the streets and the kitchens where he was raised.

Di Piero is a war child, born in 1945, and in "Pocketbook..." he relates how he grew up by Watkins and 21st, where the Italian American working poor of Philadelphia were separated by a single block from African Americans no better off. Swiftly the essay gets into the tensions of that juxtaposition, classic tensions for urban America in the middle of the previous century:

> The black working people...though physically closer to us
> than any other group, in language...were demonized and

made the most remote and adversarial. Ethnic and racial tags made up our richest vocabulary.

As for "Gots Is What You Got," the title derives from roughly the same vocabulary, an Italian obscenity garbled by the American-born generation; a fitting translation would be "you got dick." In this essay, Di Piero confesses that the interior language on which he draws for poetry "never did shed [its] tribal legacy of contrariness…festive abrasiveness and chafing hilarity."

But in the years since that essay, that legacy has served this author better still. Two of Di Piero's recent collections, *Skirts and Slacks* (2001) and *Brother Fire* (2005), both have major sequences set in South Philly. In 2007, too, the poet's sumptuous career retrospective, *Chinese Apples*, includes nearly all these poems. In the *Selected*, however, these sequences lack the structural balance of their original publication. In *Skirts* and *Brother*, they're bookends: the opening third of the earlier book and the closing third of the later one. Together, in any case, these sequences notch a new benchmark for the poetry of ethnic, urban America. This essay will first comment on these poems generally, their linked subject matter and their manifold excellences, and afterward I'll detail one telling resource for them, namely, the way their "tribal contrariness" depends on a more or less African American Other. If Di Piero has broken through to a new level of power, in what could've been a mere sentimental journey, part of the reason is the close presence of something shadowy, carnal, and violent, looming close enough to make every epiphany more nervous and humane. This presence is often expressed via signifiers for African American city culture, skillfully explored in the poet's language and imagery, as a source of strength. When he works in what we might call ghetto slang, colloquialisms associated with urban African America, he accords it the respect of careful placement, at key junctures.

Overall, in these two sequences, the poet returns to his home ground with a vengeance, and that last word is no figure of speech. Both style and material call to mind Edmund Wilson's "incurable wound," eternally bleeding. The opener in *Skirts and Slacks* ("Philly Babylon," the first half of "Cheap Gold Flats") visits his mother's deathbed and, though it concludes with the words "forgive me," pulls off a half-drunken skewing of the expression. Then toward the end of *Brother Fire* the poet recalls saying his Hail Marys down on his knees beside that mother, as she stood ironing in their rowhouse basement; lines alternate between frustration over a "deity of hurt and rue" and sympathy for a parent who, he comes to feel, is as humble as he ("Prayer Meeting").

Di Piero fits this self-exposure into flexible form. Line-length serves as a defining factor for each piece, but runs shorter in one, longer in another. The poet mixes his pacing only in the longest poems, for instance during his attempt to revisit the local library in "The Apples" (in *Skirts*), and here the staggered lengths suit the poet's rediscovery of our transitory nature. City budget cuts have hacked away at the timeless dimension of words, and the library entrance is blocked by a cawing baglady.

While that poem's intimations of mortality emerge in stanzas of nine lines, a number of powerful pieces present a single unbroken utterance, like "Ortlieb's Uptown Taproom" (in *Fire*). A page-long meditation, "Ortlieb's" pits a brewery worker's routine against a carefree Beyond; the roadhouse band lifts the worker into recollections of Christmas-morning bagpipes back in his Italian home village. Other South-Philly meditations take shape in stanzas of three, four, or five lines, and stresses fall now three per line, now four. Both "'Philly Babylon'" and "Prayer Meeting" offer a jazzy American variation on blank verse.

This formal concern, insisting on coherence within individual pieces while allowing freedom across the sequence, contributes significantly to Di Piero's suppression of cliché. A heated emotional honesty informs both recollections of the old neighborhood and descriptions of what it's like to return. But the impact of the South Philly poems depends primarily, of course, on language. Here Di Piero's technique rises to tour-de-force levels, while never lacking for the common touch; this paradox depends especially upon his artful use of active verbs. Indeed, the essay "Gots Is What You Got" makes special mention of verbs, when dissecting what he picked up from the talk across the stoops and countertops of his childhood: "Tenses mix," he writes, "coalesce, bang, and sag."

And in a piece from *Skirts* that I'll consider more closely in a minute, "Leaving Bartram's Garden in Southwest Philadelphia," the poet first notes how "new-style trolleys squeak down Woodland," they ride on tires now rather than rails, and a few lines later he recalls what he glimpsed at one of the windows in the home of the Quaker botanist: "A redbird gashed the sunned mullioned glass." Then toward the poem's end, as his trolley moves through the dicey neighborhood close to the park, he doesn't miss how "[t]he brownbrick project softens in the sun," and "[t]agger signatures surf red and black / across the wall." Di Piero's craft likewise trolleys; it sways and rumbles, the better to illuminate "whatever is authentic," as he argues in "Gots," and the authentic itself dwells in a "commingling of abstract… formal beauty with the given language textures… of my culture." When that commingling comes off, cultural referents from Dante to disco all seem entirely apropos to a troubled ethnic enclave perceived with both a gimlet-eyed irony and, as in "Bartram's Garden," newly forged awe at the oneness that embraces plant life, bird life, public transporation, and the art of the streets. As Philip Levine put it in a review for *Ploughshares*, Di Piero revels in "the texture of American cities."

That last referent I mentioned—the art of the streets—means that this "Garden" ends in the ghetto. Transcendent connectedness here arrives prompted by homeboys, perhaps gangbangers:

Tagger signatures surf red and black
across the wall, fearless, dense lines
that conch and muscle so intimately
I can't tell one name from the other.

A poem that begins in a home that dates from slave times (though
Quakers like Bartram, not coincidentally, were opposed to slavery)
concludes with a distinctively cross-cultural, cross-racial re-imaging
of the bird at the old hand-set window (with one more flourish of
verbs, "conch and muscle"). The feeling also receives a stray borrowed
assertion, in italics, perhaps a glimpse of an ad outside the trolley
windows: "*I'm in the weave.*" At climax, however, this happy notion
is embodied in the work of quasi-criminal urban youth. Need we
even say youth of color? In most media, to be sure, the image of such
young people is distorted into something thuggish and primitive. A
talent like Di Piero however—at full late-career command—inverts
this signifier for the Other so that it expresses a concept quite the opposite, namely, the Universal.

The device, to be sure, performs a traditional function of poetry,
locating the intangible in the down to earth. But when the poet and
his grown siblings converse across their mother's corpse in "Finished
Basement," the latter half of "Cheap Gold Flats," poetry's function
is allied with that of rhythm and blues. The piece ends with Mom's
presence made eerily tangible, fingering the poet's neck, but at the
beginning a very different sensation emerged from the walls behind
him: "Disco tracks / jump inside the paneling." A few lines further
on, when the poem turns more directly to the deceased, it first sharply summarizes the children's conversation with two words: "Yackety-
yak." A song by the Coasters, a crossover hit, takes our narrator from
chattering denial to a chill sensation of the Unknowable.

The first piece in the *Brother Fire* sequence, "Ortlieb's," also depends on black-music signifiers. Tonight the taproom features a sax
player in a Hawaiian shirt and "porkpie," the onstage gear of Charles

Mingus and many another jazzman. When the immigrant laborer who enjoyed the show later recalls the bagpipes of his mountain home, he hears their "goatskin bags call like animals," dark and atavistic, "like our flamingo sax, in his ecstasy tonight." One could say that this piece expounds on a folk-cultural manifestation of the genetic link between Africa and Southern Italy; in the "Gots" essay, we learn that Di Piero's mother came from Naples and his father from the Abruzzo. But then again, like any poem, this one has more to do with ecstasy than with sociology.

"Prayer Meeting," later in *Fire*, seems to eschew signifiers of black urban America—until one looks again at the very title and subject. An overworked mother and her child call on their Lord, together, aloud, one knocked to his knees by the Spirit and both half-mumbling, half-singing as "God jerked alive / in repetitions." As Di Piero evokes the setting at the poem's close, it can't help but recall the furnishings in any neighborhood of outsiders and menials; mother and son pray under "splintered rafters weeping / wan work dungarees...."

Another piece in the second book, "Lightning Bugs," constructs a metaphor that's hardly original; the easily trapped insects stand for our inextinguishable desires (desire imbues all *Brother Fire*; the book adapts this larger metaphor from a canticle of St. Francis). What saves the poem from sounding hackneyed, then, if not the sharp voice of what sounds an awful lot like an African American mom, calling down the block at twilight? *"Jo-Jo, / where you? Time to eat."* At the end, bug and poet come together as a lurking B-&-E man, as he imagines the creature "a sensor house-light's / weegee when I pass..."

The last poem in *Fire*, the last in both Philadelphia sequences, presents a portrait of the artist as a young Civil Rights sympathizer. "The Kiss," which appeared in the *New Yorker*, recalls a preadolescent visit to Father Feeney. The priest calls the boy "my dear" and awards him a kiss, on the cheek but nevertheless uncalled for, while at the same time briskly disabusing his young charge of his desire to join the clergy. Thereafter, amid the subway's "Golgotha air of piss and smoke"—the adult poet, clearly, still wonders about the Father's steaming crotch—the youngster sees in the evening papers "black people / hosed down by cops or stretched by dogs," and at once he asks himself again the question asked some minutes before by his priest: "What was I running from?" So the fearsome shadow-self is suggested by the Father but witnessed, this night, in pictures of the people who Di Piero's neighbors demonized, and this carries the poet to his true calling, here as in an earlier poem made manifest on the surfaces of the city:

> ...I believed the wall's
> filthy cracks, coming into focus
> when we stopped, held stories I'd find
> and tell.

Like Dedalus before him, the Di Piero of the South-Philly sequences has heard God in a shout in the street. This shout may take visual form, like a tagger's scrawl or, in the first stanza of "The Kiss," "summer hammerheads / whomping fireplugs." Nonetheless it's an outcry from the inner city, the black inner city. The loss of his parents may have gotten him into these poems, these visions, but in a number of cases, what gives them meaning and power comes from the people his parents warned him against.

—Presented at MLA Convention, Philadelphia, 2004
—Essays on Italian American Literature & Culture, 2010

COMING TIDE

A SLASHER SEEKING RESPECT: BRIAN EVENSON & THE OPEN CURTAIN

Publishing these days can seem like a twelve-step meeting, everyone sharing their pain. But I doubt there's a memoir that's revealed something so twisted as the following—the more so for being part of a wedding ceremony:

> They moved from signs and tokens to the penalties—promises that one would never reveal the signs and tokens, even at the peril of one's own life. If you were put in a position where you were forced to reveal the signs, you were apparently supposed to kill yourself. [The bride] was made to draw her hand across her throat as if it were a knife. She was made to pull her hand across her chest and then let both hands fall, as if she had opened her chest to let blood spill down her ribs. Later still, the back of her thumb traveled symbolically from one hip to another, slitting open her loins.

A wedding! And later the groom goes behind a curtain, where he assumes "the role of God." He reaches through iconic slits in the veil to imbue his bride with righteousness; only then can she can open the curtain.

The passage would seem to describe the rites of some Stone-Age tribe, but the setting is Utah and the time the middle 1960s. The rituals are those of the Latter-day Saints, and though the passage comes from a novel, the author assures us the details are accurate. Brian Evenson goes so far as to invite a search of the internet to check his facts in his "Afterword" to *The Open Curtain*. Not that Evenson has left behind the horrific imagination on display in his six previous books of fiction. His short stories, especially in *The Wavering Knife*, establish him as a worthy heir to Poe. He's got the braininess of Poe, too, with epigraphs from thinkers like Gilles Deleuze and a canny ambiguity about surfaces—is this a picture of a corpse, or a corpse itself? Yet some of his most chilling dramas call to mind Raymond Carver, of all people, in that they keep their bloody dementia in a lunch pail or a kitchen drawer. *Open Curtain*, his first full-length novel, has most of the same gruesome elements, in particular damage done by knives. Call it a slasher story seeking a higher purpose. I'm not sure the book achieves that purpose more than intermittently, but regarding the rituals of the temple, I'm utterly convinced.

Evenson was raised a Mormon and served in his community clergy. In time however he struggled with the faith, losing his job at Brigham Young after conservatives attacked his first book, the '94 story collection *Altmann's Tongue*. In 2000, at his own insistence, he was excommunicated. Yet a restless Mormon spirit rattles its chains behind the torture and blood-letting that occupy his imagination. As Ben Ehrenreich put it in *The Believer*, Evenson develops "violence shorn of all context…that might render it meaningful." For comparable dissociative slaughter you might look to Robbe-Grillet (indeed, Evenson holds a doctorate in critical theory)—but before an ego can dissociate, it must first be connected. Consider De Sade, driven to excess by a break with Catholicism.

De Sade's Justine, however, seeks bliss, and that's a phenomenon foreign to Evenson. He rubs his wounds with alkali. His narratives inhabit a sparse and arid landscape in which motivation is a mirage; when a man kicks a pregnant woman bloody (in the haunting *Dark Property*, '05), it's not all about Mormonism. But in the new novel, the faith is central as that wedding curtain. As the afterword puts it, the book addresses "the relationship of Mormon culture to violence." Thus the new narrative is grounded in a recognizable Provo and environs. There are Vespa scooters and adults who use the word "denial" to define a psychological state.

Rudd Theurer never becomes an adult, he's nineteen at novel's end, but he could be an expert on denial. If Rudd is the slasher here, if he's committed or plans to commit some horrendous bloodletting, the facts must be patched together from what shows around his mental lacuna. His perspective, that is, provides an iffy surface for a novel, and Evenson asks us to walk out a long way on it. The sole alternative to the pervading sense of illusion is classic I-hate-high-school stuff. Rudd doesn't get along with his mom, either. The father was more interesting, a suicide, but what little we learn of him comes from others.

So the boy reaches out to another teenager, Lyle or Lael. The Bible-haunted protagonist prefers the latter, especially since L. could be Rudd's illegitimate half-brother. Rudd's mother of course has nothing to say and Lael is equally laconic, as is *his* un-partnered mom. Nonetheless the boys take scooter rides together and veer quickly into trouble. The brother-surrogate has a violent streak, further inflamed when—as if imagined into being—he shows up beside Rudd to do research for a paper about a turn-of-the-century murder. The case may involve Mormon "blood sacrifice," a gruesome means for cleansing the soul.

But then, it was Rudd's paper. Is he the one drawn to grue? And which of these boys insisted on digging up the father's corpse just to see the gash across his throat?

The worst that Rudd and Lael get up to may be something else, may be horrendous indeed, but this too is reported indirectly. The news reaches us via the second piece of damaged goods here, a character with one name only, Lyndi. The amputation seems appropriate for the surviving member of a slaughtered family (and Rudd's last name gets likewise mangled, whenever his identity shifts). Lyndi has a few months on the main character in age and a few degrees of greater sanity. But with all other intimate connections severed at one blow, she's drawn to the boy as soon as she spies him in the hospital, the comatose survivor of the holocaust that took her family—though again his story seems dubious.

The "love affair" that follows may be a waltz of the lame and halt, but it's got more heart than anything else in the novel. It's a convincing character drama, a breakthrough for a writer who has traded primarily in shock and smarts. But such drama requires that its participants feel like free agents, however hobbled, and by the end of the wedding ceremony these two have again become slaves. The author lays a heavy, bloody hand on his creations.

Lyndi goes through the open curtain into "what she was certain would be a disaster," and it proves to be just that, with the dead and the living commingling in a nightmare pattern. An interesting effect, granted, but it requires a lot of blackouts, some of them awfully convenient. Even Lyndi has lapses of memory, and they just don't fit her personality. In the same way, when the final pages wheel in a creaking *deus ex machina*, this robs the girl of agency—if she lives, it's only coincidence. More's the pity, the developing horror is expedited by the cliché of a do-nothing cop.

I could go on grumbling, but I don't want to slam so feverish an imagination for trying to operate in a cooler zone. I don't want to fault Evenson for the challenge he's taken on, a challenge reflected in epigraphs, this time, from the solid storytellers Truman Capote and Shirley Jackson. Evenson's language too is toned down, an American plainsong. Indeed the afterword claims that the novel is a "departure"—though not in aesthetic terms. Rather Evenson says this will be his "last Mormon-themed book," and therefore he tried to be "respectful." *Respectful*: the word worries me. A talent like this should take on realism with the same savagery as he's attacked other modes.

—*American Book Review*, 2007

"CALVINOESQUE" & "WAR-INFLECTED:" ZACHARY MASON & THE LOST BOOKS OF ODYSSEY

More than a generation has passed since Italo Calvino's *Invisible Cities* (English translation 1974) set a new literary standard for disruption, gamesmanship, and transcendence. The novel was a cat's cradle, weaving together conversation and meditation, history and high math and myth, all in a form never seen before yet coming off as naturally as "once upon a time." Fairytales indeed were one of Calvino's sources—but more fascinating is how his story-surrogate has itself become a source, these days, widely imitated among the English and Americans. "Calvinoesque" has entered our critical lexicon, crowding up behind "Kafkaesque" and "Nabokovian," meaning a highly imaginative prose work built of theme and variations rather than narrative. Examples include Carole Maso's *Aureole* ('03), a dance of eros and memory, and it's Maso who must be thanked for the latest offspring. She selected Zachary Mason's *The Lost Books of the Odyssey* as the prizewinner in the Starcherone Books contest.

But while we might recognize the form and materials of *Lost Books*, with its piecemeal configuration, its close knit of appropriations from cultures actual and made up, nonetheless we've never read another novel like it. Mason appears to have previously published nothing more than a couple of online excerpts from this same book—though research can be deceptive, since the author's indulging in a literary version of *Where's Waldo?* [1] More on that later; at first encounter what matters is the masterly balance of the interlocked mosaic he's constructed, and the miniaturist's skill he demonstrates with every piece. I've rarely come across such an assertive debut, at once a game brought off winningly and a disturbing vision beyond all fair play.

The timeless elements are those of Homer. We have a hero skilled with tongue, sword, and phallus; we have the wrath of the ocean-god Poseidon and the warrior Achilles, the loyalty of the wisdom-god Athena and the wife Penelope. Then comes the postmodern collage, enabled by a pair of splendid inventions. First this author posits the lost books themselves, composed by a sect called "the Homerids" and "known only in encrypted form," and second he imagines a recent breakthrough in "archeocryptography," working from a "mimeograph of a British Museum copy...itself an early Renaissance copy of a (most likely) Roman copy." This much is explained by Mason's Mr. Chips, in a parody introduction that goes down easy and concludes with the obvious: "mysteries remain." Among those mysteries is how recurrent topics like "Words" or "The Gods," which number eleven, can be parceled out evenly among forty-six decoded *Books* (the number of squares on a chessboard, inverted). We begin undone, informed yet ignorant.

We begin, that is, as much shaken as charmed, and it would be wrong to present this novel as purely playful. *Cities*, after all, horrifies us with the stench of the urban inferno as much as it entertains us with the strut work of the Fibonacci series. So too, throughout the *Lost Books*, the reversals and ironies raise a chill. Reversal is the theme, and I daresay this *Odyssey* comes up with more ways of eradicating identity than a ten years' war. A few of the extrapolations out of conflict and return occupy a single page, more commonly they run on for four or five, but in all of them king and usurper, monster

---

1. The game was dropped in the later, large-press edition, but it's pertinent to this piece. My original review also included more "Calvinoesque" examples.

and hero, the quick and the dead trade places. A number of times, by turning tables, an alternative Odysseus will arrive at a happy ending. But nothing here constitutes simple reassurance or the restoration of the old order.

Carole Maso, in her endorsement, describes this author's manner as "war-inflected." The praise seems apt for a book in which the first story (the clearest homage to Kafka) ends with an assassin "holding a razor flecked with…blood"—or so he claims. In the last piece (which would be the most Calvinoesque, if it didn't owe so much to Barth's *Lost in the Funhouse*), Odysseus keeps giving away his weapon and then facing another murderer. In two stories we finger the "vitreous humor" of the Cyclops' put-out eye. Others render Sisyphean hells or moments *in extremis*:

> Waterlogged, frozen, exhausted, Odysseus clung to a spar, dark waves surging over him. He could not help but think that this was happening to someone else…being consumed by the sea…

War-inflected, yes, but brought off with a luxuriant formality. In these *Books* Odysseus shuffles off his mortal coil with a certain reserve, never reticent but always correct. The tonal control helps allow for well-placed anachronisms like psychotherapy, as this hero's return becomes "a sequence of images that could…fit almost anywhere." A similar trick occurs at the end of the drowning episode, when Mason shifts into the voice of the goddess in order to refresh the cliché of our life passing before our eyes:

> Runes of ephemeral fire.…A twilight forest haunted by beasts…An onion, an ocean, a palimpsest, a staccato machine of oiled iron gears. These are among the metaphors with which I describe myself, like a hand trying to grasp itself by reaching into the mirror.

That mirror held up to nature is of course yet another metaphor, and appropriately one that goes back to a Greek. Mason's novel would be the latest to refute Aristotle, and one of the liveliest, with bright thrills that flutter amid the intertextual dapple. Then too, this author places himself in his hall of mirrors; his bio makes him out to be a composite of Nabokov's John Shade and Homer's wily voyager. A bit of research may turn up the actual Zachary Mason, a computer technician in Silicon Valley. But why bother, when ferreting out the man's ID detracts from the impact of his paradoxical monument? A mash-up very much of the moment, with one ingenious proof after another that nothing is as it seems, *Lost Books* winds up asserting the eternal value of ambiguity—one of the core reasons we keep turning language into story.

—*American Book Review*, 2008

CATHARSIS IN BEBOP: GILBERT SORRENTINO, THE FINAL NOVELS, & THE REDISCOVERY OF FEELING

Even in death, Gilbert Sorrentino goes his own way. *The Abyss of Human Illusion*, published posthumously in 2009, caps his output at twenty novels, but the math is complicated. Till cancer took him in 2006, Sorrentino never quit rejiggering what constitutes a novel. Thus his '09 title isn't some hash of the papers he left behind. *Abyss* appears with a forward by the author's son Chris (himself a novelist), in which he admits to minor emendations but insists that the work was finished, its final adjustments made by hand. The argument's persuasive, but not nearly so much as the text, which everywhere bears the old man's trademark.

This is another novel without narrative—fifty Roman-numeral'd prose shards, otherwise discontinuous, in which form rather than content generates momentum. A few pieces appeared in '07 in the magazine *Golden Handcuffs*, but in hard copy, we see that each is a bit longer than the previous. *Abyss* begins in flash-fiction and ends in three or four-page summaries of failure in various forms, something like the digressions establishing background in a conventional novel. Dream passages occur at what seem to be regular intervals, another touch of a guiding authorial hand, but even in dreams the material's drawn from the ordinary. A structure that recalls *Invisible Cities* or *If on a Winter's Night a Traveler* has none of Calvino's fantasy. A few lines of "Commentary" follow each section, and these if anything underscore the fiction's basis in the real, as in this gloss on "highball:" "In this instance, Canada Dry ginger ale and Seagram's 7 blended whiskey. The term 'highball' is no longer in general use." Everywhere, the text goes out of its way to name names. In the process, naturally, it also punctures pretension and so supplies plenty of humor, never more so than when the subject turns to art or literature. Even the two artists of genuine gifts, here, exemplify what's fraudulent about their calling. They live out the melancholy recognition implied in the book's title.

A melancholy anyone can recognize, too: that of *feelings never expressed.* Old or young, the people in this text deny what they want; ill will and discouragement accumulate till they quash the life force. All about bringing what's hidden to light, *Abyss* has no place for a bad sentence, though it weaves through diverse perspectives and rhetoric high and low: "He was no better, no cleverer, no more insightful than any shuffling old bastard in the street, absurdly bundled against the slightest breeze." Then too, Sorrentino's final quintessence sets its most moving anecdotes in his imaginative homeland of mid-twentieth-century Brooklyn. The players may transfer to Manhattan, but they never escape the beaten-down working class among whom the author was raised, and toward whom his brutal honesty is a form of empathy. He does urban realism as metafiction.

The man dedicated his career to the assault on expectation. In some cases he attacked head-on: no other serious writer generated such creative energy out of savaging the publishing industry. As early as 1971, referring to mid-Manhattan's Powers That Be in *Imaginative Qualities of Actual Things*, he sneered, "You could die laughing," and he went on dying for another thirty-five years. Nor was he reluctant to bite the other hand that fed him. Though he taught for almost twenty years at Stanford, his "Gala Cocktail Party," from *Blue Pastoral* (1983), won a Pushcart Prize for its skewering of phoniness in the Academy.

In an essay on William Carlos Williams—his enduring inspiration—Sorrentino insists, "America eats her artists alive." The culture, that is, celebrates creative spirits who produce "trash." "Writing is most admired when it is decorously resting...the more comatose, the more static a mirror image of 'reality' the better." So the great majority of his countrymen "employ language and techniques inadequate" to the times, creating drama via hand-me-down emotional signals, interactions across "a sea of manners." In John Updike, to name one of his bête noirs, catharsis was nothing but a papier mâché of chewed-up and regurgitated convention. Trash.

Such contrariness finds its most direct expression, naturally, in the essays of *Something Said*, first published 1984 (expanded and reissued 2001). Getting beyond the sham that passes for represented reality also animates his dozen books of poetry, the best perhaps *Corrosive Sublimate* (1971), as well as the stories collected in *The Moon in Its Flight* (2004). Still, when it comes to the man's novels, the work on which his reputation depends, one has to ask—well, how's *he* do catharsis?

Innovative as he was, Sorrentino never suggests that a reading experience of two hundred pages or so can depend entirely on formal qualities. He recognizes that a booklength work in a language-based art form can't help but engage the passions, and his rave review for William Gaddis's *JR* bears a title that's all about the passions: "Lost Lives." His complaint about the common run of contemporary novels lies elsewhere, in the notion that they perform an emotional charade, as dated as the Gibson girls that decorate a creaky carnival ride (to borrow a pertinent metaphor from John Barth's "Lost in a Funhouse"). All right then—what does he offer instead? Does his work construct a new apparatus for finding what hurts and making us share it?

Born in 1929, the product of immigrant Brooklyn factory workers, Sorrentino studied the literature of the English Renaissance, before and after a stint in the Army. He never took a degree, however, and he's best appreciated as an autodidact who served his New York apprenticeship amid "an incredible artistic ferment" (to quote from a 2001 article in *The Review of Contemporary Fiction*). A jazz buff and a regular at the Cedar Tavern, the hangout of the Abstract Expressionists, Sorrentino moved in circles that included, by end of the 1950s, both Williams and the other figure with whom he's most closely identified, Hubert Selby, Jr. He helped edit two cutting-edge magazines, *Neon* (where Selby was co-editor) and *Kulchur*, while paying work came with Grove Press and elsewhere. The first collection of poetry appeared in 1960, and his debut novel in '66.

The author made revisions for a new edition twenty years later, but from the first *The Sky Changes* was notable for its prose. Even a brief sample conveys its striking combinations, coarse yet subtle, extending deep sympathy yet casting a cold eye:

> They had another drink, and C told him how happy he was that his wife and P had finally decided to make it together, because he was good for the kids, and the husband agreed. So they lied warmly to each other and their friendship resumed where insanity and despair had cut it off.

Such a sample also demonstrates how *Changes* does without full names or direct quotation while also toying with chronology and Authorial intrusion. Nevertheless the novel presents a recognizable crisis, a divorce story. Then in 1970 and '71, moving at a formidable clip, the author produced *Steelwork* and *Imaginative Qualities of Actual Things*.

These establish the mode at which he excelled: the community portrait. Portraits of misery, what else? Both books, however, fillet out any trace of bathos with deft cuts of hilarity and frankness. Also helping defeat sentimentality are the disrupted time sequence and, going further than *Changes*, the absence of any central narrative.

Rather both novels achieve the equilibrium of a great bebop work-out, in which every fresh racket loops back eventually to the head. Not for nothing does *Steelwork* begin with the Charlie Parker rave-up, "KoKo," its "great blasts of foreign air" disrupting the afternoon of two young men in Brooklyn, 1945.

Brooklyn, to be sure: Sorrentino would seem autobiographical if his work weren't so discontinuous, the solos of *Steelwork* scattered across fifteen years of depression and war and amid half a hundred players. "Gibby" and others recur, occasionally, but a more fitting model than the *Bildungsroman* would be the American immigrant tragedy, the stuff of Henry Roth. Among Sorrentino's people, up by your bootstraps does nothing but expose you to worse punishment (indeed, *Steelwork* remains his most violent novel). But then *Imaginative Qualities of Actual Things* rejects even that typology, as it crosses the river to join the turn-of-the-'60s Manhattan art world. Or the world that it wishes it were—everyone's on a budget and most prove to be frauds. Here Sorrentino works with a smaller group and a central consciousness, an unnamed narrator spinning loose-limbed anecdotes. This author figure fully comprehends what a bunch of losers he's got as friends, even before they begin to betray each other. He needs only a single paragraph from an old letter to realize that one of the group, the short-story writer, Guy, has genuine talent. But the narrator sees as well that Guy's a tormented closet case, without the spine to stand up to the Brahmins of publishing. In the end, the author can transcend his context only via his text.

Both books interpolate all sorts of borrowed language. Sorrentino's natural poetic intensity opens up to allow bits of journalese, advertising, ethnic slurs, whiskey blather, and the sweet nothings of loveless sex. The shreds in the latter novel's patchwork tend to be more colorful, the combinations more gleeful, a difference implied in the titles. *Imaginative Qualities of Actual Things* comes from Williams, *Kora in Hell,* and the text also repeatedly references the poet's famed passage "[i]t is only in isolate flecks that/ something/ is given off" (from "To Elsie"). Indeed, those lines might speak for everything Sorrentino wrote, though he would touch his old mentor for a title only once more, in his penultimate work *A Strange Commonplace*.

"To Elsie" is, among other things, a miracle of empathy. The poet gives expression to a reality far more brutish than his own, and Sorrentino's assemblages from '70 and '71 share the same purpose. They forge wincing connections with their battered creatures, all the more striking when it also fetches a startled laugh. The work moves us to pity and terror, no less, *Imaginative Qualities* especially, though none of the wannabes who populate the book possess what Aristotle would call tragic stature. A signal case occurs when the omniscient storyteller struggles to make sense of Bunny, a pretty hanger-on, briefly and brainlessly married to Guy:

> It would've been better had I simply not got involved with Bunny, she's hopeless. I'll bet you a dollar that she gets a job in a publishing house assisting a hip young editor....She's one of those bright, lovely, intelligent people who should never have been born. We'll finish with her postmarital career by putting her in a Connecticut motel one December afternoon, with a gang of young, creative professionals, half-drunk. She's in the middle of a laugh, those perfect white teeth. They're all watching the Giant game. Bunny, who is now called Jo, suddenly recalls Guy's absolute contempt for football: "For morons who like pain." She looks around at her friends and hands her empty glass, smiling, to her escort. Her heart a chunk of burning metal. She will marry this man.

The scene, in narrative terms, comes out of nowhere and goes nowhere. We never again encounter these young creative morons. Yet within the fiction's abstract-expressionist whole, the moment's a climax, its agony piercing. And within the career of the author, this pair of novels presents a creative peak.

Fifteen more books followed, none much resembling what E.M. Forster would call a novel, but two or three often mentioned as Sorrentino's greatest. Chief among those would be his next big project, *Mulligan Stew* in 1979. His longest standalone work at nearly four hundred and fifty pages, the novel afforded his lone brush with wider recognition, in part because the means of publication courted controversy. The book appeared on Grove Press, where Sorrentino had been employed, and the text was prefaced by the rejections the manuscript had received elsewhere (names were changed, but thickheadedness left untouched). Reviewers, predictably, couldn't resist, and most were respectful. Almost thirty years following its publication, in a brusque *New York Times* obituary, *Mulligan Stew* was the only Sorrentino book mentioned by name. It's also the lone title that Frederick Karl examined, free of deadline pressures, in his critical omnibus *American Fictions 1940-1980*. Karl's response was mixed overall, but not when it came to the novel's madcap lists. He understood the usefulness of this device, first indulged in *Steelwork* but here exploited to the hilt: now enumerating the clutter of an old barn, now the inventory of mail-order sexual aids.

Lists provide a sort of safety valve when an iconoclast means to tell a story. In the *Stew*, Sorrentino presents a metafictional switcharoo in which the novelist Tony Lamont declines into madness while his characters attain freedom and power. A more ordinary Big Book would shape the reversal around mounting tensions and confrontations, but this one embodies the breakdown of "lonely, lonely Lamont," by and large, with lengthy rounds of parody. The lists function as part of the comedy. They free the man behind Lamont from the sort of narration he found counterfeit and embalmed, even as they send him into verbal performances not unlike those found in a conventional climax. The novel closes with just such a bang, six pages of gifts (to people never mentioned previously), tokens perhaps for Lamont's parting: "To Helena Walsh, the goatish glance of the cockeyed lecher; to Twisty Abe DeHarvarde, shimmering hose of glittering glows."

Astonishing lists, and Frederick Karl grasped their purpose, but he found other elements of the *Stew* disappointing, indeed "unimaginative." The tangle of underappreciated authors invented and actual wore him out, as did all the "fraternity-house male-female antics." Such misgivings, from our present perspective, seem right. Sorrentino isn't comfortable spending so long with just one character, and his comic games start to feel like he's drumming his fingers—especially compared to the impact of what he delivered next.

What impresses one most about *Aberration of Starlight* isn't its squib from Philip Roth, or its appearance the short list for the 1980 PEN/Faulkner Award. Rather, what stands out is its anomalous material, very nearly straightforward realism. The prose is flexible as ever, but within careful restraints; the present action occupies a single weekend in New Jersey, and the voices, both interior and spoken, are those of a few New York wage slaves at a cheap resort. It's the end of summer 1939, and a Holocaust looms for these people as well, though this gloomy little masterpiece generates suspense not with war stories but via a literary experiment. Its devastation coheres only as we work through four successive points of view. Their order has the inevitability of aging: first a boy, then his divorced mother, her Saturday-night seducer, and the boy's grandfather. The text's brief spate of pornography feels apropos, unlike in the previous novel, since the character enjoying the fantasy is a salesman on the road. As for the actual sex, it may be Sorrentino's most fully rendered, though unhappy and deluded, the participants more fragile than they'd ever admit: "She was covering herself up too, smoothing her dress. ... 'I love you,' he whispered, and they kissed again, chastely, but...[h]e wasn't complaining, hell no. A hand job from a doll who's almost a nun on the first date? Tom had no beef, kiddo."

For the author, however, what mattered proved to be the experiment. Over the next twenty years, Sorrentino's prose not only embraced radical alternatives to plot but also eschewed character tensions or other gateways to mimetic connection. Granted, he'd always flirted with such extremes. Between *Imaginative Qualities* and the *Stew*, he brought out the pamphlet-sized *Splendide-Hotel* (1973), its title drawn from Rimbaud and its form based on the alphabet. *Hotel* has a swift and satisfying zaniness, but its author took his recreation far further, throughout the 1980s and '90s. With all due respect for Robert Coover (more respectful about narrative) or Kathy Acker (more direct in her social critique), it's fair to say that, starting with *Crystal Vision* in '82, Sorrentino subverted fictional norms more thoroughly than any American of his stature. By 1997, the late philosopher-critic Louis Mackey (himself a boundary-blurring figure, with cameos in two Richard Linklater movies) could claim that Sorrentino had brought off "the ultimate postmodern novel."

In *Fact, Fiction, and Representation: Four Novels by Gilbert Sorrentino*, Mackey provides an exegesis of the '80s threesome *Odd Number, Rose Theater*, and *Misterioso*, and he argues that these small- and smaller-press publications amount to the "culmination" of the author's project. The novels have since been repackaged on Dalkey Archive as the opus *Pack of Lies* (Dalkey keeps most Sorrentino in print), and indeed, it will be many generations before literary evolution produces a more bizarre adaptation. These scattered dregs of a murder mystery prove delightful at the level of the sentence, full of panache in a breathtaking variety of tonal hues. Any number of passages set you chuckling, and comedy is part of the trilogy's *raison d'etre*, given how Sorrentino's downbeat vision tended to constrain him whenever he worked in a realistic mode. But it's comedy without humanity. The sexual hijinks have a sterile affect, involving names rather than people, names often recycled from earlier books. As for narrative coherence or its surrogate, an attentive reader will detect the occasional hint of pattern, but it takes an acolyte like Mackey to divine each fiction's organizing principle. The climactic *Misterioso* is nothing so inviting as the eponymous Thelonius Monk tune. Rather, it's arranged according to an obscure seventeenth-century catalogue of demons, their names and others' worked into a double-alphabet, one proceeding backward and the other forward.

Pack of Lies does amount to a culmination, but one of baroque idiosyncrasy. For my money the more rewarding distillation of this author's sensibility came a few years later, in the three books that preceded *Abyss*. These were *Little Casino* in 2002, *Lunar Follies* in '05, and *A Strange Commonplace* early in '06. Each seems a legitimate candidate for that hard-to-determine honor, The Best of Sorrentino, and *Little Casino* returned him to the PEN/Faulkner short list. Nor does the posthumous novel (though a bit weaker overall) reject what distinguishes the previous three, namely, their reassertion of emotional content, even in constructs that have no truck with convention.

Each exhibits great skill at stylistic modulation, but none indulge the excesses of *Stew* or *Lies*. Sorrentino's done with sex-capades, his new plot-surrogates instead sophisticated yet apprehensible. The texts provide the sense of perceiving and completing a whole, a central pleasure of the medium, though via devices far from ordinary. That sense derives in part from devices like the number and the titles of chapters, and I'll talk about one such case in a moment. But the developmental and unifying elements also include, for instance, the recurrent suicide fantasies of *Strange Commonplace*. Four decades into his vocation, that is, this tireless innovator found ways to approach the passions as yet another territory of the new. About those passions, to be sure, Sorrentino remains a cleansing agent; he strips away the veil of *politesse* and exposes what his people would prefer to deny. Nevertheless, his last books value the identification with another's suffering as a core purpose for art made of words. In *Abyss*, an old writer finds he can't quit despite his sober awareness that his work "proved nothing, changed nothing, and spoke to about as many people as one could fit into a small movie theater." Still he continues "to blunder…until finally, perhaps, he would get said what could never be said."

But before I blunder myself, turning all warm and fuzzy, I need to test my hypothesis against *Lunar Follies*. If I mean to say that in his final novels Sorrentino recommitted to something like opening a window on the soul (the very idea!), then this effort from '05 presents my steepest challenge. As the title implies, the book is out there. Plot, protagonists, chronology are nowhere to be found. *Casino* and *Commonplace* revisit the broken families of mid-century New York, their meager lives undergoing biopsies of two or three pages each. *Strange Commonplace* brims with haunted figures; it makes a lovely valediction. But *Lunar Follies* hardly has people in it at all.

The book collects trash, the kind of thing its author spent a lifetime contending against. The "folly" refers to the detritus of the art world, as Sorrentino dreams up catalogue copy for exhibits beneath contempt, as well as numbskull reviews, vicious gossip, and so on. There's also an academic deconstruction, hopelessly clotted. Stranger still, each chapter or whatever you'd call it is titled with the name of some lunar landmark, some fifty-three mountains and seas, arranged alphabetically. Nonetheless, this mooncalf wears a leer we know well. From the first page, "It's on to the snow-chains story; the heat-wave story; the story of the tough coach and his swell young protégé; the killer-hurricane (with puppy) story…"—it's on, that is, to brief but scorching rounds of parody, in contexts always easy to grasp. In this opening instance the butt of the joke is narrative itself, story, and that's a pertinent target, certainly. But throughout the rest of the text the particular art form matters less than the degradation it suffers, in one piece of *poshlost* after another, where the wit swiftly clusters and explodes. As Sorrentino's moon illuminates his detested "sea of manners," it's more satire than parody, it invites participation. Likewise, though the book is densely intertextual (as one might expect given the subject), a reader doesn't need to catch all the isolate flecks to appreciate the fun. Consider, for instance, the list of personalities in what appears to be a photography exhibit. The chapter has an Italian name, "Fra Mauro" (the moon highlands where Apollo 14 landed), and the exhibit is titled "Our Neighbors, the Italians:"

> Familiar Carmine, who cursed out a Puerto Rican mother,
>   hey, why not, they breed like animals.
> ...Benign Giannino, who once read a book for fun.
> Garish Richie, who has a mouth he shoulda gone to law school.
> Exuberant Frankie Hips, who don't mind moolanyans if they
>   mind their fuckin' business.

No-nonsense Gil Sorrentino, who worked a dig at ethnic solidarity into nearly every one of his books... Wisecracking Sorrentino, who was rarely so eager to have you follow his snarling tune. Yet it's not the rhetoric of *Follies*, but rather the structure, that best demonstrates how the writer developed new apparatus for catharsis. Most of the book's longer sections, wouldn't you know it, occupy the passages named after those wide-open spaces called the moon's seas, and since these start with the letter S, the novel reaches a kind of climax, with its late entries among the most complex. Among the least comical, too. "Sea of Clouds" touches on "regrets" and "gravestones" before concluding "Don't see nothing too goddamn funny *here*;" other "Sea" chapters offer little or no satire, instead casting shadows of mortality over the project they're concerned with. So they create, of all things, an epiphany, a pang of insight. In this surrogate climax, the elements dramatize how paltry would be the gain, a few bucks or a few strokes, from even the oiliest con. They assert, with Flaubert, that of all lies, art is the least untrue.

To argue that Gilbert Sorrentino's book-length prose was ultimately about what's *true* might seem a dubious exercise. In the first place, anyone can see that his novels never pandered to the marketplace, and in the second, the last thing I want is to pester him in his grave. To him the T-word was a signifier long perverted by abuse, and so he constructed his novels to enlarge their field of discourse, to put as much distance as he could between himself and that abuse. Maybe, by dint of that wide-ranging exploration, he also located some fresh ground where once again truth could be itself, vulnerable and volatile. That's my contention, anyway: that this author came home now and then, and when he did he found it a place of greater power and durability precisely because he'd first gone on so far an odyssey.

—*The Believer*, 2009

DANCING ON THE HEAD OF A PIN: DAWN RAFFEL & FURTHER ADVENTURES IN THE RESTLESS UNIVERSE

A critic's conundrum: the book that's easy to praise but hard to describe. Consider, for instance, Dawn Raffel's new collection of stories, *Further Adventures in the Restless Universe*. I can say confidently that it's difficult to imagine this sort of thing done better—indeed, two or three of the pieces strike me as nothing short of masterful—but to put a name to what she's doing remains desperate work. Of course labels exist in the reviewer's lexicon. "Minimalist" is the brand that tends to get respect, since it's worn by the likes of Raymond Carver, but the designation remains awfully loose, and comparisons to Carver would badly misrepresent Raffel. On the other hand, newer nomenclature like "short-shorts" seems worse, a pet name. Nor am I comfortable working up some fresh coinage, like "fiction of the resonant ellipsis," since the definition would take up half the review at least. The emphasis here must be on Raffel's new contribution, worth celebrating whatever its category.

Further Adventures runs a scant one hundred pages, and a few of its fictions take up less than one of those. The opener, "Near Taurus," comprises just twenty lines of print, in eleven paragraphs, with three brief quotations. Yet "Near Taurus" relates a tale recognizable to any lover who fumbled his or her initial play at passion. Indeed, these few remaining bones from an unconsummated teen romance are arranged for their mythic association. It opens with a variation on once-upon-a-time, "After the rains had come and gone…" and then ends with both fable and weather, closing the circle, "our naked eyes turning to legends, the dirt beneath us parched."

The best of these *Adventures* share this magic, making immensities appear out of next to nothing. If that staple of commercial fiction, the mutigenerational family saga, can dance on the head of a pin, then that's just what's happening in a story like "The Interruption." The piece has no less a sweeping historical canvas than the Holocaust, but the references are glancing, indeed. The whole story's a phone conversation between sisters, the American descendants of a destroyed *shtetl*, but the worst tragedy of the previous century is reduced to the following, which at least is of one of the longest utterances from either protagonist:

> This was all before the war. Meanwhile, the cousin said— meanwhile the lover who'd left her married someone else and had a family with her. Of course—you know. The lover, the children—none of them survived. And now that I think of it, the family in Poland…what?

That last question, more's the irony, refers to the eponymous "Interruption," a call coming in on another line. The sisters here are trying to connect despite a twenty-first-century American threat to family, less dramatic but still destructive. The story's last line, with a finger "on the button," is "Forgive me."

Along with stories like "Our Heaven," "The Interruption" helps to sketch a family-saga structure for the whole of these *Adventures*. The opener is that fairy tale of first love (yet lacking in sensuality, beyond the feel of grave-dirt), all move by fits and starts to some momentary reassertion of family (even when you're about to put family on hold), and the closer, "Beyond All Blessing and Song, Praise and Consolation," features a big middle-American get-together, with three or four generations around the table and ghost-quotation from the verse on the Statue of Liberty (though the story's Earth Mother dies, and the conclusion's rich with prevarication: "We cannot look. We cannot but look.") Raffel's toolkit is so spare, her constructions leave plenty of gaps, and into these rush clusters of ambiguity. In particular, the abbreviated exchanges between mothers and sons teeter on the verge of collapse into permanent dysfunction. Still, despite the threats in its offers of dessert or a toy, the hiccups in its sweet-talk, *Further Adventures* may be best seen as a striking new constellation put together from the scattered pieces of our country's diasporic families.

Speaking of constellations—and note: Raffel turns up her title in a story set mostly in Chicago's Adler Planetarium—it's the distance between the stars, the narrative gaps, that most usefully distinguish this minimalism from that of most Americans struggling under the trademark. Carver's most famous piece, "What We Talk About When We Talk About Love," needs every one of its phatic conversational fills; as the title implies, the work picks over every inch of our talk in order to glean its most cutting shards. But these *Adventures* leave out many more hems and haws than Carver would (or Beattie, or Mary Robison…), and it never develops a scene so fully as the liquid dinner of "What We Talk." Quite the opposite, one of Raffel's most impressive pieces, "Seven Spells," is all about the *holes* in the narrator's experience: her fainting spells. The numbered episodes subsume dialog into a concussed summary, yet this same fractured streamlining adds flavor to the experience, heightening the vitality by underscoring its fragility. Not for nothing is the last phrase "the uses of salt."

Other elements set her minimalism apart, such as the pronounced strain of legend and fable. What matters more, in the end, is how this sharply cornered storytelling cuts to what Flannery O'Connor called "the nature and aim of fiction" (in *Mystery and Manners*). In particular, Raffel's work raises questions about the distinction between fiction and poetry. Story after story depends on subtle verbal manipulations like that of poetry, a word at the end that rings changes off a phrase from the start, and the stops and starts can suggest stanza breaks, more about development of an image than increments in narrative movement or psychological penetration. Well, then, what defines Raffel's endeavors as fiction, other than typography and layout? The question, as she frames it, presents no easy answer. Certainly one notes the absence of regular rhythm, still the secret heartbeat of nearly all poetry. Certainly a few stories, such as "Coeur," have more character-based conflict and growth than most poetry. But by and large the ambiguities that pervade and enliven this collection extend to the very form the work claims, they clear new ground for that form, and if you ask me that's the most exciting of these *Adventures*.

—*American Book Review*, 2011

MAKING CLAIM TO QUIXOTE: ROY KESEY & PACAZO

Is the sheer bulk of a book worth celebration? Roy Kesey has never gone beyond novella-length before, but his new *Pacazo* runs more than five hundred pages, bulging with detail and incident, with everything from midnight snacks to invasive insects. It's a shaggy-dog tale, one that eventually—boldly—invites comparison to its great progenitor, *Don Quixote*. In cutting a classic wide swath, *Pacazo* exposes itself to risk, a tricky balance between hilarity and horror. By and large, though, this rangy novel earns its claim to the old knight's inheritance.

The setting is 1990s Peru, in a backwater that a lesser author would've termed a "sleepy university town." Kesey, however, knocks the setting's quiet and refinement into laughable loops of inefficiency and sloth. There's the traffic, the streetlights, and in particular the narrator, the American ex-pat John Segovia. This man can come across as a slacker, a perpetual grad student, fat and sloppy and lacking a visa. Nonetheless, he's lucked into a university job teaching English. He's won the hand of the lovely Pilar, and they've wasted no time having a baby—but shortly before the novel opens, the wife dies horribly: raped, beaten, and abandoned in the desert.

The latter-day surfaces, that is, don't mask the Woeful Countenance of the Cervantes model. Comic and tragic live cheek by jowl, to choose an appropriate cliché. Their jostling even disrupts individual sentences. Before Segovia finishes a sentence, his thinking (much distracted by his baby, besides everything else) can rummage through widely disparate subjects. When he's out on one of his dubious quests to solve Pilar's murder single-handed, his investigations give way not just to memories, as you might expect, but also to musings on the bloody exploits of the conquistadors. Such juggling challenges the reader, certainly, but the balls in play stand out vividly, most of the time, easy to differentiate. Meanwhile, the meditations on Pizarro or De Soto prove oddly fitting. Segovia, we learn, may himself be a descendent of a sixteenth-century Spanish adventurer, and he originally came to this country to study history. Besides, the conquerors' excesses seem like terrifying kin to Quixote's straight-faced bumbling.

In *Pacazo*, bumbling and terror emerge also from an environmental disaster, a catastrophe with broader ramifications than the narrator's personal loss. El Nino arrives about mid-novel, in all its muck and headbanging, and brings with it extraordinary houseguests: "a moth...with wasp eyes and a long black nose and a tail that flexes and expands something like a horsehair brush and something like a mace." Plenty of knockabout action ensues, as well, some involving whole frightened mobs, and we're reminded how often great novels of the past featured some storm or flood or blizzard; such stuff used to be a chestnut we could count on, and here Kesey restores it to the menu. Better yet, *Pacazo*'s bad weather always amounts to more than mere spectacle. The high water also sweeps away all the so-called evidence Segovia has gathered concerning his wife's murder. He's forced to recognize how "anger is a form of nostalgia."

This revelation doesn't cure the narrator. The novel's latter half hangs on the hard choice he faces: either resign himself to the battered pleasures of this New World (including an independent-minded new lover), or plunge into a madness impenetrable as the Amazon, searching for his private El Dorado. Does such a quandary sound improbable? Perhaps, but it's precisely such hyperbole that energizes this author's imagination. He's most agile on the fine line between the Three Stooges and a splatter flick:

> I stretch the turkey's neck across the block...the machete falls...and the turkey seems to explode in place. Blood spurts into my face...the turkey's head limp in my left hand and its body wrenching out of my right, both wings free and beating and blood spraying from the neck as the turkey ricochets from rector to student to gardener, blood jetting into our eyes and hair and open mouths, the guest lecturer still swinging...

A "guest lecturer," yes, performs this butchery. The scene takes place at the university. It offers a comic foreshadowing of the violence at the novel's climax, and in both cases Segovia functions as a guest himself, shanghaied into bloody business. *Pacazo* thus presents a special case of the gringo out of his element. When such protagonists turn up in B. Traven's *The Treasure of Sierra Madre* (1927) or Robert Stone's *A Flag for Sunrise* (1981), they suffer more sober comeuppance than here.

But the humor isn't all that sets this new novel apart. This visitor also displays unusual appreciation for the country he now calls home. Segovia seems to have all of Peru's tortured history at his fingertips. He knows better than to call his eponymous animal by the schoolbook name "iguana." Such a pan-American sensibility remains rare in U.S. fiction, and it allies Kesey with such notable exceptions as John Sayles (especially in *Los Gusanos*, 1991) and Jay Cantor (the unjustly neglected *Death of Che Guevara*, 1983). Kesey, to be sure, has always been a sensitive voyager. His novella *Nothing in the World* (2006) snares its protagonist in the last paroxysms of the former Yugoslavia, and the collection *All Over* (2007) succeeded best in its prize-winning story "Wait," a fantasia of the international community that springs up during an airport delay prolonged to surreal extremes. *Pacazo* marries the freewheeling cool of the latter to the sympathetic darkness of the former and generates a fresh and powerful reminder of what fiction can accomplish at full length.

—*Bookforum,* 2011

ECSTASIES IN COUNTERPOINT: PAUL HARDING & TINKERS

Any new novel worth thinking about raises old questions, and in the case of Paul Harding's often-impressive *Tinkers*, the question is: how much ecstasy can a person stand? A first novel of admirable risk[1]—unconventional in subject, structure, and sentence—it begins in a kind of ecstasy, with the deathbed hallucinations of George Washington Crosby. These visions, by authorial magic, swiftly carry George back into the perspective of his own runaway father, Howard.

George was still a boy when the father disappeared at the turn of the previous century. That simpler America provides the setting for what action the story offers, a world of woods and farms and solitude, and the season is nearly always unstable, fall or spring. Howard gees his mule down rutted roads, now in Canada and now upstate New York, trundling through a sales route but never turning a profit. He struggles too with a hard-hearted country wife, Kathleen, and falters as a family man, never connecting with young George. The father's core problem, we discover, isn't his heart or his psyche but his nervous system. He suffers epilepsy, and he knows his Kathleen could never stand the shame should his children or his neighbors see him struck down by a fit.

---

1. For all its risks, *Tinkers* captured the Pulitzer Prize in the Novel, only the second winner ever on a small press. This review, one of few on initial publication, was for a venue well off the beaten path.

That's about it for plot and tension. Of course I'm keeping my reviewer's hand over a twist or two, but I doubt the suspense in *Tinkers*
could be spoiled. What matters isn't event, but immanence:

> Summer would anneal the chilled earth, but for now the water
> was so mineral and hard that it seemed to ring. Howard heard
> the water reverberating through the soil and around the roots.
> Water lay ankle-deep....Puddles shimmered and...looked like
> tin cymbals. They looked as if they would ring if tapped with
> a stick. The puddles rang. The water rang.

The ringing doesn't stop, either; the next three lines repeat the verb
twice more. Throughout, Harding's performance tends to the baroque, no matter that the landscape is wilderness. Transcendent
states of mind—a few of them, like the passage above, on the verge
of epileptic seizure—take the form of the winter sky-sheen behind
barren trees, or of wind and insects in chorus as evening comes on.
A defining forebear for this novel would be *Walden*, which likewise
made poetry, affirming poetry by and large, of woodsy detail. *Tinkers*, at its best, pulls off a re-entry into the Thoreauvian mindset,
with both hunter-gatherer turmoil and horse-and-buggy challenges.
It includes a spooky round of anecdotes about a mythic Indian guide.

However, the novel also whips up its rhetoric when the subject is
clocks. In one list of clockmakers:

> We find a humble and motley, if determined and patient,
> parade...all bent at their worktables, filing brass and cali-
> brating gears and sketching ideas until their pencils dissolve
> into lead dust...all to more perfectly trans*form* and trans*late*
> Universal Energy by perfecting the beat of the...wheel. Lis-
> ten, horologist, to the names of their devices: verge, dead-
> beat, tic-tac...

Now, this second example of Harding's rococo doesn't depend on repeated words but parallel syntax. Indeed, in these pages there's a different protagonist, not Howard but his now-dying son. George had a passion for antique clocks, and just about the only time we see the adult character in action (as opposed to the boy, defined against his troubled father), he's repairing clocks. Then too, the lines above purport to be not George's own but a section from an eighteenth-century treatise on clocks. *Tinkers* interpolates a few such pretend-quotes, as well as a few imitation-scientific enumerations ("*Crepescule Borealis*: 1. The bark of birches glows silver and white…2. Fireflies blink in the thick grass…").

The pervading effect is contrapuntal. At one point everything's in smithereens, a victim of family dysfunction and brain seizures, so that Howard sits helpless, "baffled by his diet of lightning," and at the next these lives are blessed by assertions of coherence perfect for their very oddity: the clock in one case, the bird's nest in another. The latter image may provide the climax, and something of a happy ending: "One's whole countryside might be fitted out with a constellation of such nests, each holding its own special treasure." The imagistic seesaw between utter breakdown and unlikely reconstruction is impressive, as well as central to the mission of the publisher, Bellevue Press, which seeks to combine medical and literary exploration.

All well and good—but insofar as Harding intends a psychological drama, he disappoints. For all its verbal acrobatics and echoes of Thoreau, *Tinkers* isn't some purely textual exercise, in which plausible character and relationships don't matter. So, as father and son protagonists, Howard and George frustrate. They come across as little more than twinned pastiches of intense moments. The problem isn't that such moments occur in a language far above either man's head, a stretch that many authors bring off, but how it can bulldoze the passions under agglomerations of metaphor. Father and son are unbelievable especially for their lack of anger. Howard's affliction doesn't appear to have left him with a mean bone in his body, nor with any drive to excel (though those traits defined history's most famous epileptic, Julius Caesar). George, so far as we can see, grows up into an eccentric-but-beloved paterfamilias, entirely unscarred by a father's abandonment and a mother's neglect. Indeed, Kathleen's relative nastiness comes as a relief, when she asserts herself about halfway through. At last we whiff the bracing stink of inadequacy and low motives.

Which returns us to the initial conundrum: ecstasy all the time. Do Harding's hosannas sometime sink to preciousness? Yes, alas, ("and each little bee settled in a yellow cup and took suck like a new-born"), and his recurrent images can seem merely redundant, as well. Yet the text remains remarkable, free-thinking and beautifully composed. The turns of phrase in *Tinkers* often had me whistling in envy, and overall the project blazes a new approach to historical fiction.

—*Gently Read Literature*, 2009

FRESH-HATCHED FREAKS: BLAKE BUTLER'S EVER & MATT BELL'S THE COLLECTORS

You can see at once that both these books are freaks. You won't even find the Caketrain prizewinner, Matt Bell's *The Collectors*, bound between covers. Its first run sold out fast, and now the chapbook or novella or whatever you'd call it is available as a free download. And Blake Butler's willowy *EVER* seems even weirder, page for page. The prose is often fitted around gray-black designs, themselves never representational, and the passages without artwork feature outlandish space breaks and punctuation.

As for things like plot or character, forget it. Both works track central figures, but neither develops tension or provides other novelistic amenities. Yet when I say that these two very-small-press books afforded me some of my most cleansing and enjoyable reading, recently—a terrific experience, no less—I have to reach for comparison to work half a century old.

In the 1950s, Samuel Beckett brought out his groundbreaking trilogy: *Molloy*, *Malone Dies*, and *The Unnameable*. These were stories of renunciation, as in the brilliant central novella, when the bedridden Malone gives up the scrap he's carried this far and lets his consciousness fade into a story. Beyond that, Beckett renounces the culture in which he came up, the High Modernism of his mentor Joyce. He insists on a new field of discourse, primarily by means of doing without. So as I read these two latest challenges to what we expect of fiction, stories stripped of their vestments, I couldn't stop thinking of Beckett's trilogy.

Bell's novella does have a setting and a history, mid-town Manhattan during the same period when Beckett was bringing out his trilogy. To establish this much, though, takes digging—and that's *precisely* the word. The abode of these "collectors" is a garbage heap. The bachelor brothers Langley and Homer Collyer were packrat-psychos. They occupied (boy, did they) an Upper East Side brownstone, and died crushed beneath their own cram: "three baby carriages, rakes and hoes...several rusted bicycles, kitchen utensils (including at least four sets of china...), a heap of glass chandeliers that had been removed to make room for the piles and the tunnels." And this is just one list, from one of the several short chapters that Bell labels "Inventory."

The Collyers, in his reimagining,[1] don't live in a place so much as a passion. *The Collectors*, keeping things in-house, burrows deep into the mind. Most of the two or three-page chapters deal out imagined snippets of the brothers' dying days, the point of view shifting between two men beyond help: Langley crippled and Homer blind. The latter's name and disability are another fact of the history, but they suggest of course the famous first storyteller, and so add an intertextual irony. Both war and odyssey stay within the city walls.

Bell visits one or two other perceptions as well in chapters set after the brothers' demise, but the feel remains claustrophobic. The style tends to lists and compound-complex constructions, such as when we get an inkling of psychology, regarding the father's abandonment: "Every stray hair clinging to a shirt collar, every scrap of handwriting left in the margins of his texts, all of it is him, is who he was. It's all that's left, but if you keep it safe then it's all you'll ever need." Hard feelings have calcified, leaving everyone pretty well paralyzed even before the accident to the (slightly) more mo-

---

1. Hardly half a year after Bell's book appeared, E.L. Doctorow came out with his own Collyers novel, *Homer and Langley*.

bile brother. That accident's the only event; the rest is inventory, including the death rattle.

Yet such a description violates the story's sprightliness. The brief volume has almost thirty chapter breaks, and these are arranged in an outline of numerals and capitals, pleasantly confounding while it's reliably repetitious. More than that, each "Inventory" embodies, in its archeological slice of the home, some smaller tragedy. The dolls in one room, uncovered at what would be the climax point of an ordinary fiction, amount to "no more a family than anything else." So while the madness of the situation remains beyond our ken, the sorrow's brought down to human scale.

The reader, you could say, becomes both cleanup crew and author. These are the two other perspectives that turn up, again imaginary; the author isn't the historical Matt Bell, no more than Homer and Langley are the historical Collyers. But a few of the passages here speak with re-animating force amid the wreckage. *The Collectors* suggests, ultimately, that there exists no better form of renewal than the accommodating art of story.

I should add that Bell's book was the runner-up for Caketrain's contest, after *All the Day's Sad Stories* by Tina May Hall. Both were selected by Brian Evenson, a compatible sensibility—and Evenson also committed a lengthy blurb for Blake Butler. Yet *EVER*, for all the correspondences between it and *The Collectors*, presents a significantly different texture. Bell suggests a fugue, Butler an aria. Both works may confine their alterna-drama to a single indoor space, but in *EVER* it's a space without a setting. There's a suggestion or two of the hurricane alleys of the American South, but the context serves primarily as a platform for surreal metamorphosis and extraordinary style.

This author's sentences at once estrange and seduce. A number of passages read like a twenty-first-century resurrection of Middle English, constructed for the ear, dependent on assonance and buried rhyme. From the second page: "In the light my skin was see-through—my veins an atlas spanned in tissue." Not much later, more pugnaciously: "Streams of night might gleam like glass. The dirt would swim with foam." Appreciation of Butler's small, scary miracle requires appreciation of such beveled prose gems, the majority of which appear between brackets. It's as if everything were a whispered aside, the bits and pieces of former lives picked out of a whirlwind.

A whirlwind would be one way to describe what happens, a whirlwind played *Largo*, but *EVER* offers nothing like disaster reporting. Earlier I noted the design elements, which rarely allow for a full page of prose, and in one sequence we read no more than a few lines on each. Yet the decorations hint of Edward Gorey, with their shadowy semi-skeletons, and a few bones of story turn up. *EVER* follows a soiled Alice through the looking-glass. The girl (unnamed, but she mentions a dress and such) is pulled through the rooms of a phantasmagoric home, right through walls, by a force she can't understand. She realizes she's up against a threat, and there's also a drifting, disturbing neighbor, yet she's fascinated, savoring details. "The next room was made of wobble. Magnetic tape streaming from the rafters, bifurcating blonde split-ends. Cashed." The remainder of that page runs blank, too, as if to invite meditation.

Unworldly as her house-tour is, the girl's ghostly traveling recalls a familiar turn of the mind. A psychological phenomenon noted by several researchers, often called "the dream of rooms." Such dreams can occur at any age, but they're most common toward the end of life, when the consciousness seeks to revisit the arenas of experience and somehow extend them to whatever's next. The correlative figures for *EVER* would be, naturally, the dying vagabonds of Beckett's trilogy. If Butler's Alice is headed for the ever-after, the victim of some place and catastrophe she can't comprehend, it's through these same gaps of mind that she slips into heaven. So too we might say that Matt Bell's sociopathic collectors, in becoming *dramatis personae*, achieve a perverse Assumption. Or perhaps fiction itself is what's rising to a higher sphere, given these fresh examples of how it refuses to be reined in.

—Bookslut, 2009

GALACTIC POLE

TOWER, TREE, CANDLE: DANTE'S DIVINE COMEDY & THE TRIUMPH OF THE FRAGILITY

I crown and miter you lord of yourself!
—Virgil to Dante, as they exit Purgatory
(Canto XXVII, line 142)

Those who read this essay will likely participate in the eighth century of discussion concerning *The Divine Comedy*. Clean copies of the finished canticles, with all their intellectual sizzle and range, their right-on humanity and intertextual strutwork, and above all their poetic command, flexible, profound, precise—with all that intact already, the completed work began to circulate in 1320, the last year of its author's life. Yet as 2020 approaches, in every creative arena, "the Poem" (as the great scholar Charles Singleton liked to call it) looms as an ever-more-common referent.

I'm not the only one to have noticed. Joan Acocella, in assessing the 2007 Hollander translation of *Paradiso* (completing roughly 3,600 pages of *Commedia* and commentary), plunged into a close reading combined with an assessment of twentieth-century Dante criticism, assuming readers of *The New Yorker* would be eager to go along. Judith Shulevitz, in an '03 essay for the *Times Book Review*, detected a similarly widening appeal in two successful recent novels, Matthew Pearl's *The Dante Club* and Nick Tosches's *In the Hand of Dante* (unfortunately, neither book proved much good, though Tosches had a fine radical premise). In '04 Harriet Rubin brought out a combination of biography and analysis, *Dante in Love*, its strengths and weaknesses encapsulated in the overheated subtitle: *The World's Greatest Poem and How It Made History*. The book earned Rubin a lengthy NPR interview, never mind that her subject was one of the most thoroughly discussed in history; on air she cited T.S. Eliot's claim that "Dante and Shakespeare divide the modern world between them," then asserted that, these days, the Florentine took up "more and more of the sky."

More and more bandwidth, certainly: new-millennial fascination with the *Comedy* results in thousands of items on a web search. But Google hardly offers the best place to appreciate Dante's present influence. The overwhelming example would be Peter Jackson's movie trilogy *The Lord of the Rings*. Tolkien's novels, to be sure, outlined a Christian redemption tale similar in many respects to that of the *Comedy*. But in the films Jackson and his collaborators make transparent, not to say ham-fisted use of effects from *Inferno* and *Purgatory*. Nor does it matter if the movies' brain trust never read a word of the original *terza rima*. What they put onscreen derived from material that's become common visual and conceptual currency, including the famed engravings by Doré.

The demonic Orcs, for instance, are summoned out of a region modeled on the Inferno's Ninth Circle, the icebound Cocytus. This bottomland lies below the tower of the diabolic lord Saruman, a potentate at once devastating yet trapped. As for images of Purgatory—which derive primarily from Dante, who dreamed up his Middle Realm out of legends of his era and phrases from St. Paul—even a secondhand familiarity with that sin-cleansing Mountain will call to mind the fourteenth-century poem at the twenty-first-century films' repeated long shots of Frodo and Sam, laboring up terrible steeps to rid themselves of evil. Also, Jackson presents a simulacrum for the Earthly Paradise at the top of the Purgatory, namely the Elf Kingdom. In this leafy domain the dominant figure, like Beatrice on the mountaintop, is a flashing-eyed superwoman.

Correlations of this kind can be forced, shoehorning any story into Dante's frame. A more serious problem may be the reverse: the *Comedy* may get cut down to iPod-size. With that in mind, I must point out that Jackson created his films without recourse to the *Paradiso*. The closing canticle enacts the poet's bravest leap of the imagination, at once lasers and lectures, gossamer material that had no place among Jackson's galumphing heavy cavalry. But elsewhere in the films the parallels amount to a telling case of the *Comedy*'s contemporary penetration into image and meaning. An extraordinary impact for an epic about an afterlife to which few now give credence, composed in a form and language fewer still can penetrate.

Thus my goal: a fresh explanation of that impact. I'll proceed by analysis of three major images in the work, each occurring at similar junctures late in their canticles. This reading owes something to Singleton and to followers like John Freccero and the Hollanders—though in the end I'll argue against them, posing an alternative to the ruling interpretation of the last half-century. After that, with Dante's three signal metaphors in mind, I'll suggest an overarching psychological or anthropological paradigm at work. My suggestion derives in part from long-ago reading of Jan Kott's *Shakespeare Our Contemporary* (1974), and in part from others like Joseph Meeker and Gaetano Cipolla. Like them, I find the Poem most telling in the interplay of its archetypes.

Extravagant as his *Comedy* is, its vastness and extremity far greater than anything in Jackson or Tolkien, Dante nonetheless puts the period to each of the three journeys within his journey by means of something small and ordinary. The word which concludes each canticle is *stelle*, stars: a glimmering diminuendo, in which the sound softens from fricative to glottal to mere breath. But of course this closer contains considerable power as well. Mark Musa, in his notes to the final lines of *Purgatory*, points out that the word suggests "the upward movement towards God." And Musa, with his blank-verse tercets in American English, makes the best translation to quote for my purposes; I cite by canto and line.

Throughout the *Comedy*, then, what guides Dante's Pilgrim toward salvation, and what affords comprehension of God's plan, often finds fragile embodiment, fragile as starlight. Indeed, the contrary holds true. Infernal landmarks are generally notable for their size, the devils and damned saddled with grotesque protuberance; the same proportions apply to the worst trials of the purgatorial mountain. Hence the dramatic problem of *Paradise*, the challenge of creating story tension in a place of infinite harmony, extends to the problem of creating images: what shape can enlightenment take when any natural form prompts connection to the Fall? Dante's best-known solution, ingenious yet everyday, is the Celestial Rose, a characterization he first awards the highest Empyrean in a tercet that begins on line 115 of Canto XXX:

> And if the lowest tier alone can hold
> so great a brilliance, then how vast the space
> of this Rose to its outer petals' reach!

The image places a measureless theater, a seat of infinite power, within a flower easy to pluck.

An impressive sleight of hand—but its greatest accomplishment may be the dialogue it helps set up across the epic, a relationship among three closing images. The first two occur at similar points in *Inferno* and *Purgatory*, and these visions in the pit of Hell, at the peak of Purgatory, and up at the lip of the Rose present, together, a marvelous paradox. Their progression embodies the opposite of what you would expect; it moves from ostensible power to ostensible weakness.

The first of these climactic images looms in *Inferno* XXXI. On a plateau above the icy bottom-most circles of traitors (still above

Lucifer, that is), what the Pilgrim sees elicits a confused comparison to a metropolis: "I soon / made out what seemed to be high, clustered towers. / 'Master,' I said, 'what city lies ahead?'" (19-21) Even after Virgil has corrected his Pilgrim, explaining that the uprights ahead are the half-buried giants who rebelled against Jupiter, the urban analogy continues. Dante first makes reference to the towers that circle the Sienese fortress Montereggioni (40), then mentions the immense bronze pine cone that, in the poet's time, stood outside St. Peter's in Rome (59).

These references join with other allusions made during the recent descent to suggest that primordial figure of vanity and overreach, the Tower of Babel. We are reminded, explicitly, that Nimrod commanded the Tower to be built; we sense, without being told, the claustrophobia of Lower Hell, gated by Dis at the top and Lucifer in the pit. The connection to Dis is implicit in the Pilgrim's very word for the skyscraper-giants. The question "what city...?" uses not *città*, but the more complicated *terra*, suggestive of an entire *"terra"*-tory or city-state.

Nonetheless Musa, Singleton, Allen Mandelbaum and others translate the word as "city," and Musa and Singleton note the reiteration from Canto VIII, when the devils atop the walls of Dis refuse the Pilgrim and his guide entrance until an angel descends and pulls heavenly rank; outside Dis, Dante twice uses the broader *terra*. Therefore the Pilgrim stumbles through the same dread city now, in the lowest circles, just as down here too, the Sodom that most often comes to his mind is Florence. Pilgrim Dante may be approaching the Devil himself, but he asks a natural question, the same as must've occurred more than once to exile Dante. Catching sight of a new hilltop stronghold: *che terra è questa?*

Now Lucifer, in the final canto, presents a tower still more frightening. Virgil however introduces him as the city we already know: "This is he, this is Dis..." (XXXIV, 20). Also he's first taken for a windmill, another down-to-earth association, though made unsettling by links to night and fog (4-6). But whatever we call the three-headed thing at the center of the Abyss, the first of such giants seen up close, Nimrod in Canto XXXI presents a deliberate foreshadowing.

Like the monster below him, Nimrod stands immense yet locked down, half-buried, and Virgil calls attention to the hunter's horn and its strap, both suggestive of Satan's leathery wings. More significantly, both creatures remain oblivious to their visitors. Nimrod's outburst "*Raphèl maì amècche zabì almi*" (70) remains impenetrable (Singleton's summary of attempts at analysis occupies two pages), and the exclamation should defy understanding, given the giant's connection to Babel. But the gibberish is most unnerving for its *near*-intelligibility, like the jabber of a psychotic in an alley. It induces sympathy—there but for fortune—even as it anticipates Satan's blind absorption in his three-headed chewing.

In the twinned towers of Nimrod and Lucifer, the threat of entrapment is heightened, just as the repeated open *a* in the giant's nonsense suggests a cry of attack. But these slum landmarks represent the worst of God's universe as much for their *self-inflicted* solitary confinement as for any freakish external affect. And we very nearly get under their skin; Pilgrim and poet crawl through the fur on Satan's haunch in order to escape.

The closing cantos of *Purgatory* have their hard-to-figure devices as well. Only a century ago, for instance, did exegesis by Edward Moore and Charles Grandgent clarify much of what Dante meant by the phantasmagoric charade up in the Earthly Paradise. We now understand how, in hallucinatory allegory, *Purgatory* XXIX, XXX, and XXXII present the elements and history of the Christian faith. Yet to unveil these systems of meaning reveals other subtleties. Consider the final tercet-plus-one of the *Purgatory*, the sonic effect of the original Italian.

When the Pilgrim turns at last toward the *stelle*, toward heaven, he's just been baptized in the *santissima* waters of Eunoë (bathing in the River Lethe lets a soul into this Eden; bathing in Eunoë enables the ascent to Heaven). He has been made new, "refreshed like a newly-leafed plant." His creator cloaks the finale in a fugue of repeating assonance and consonance:

Io ritornai da la santissima onda
rifatto sì come piante novelle
rinovellate di novella fronda

Puro e disposto a salire le stelle.

No English translation captures the nuance. As if anticipating the games that Vladimir Nabokov later played with the name of his imaginary child-lover, in the first lines of *Lolita*, Dante here opens the mouth wider with each softening syllable of the repeated *no-vell-lahh*, while at the same time playing conceptually off the repeating flow of a river's current (*onda* means "wave"). Also, most English renderings are hampered by using "tree" for *piante*, actually the more generic "plants." Not that Musa and Singleton and others don't have reason for choosing "tree," though the Italian is another common Latinate, *albero*. Nonetheless, translators wish to draw out the correlation between the Pilgrim's newly blooming spirit and the Tree of the Knowledge of Good and Evil.

The poem's protagonist spends much of the thirty-second and thirty-third cantos of *Purgatory* (the final cantos) meditating on that Tree. Already a "miracle of height" (XXXII, 41) it goes through miraculous changes at the hands of Beatrice and her angels. Though the Pilgrim understands this mountaintop is Eden, he first spies the tree "stripped of leaf and fruit" (39). Then later, like his own revived soul at canticle's end, the tree erupts magically into bloom at a touch of the "pole" (49) that is Christ's cross and faith. Still from its first leafless appearance this Tree is identified, in the original, as "*una pianta*" (37).

Now, surrounding this tree on the peak, just as down in the meadowlands at Purgatory's foot, one finds a number of other trees, all unremarkable. In the canticle's first episodes, they offer simple shade as souls rest in preparation for the challenges upslope. Then after the Pilgrim enters Purgatory proper, as he climbs its ever-steeper terraces, he encounters only two trees of any note. Both are said to be offshoots of Adam's and Eve's *pianta* on the mountaintop (XXIV, 117), but Dante calls the first *alber* (XXII, 131) and the second *pomo*, a shorthand for apple tree (XXIV, 104). These stand on the Terrace of the Gluttons, where former profligates stagger along emaciated, more Gollum than Frodo. The plant life, full of tormenting fruit, engages the poet's imagination wonderfully: the first grows upside down, a renunciation via botany, and both harbor magic voices of warning.

All this presents a distinct contrast to the outstanding "plant" up beyond the River Lethe, the tallest tree there and the one honored at first encounter with a chanting circle-dance by Beatrice, her angels, and a monstrous but gentle menagerie. Despite such company, Eden's tree at first carries a faint suggestion of Nimrod's and Lucifer's towers: an immense yet barren upright, silent and "stripped." Dante could hardly have conveyed a more vivid contrast to the rest of the Earthly Paradise, that "heavenly forest thick with living green" (XXVII, 2), or to any of the trees down the mountain. This one stands as a naked totem for Original Sin, no particular fruit or species, but rather a root genus.

Then immediately following this mute allegory of the Fall, the *pianta* goes on to represent the Resurrection. In expressing this aspect of his metaphor Dante allows his fancy free rein, unleashing the canticle's last surreal excesses. This begins with the most bizarre of the local fauna, the griffin-Christ, which touches Adam's tree, "returning to it what it once brought forth" (XXXII, 51, and the line in Italian offers another gem of sonic balance: "*e quel di lei a lei lasciò legato*").

After that the pageant turns carnivalesque as anything in Rabelais—while never losing control of the humble central image. Beatrice sits protecting the roots, and the plant is spared the worst developments. Those take place in the chariot, and show us again the infernal tower: a whore on a throne "like a fort / high on a hill" (148-49).

The interrelations glitter, impossible to miss even amid passages that remain obscure. In *Purgatorio*'s final canto, for instance, Beatrice speaks in riddles, using numerology to prophesy better times; Pietro Mazzamuto has taken the best stab at explanation, but for my purposes, what matters is how easily such arcana could've overwhelmed the work. This *Comedy* could've been reduced to a *Da Vinci Code*, but Dante provides consistent relief from the abstruse via the anchoring figure of the Tree. Beatrice herself at one point simplifies matters by a reference to the "*pianta*" (original, 57). She tells her guest that when he writes about these visions, above all:

> ...be sure you that describe
> the sad condition of the tree you saw
> despoiled, not once but twice...
> (XXXIII, 55-57).

That double despoiling provides stinging expression for Dante's outrage over the corrupt church. Yet before a thing can be polluted, it must once have been pure, and the true power of this canticle's final scenes derives not from angry invective that requires a footnote, but from a pleasurable experience as universal as a day in the park. For all his high dudgeon and esoterica, the poet never neglects the soothing and uplift that the episode must convey. Readers never lose sight of the luxuriant setting, diametrically opposed to the rubble-strewn lower Inferno; we're never far from a restorative nap amid wildflowers, a midsummer's night dream.

———

Paradise, in general, takes us a long way from such familiar points of reference. The realm of the Blest is something else again, all startling illuminations, keen but harmonious explanations, and darting movements over vast spaces. More than once the effects suggest computer animation or internet hyperlinks, several centuries ahead of their time—but then the subject has no truck with time; it exists outside of time. Nor should anybody confuse the actual Paradise with its faint simulacrum, the Earthly Paradise. The Empyrean, the subject of the final cantos, has flowers and waters that recall the peak of Purgatory, but these too have gone unearthly.

The example most pertinent to my essay is the Pilgrim's first glimpse of the "stream" that forms the border to Highest Heaven, in Canto XXX. In keeping with the mad experiment Dante conducts throughout the canticle, his attempt to embody experience that's beyond the body, this stream is not a stream, but rather a flowing ribbon of mosaic, its bits now jewels and now flames, a thread of infinite innocent sensuality and envy-free abundance, all distilled somehow from the Celestial Rose beyond.

In the Italian, the initial description resounds with the *r* and *v* of *primavera*, the ruling rhyme of the first tercet. The rolling of the lips may suggest flowers bursting at springtime. But in any language this foretaste of utmost Divinity takes us to strange waters:

> And I saw light that was a flowing stream,
> blazing in splendid sparks between two banks
> painted by spring in miracles of color.
>
> Out of this spring the sparks of living light
> were shooting up and settling on the flowers:
> they looked like rubies set in rings of gold. (61-66)

Miracle builds on miracle, with sentient glimmers that leap onto starflowers that turn to heirlooms, meanwhile incorporating allusion to both the Old Testament (Daniel 7:10, the "swift stream of fire") and the New (Revelations 22:1, the "river of the water of life, clear as crystal"). So image, sound, and concept come together to enhance the crossing of a final heavenly boundary. From here the Pilgrim will rise out of the nine widening spheres of Paradise and into the linked petals they all form together, impossibly but perfectly, at their zenith.

So too, over the next several stanzas, the poet takes care to have this crossing express again, as in the first canto of *Paradise*, just how his Dante-character can understand so much that's beyond ordinary understanding. After the Pilgrim drinks from this impossible stream, "the sparks and flowers changed / into a greater festival:/ … both courts of Heaven in their reality." (94-96) Here again, that is, our traveler has managed to "transhumanize"—as Musa renders *trasumanar*, Dante's remarkable neologism from Canto I, 70. Simply to enter Paradise, back in the first canto, he needed to transcend to a fresh level of apprehension, and now here in Canto XXX, on the verge of his greatest epiphany, he needs to acquire his fullest powers of perception. Therefore the Pilgrim undergoes a "transhuman" baptism, more potent than the earlier cleansings in Lethe and Eunoë.

For its creation of one heightened perspective after another, Musa declares in the Introduction to his translation, *Paradise* must be counted "the most 'artistic'" of the three canticles. Yet Dante understands as well that the art of the last thirty-tree cantos can never violate the drama of the sixty-seven that came before. The experience, however epic, must retain aspects of human scale. Thus I will focus on another concluding image, which in dialogue with the two others I've looked at sets forth a fundamental human concern, a psychological essence. Once more I'll begin with a problem of translation.

The word that concerns me, "*lume*," occurs in the first line of the tercet quoted above (XXX, 61). The Italian doesn't translate as "light" in the standard sense, though that's the English word used by Musa, Singleton, and Mandelbaum, concurring in the same way they did with "tree" toward the end of *Purgatory*. Nevertheless, for "light" plain and simple, Italians use *luce*. *Lume*, which occurs a number of times during the book's closing cantos (the next iteration comes at line 100), connotes a relative weakness and smallness, an evanescence, as in the expressions *lume a olio*, an oil lamp, or *a lume di candela*, by candlelight. Nor is Dante's reliance on such a term explained simply by the technology of his time. He knows what *luce* is, and in XXX, 59, he seems to set it up in opposition to the softer word, which follows soon after. In 59, speaking of the heightened perception Beatrice is helping to create in her guest, he asserts "*nulla luce è tanto mera*," no light is so bright. Yet a few lines earlier still, in order to prepare her guest for such resplendence, the hostess uses no sun image but rather that of *il candelo*: "So is the candle for Its flame prepared." (54)

Once the Pilgrim's candle has been dipped into its stream of flame, in Canto XXX, his first impressions of the highest Heaven beyond are full of biplay between the all-powerful *luce* and the more confined and temporary *lume*. In XXXI, 22, we have the "*luce divina*," and in 28 "*trina luce*," "Triune Light;" both are direct references to elements of God. In line 50 however the Pilgrim sees the faces of the Blest "*d'altrui lume fregiati*," which Musa translates as "adorned in borrowed light," and in 126, alongside one of the *Comedy*'s several references to Phaeton and his tumbling chariot, the narrator describes how "*il lume si fa scemo*," dressing the smaller light in an idiom meaning to trick, to make a fool of someone. In any case an accurate translation conveys the sense of light that's indirect or second-hand. It's not the thing itself, powerful enough to knock Phaeton from the sky.

Scholars have noted the pervading use of reflection and refraction. Singleton explains how, in the penultimate canto, the newcomer to the Celestial Rose discovers he's "been seeing by reflected light all the while." Such a process of discovery makes a natural correlation with the Pilgrim's continuing need to transhumanize; as he approaches each new aspect of the Divine Plan, he must first habituate himself to some smaller-scale model. The process carries through to canticle's end, since it's only in the last tercets that the pilgrim can look upon God Himself. But my own reading doesn't concern that supreme illumination so much as its flickering domestic stand-in.

When Pilgrim Dante looks finally into the "Light Eternal fixed in Self alone" (XXXIII, 124), poet Dante rises to the occasion via an alliterative tour de force that depends in large part on its manipulation of the light image—or more precisely, the degrees-of-light image. In this line the indivisible Alpha and Omega is addressed "*O luce etterna*," but soon after that the visitor treats God made flesh, the man Jesus, in terms more vulnerable: "*come lume reflesso*," "as light reflected" (128). The Godhead shines without source and without end, whereas Its earthly embodiment glints and is gone, and over the final cantos of the *Comedy* the recurrent opposition of sunlight and candlelight creates dramatic tension. The counterpoint nags at the revelations; the play on words evokes, like Dante-Derrida, the tenuousness of mystic experience.

Noting this tension, this insubstantiality, Freccero and others go to the extreme of suggesting that *Paradise* describes an exposition unique in all eternity. This one time only, runs the argument, have the Elect descended from their Empyrean chorus to instruct this one special visitor. This reading has some textual support, but it strikes me as making too much of the Pilgrim, and calling attention to the poet who made him, a poet elsewhere so clear-eyed about sins of pride. I prefer to emphasize how in Dante, God's house is free of blast and thunder.

The quiet lapping of *luce* and *lume* works against inflated rhetoric about omnipotence or righteousness. Had our narrator gone for a more stentorian effect, like an Italian Isaiah, we would've come to a briar patch rather than a rose, a place that would brook no transhumanizing. But Dante plays up the quieter side of his light-dialogue, with rhymes like *candela* and *favilla*, spark. So too, even in *Paradise*, Dante gains a sensory grounding from the canticle's closing image.

The obvious association, for this play of illumination and murmurs, would be a late-night Mass or novena. But the dappled conclusion of *Paradise* also suggests another context, earthier, and calls up notions that run counter to much of the past century's Dante scholarship.

I mean that the softer light of Highest Heaven, in concert with the garden-tree and the slum-tower, enact something more ambivalent than a "conversion narrative." The conversion story, the essence of Singleton's insight, certainly demands the respect of anyone who cares about "the Poem." The Bollingen translator claimed that Dante gave us an "allegory of theologians" rather than a mere "allegory of poets," and thus his odyssey has its "proper end not in the life after death, but here in this life" (this in a 1954 essay, "Dante's Allegory"). So Singleton, and most twentieth-century thinkers with him, see the work as principally an imaginative reframing of its creator's journey back to faith from the dark wood of exile. According to this interpretation, Dante's verses had the same root purpose as Scripture: a means to Divinity for both author and auditor.

Of course I am simplifying. That's what happens to any system of thought under the wash of sixty or seventy years, and with 2020 in sight, Singleton's analysis begins to feel simple, indeed burdensome. It makes me uneasy to see the conversion reading lowered into place like an inviolable monolith in the notes to Robert Pinsky's translation of *Inferno* (otherwise very fine, *tempestoso*).

With regard to the final epiphanies of *Paradise*, then, I must point out their impossible-to-overlook intimations of what used to be called "the act of love." The glowing eyes and flying sparks limn a growing closeness and can't help but suggest a tryst by candlelight. Not just any sort of tryst, to be sure, nothing juvenile or prurient. Rather, given the context of talking with the dead, combined with the narrator's much-remarked-upon aging (especially at the beginning of Canto XXV), the correct association seems to be some youthful romantic encounter recollected years later, an embrace in the dark once fumbling but now—as the candle of our sensual being gutters—transcendent.

I make this connection fully aware that the author knew conversion. Dante's revival of faith makes itself felt on first reading, in the difference between the teeth-gnashing *Inferno*, begun when he was only a few years out of Florence, and the awed receptivity of the later *Paradise*. And even in the earliest chapters, Dante gives carnal desire its comeuppance, most famously in the case of Paolo and Francesca (*Inferno* V). Likewise toward the close of *Paradise*, when the poet requires some emphatic expression of desire and contact, he speaks of a baby at its mother's breast (XXX, 82-84). Nonetheless, at a number of points in those final cantos, it requires no great stretch to imbue the transcendent experience with the ardor of a mature lover, a desire purified by time. Doesn't Master Virgil claim, at the center of the journey: "Natural love can never be at fault"? (*Purgatory* XVII, 94). And higher up the mountain doesn't a second philosopher-poet, Statius, reiterate the point? A clarifying latter-day companion piece would be *Krapp's Last Tape*, Samuel Beckett's piercing rejection of epiphany. In this one-act, an old man fast-forwards through his younger self's recorded pontifications about meaning; he prefers to hear, again and again, a few words about a lost lover.

At the end of the *Comedy*, I believe, "natural love" participates in "the Love that moves the sun and the other stars" (XXXIII, 145). And that participation reveals, further, something intrinsic to the work's lasting impact. The concluding images from the end of *Inferno* to the end of the whole—from tower to tree to candle—delineate a consistent movement away from power.

In worldly terms, each of the metaphorical objects is more fragile than the last. Dante first leaves pride and its towers behind, he leaves it to those who feel nothing beyond their own grudges and lusts, and then next he embodies pride's cleansing in the flutter of a newly blossoming tree, and then finally he locates the greatest force in the universe in the frail and transitory glow of a candle. It's a reverse *Pilgrim's Progress*, distinguished by a steady agitation against ordinary representations of the Almighty. It's an epic demonstration that the truth and the way dwell in the meek and the low.

The continuing power of *The Divine Comedy* depends, in large part, on the importance it awards frailty in its scheme of the eternal. The Poem can still upset expectation, via this tension between the power it seeks to express and the fragility in its instruments of expression. Not all devices in this rare epic partake of that fragility, to be sure. The organization for instance remains more formidable than anything in all but the smallest handful of literary artifacts (Joyce's *Ulysses* comes to mind). Still, as I move from textual specifics to general conclusions, I am guided by the *Comedy's* tension between mighty themes and lowly embodiments. It says something, for instance, that the comparison with Jackson's *Lord of the Rings* is essentially one between crowd scenes and intimate encounters. Jackson crams the screen with armies; Dante pauses for a whisper.

Which brings me to my overarching theory of the work—perhaps psychological, perhaps anthropological. The idea owes something to Jan Kott, and to Joseph Meeker's *The Comedy of Survival*, a central text in what's come to be called literary ecology. I'm also grateful to Gaetano Cipolla and his brief essay about teaching the work's mythic archetypes. In any case, I start with the term "Comedy," a word many an explicator has wondered over, and take Dante's masterpiece to be at heart a parable of survival, of getting through and getting on—and so a conversion narrative in a different sense, in which conversion can never be a lone, fixed entity, but rather a process of lifelong iteration. The conclusion of this Pilgrim's journey is itself an iteration, since we know that our visionary won't remain floating on air before "the wheel in perfect balance turning" (XXXIII, 143). Rather he must tumble away, an out-of-balance pinwheel.

Or Phaeton, young and proud, dumped from his chariot with no one to blame but himself. Indeed, how often the *Comedy* entails a fall! When our narrator isn't collapsing physically, as at the end of the Paolo and Francesca episode, he must apologize for a mental breakdown, and his apologies multiply as the story goes on, as his vulgar Italian and bookworm's analogies prove ever more unequal to his task. Yet his quest survives each stumble, and so it takes on the pattern of comedy combined with parable. Culture cannot exist without such parables, their major players at once hero and clown, here Quixote, there Shine the Signifying Monkey, and more recently Beckett's Unnameable: "I can't go on, you must go on, I'll go on."

But of course Beckett's trilogy, another that goes beyond the life of the body, is also a comedy in the ordinary sense; it makes us laugh. The same can be said of *Quixote* or any other picaresque, whereas Dante's voyage offers hardly a chuckle. Our protagonist may fall— and the monolith of the conversion narrative along with him—but it's never a pratfall. This artist doesn't amuse, he fascinates: now poignant, now uncanny, now brilliant. The exception that proves the rule comes in *Inferno*'s Malebolge episodes, but even then it's the demons who play the stooges, with locker-room nicknames. The Pilgrim and Guide carry on with horrified rigor, and what I'm proposing doesn't ignore that rigor. Rather, I'm calling attention to its compassion, its humanity.

Human fragility, never so obvious as when we insist "I must go on," lies at the root of why the *Comedy* has become so much more than a lovely literary antique—another *Orlando Furioso*, say, also a "Comedy of survival," and in fact constructed on Dante's model. The difference can be seen most clearly when we consider the Poem the way Kott looked at Shakespeare's drama: as representations of the psyche in development. With *Shakespeare Our Contemporary* in mind, the three images I considered emerge as signals for critical stages in spiritual and emotional growth.

The psychological principles that underlie my reading are best known in their framing by Carl Jung. It was Jung who argued that every individual has his or her "Shadow," a realm of things we'd rather not know about ourselves, extremes of our nature and our desire, horrifying yet impossible to dismiss. By extension, the primary work in achieving wholeness as a personality is that of embracing and integrating the Shadow. Then too, Jung was one of the thinkers who helped refine and articulate the idea of the Unknowable, intrinsic to how our species understands the world. Every civilization recognizes the existence of the Unknowable, some all-encompassing essence out beyond the ken of the wisest sachem, or of the most whole and actualized personality (beyond, too, Jung's own dubious explorations of the "cosmic Overmind"). To describe the Unknowable as God is actually to diminish it, as observant Jews would say about writing His name.

The Divine Comedy embodies these three aspects of human growth and potential via a sequence of illustrations or signifiers so fitting as to seem arranged back at the dawn of Jung's Collective Unconscious. One might use an older locution; one might say, concerning this archetypal sequence, that the *Comedy* "images them forth." In any case the context requires, surely, explication in poetic terms.

The tower terrifies, it houses our most fearsome icon of self…and yet at the same time it shows us the walls that must come down while we do the work of wholeness, a many-step program that will turn a naked stump in the middle of our life's road to something fully realized and alive, of hopeful green stuff woven…and once that high yet still earthly goal has been achieved, once we've embraced the totality of our embodied spirits, then the candle emerges clearly ahead, the still, small flame that leads us on to our true calling, to a permanence and value we cannot name yet can never cease believing exists…and throughout these passages, this evolution toward a happy end, progress takes the form of renunciation, of putting off our worldly armor and becoming ever more vulnerable.

Tower, tree, candle: shadow, wholeness, hope. A sturdy chain of meaning, that, one with the strength to haul *The Divine Comedy* across a near-millennium by now and to ground it firmly in the consciousness of a time like our own, mad for individual self-actualization. Yet as I finish laying out the argument it also begins to seem a bit simple. It begins to sound, almost, like the string of platitudes out of an Oscar winner.

Naturally, I have assurances that my work is nothing so superficial, no pop-mythic imposition on the text. I remember my reading lists, my decades of dedication. My analysis doesn't exclude Singleton's, no more than his negated the so-called "romantic" interpretations of De Sanctis and earlier critics. Nevertheless, after so much of this *Comedy*, I find myself feeling like the joke's on me—like I'm merely playing the role I was born to, as a younger disciple, when it came my turn to wrestle with so protean a narrative. So this journey too ends in freefall. The seeker has only a moment before the miracle and then staggers dizzily away. The best he can hope for is that when he returns to himself he can still count on so rich and sagacious a text as a companion.

—*Southwest Review*, 2009